Carl B. Stokes and the Rise of Black Political Power

Carl B. Stokes
and the Rise of
Black Political Power

LEONARD N. MOORE

University of Illinois Press

URBANA AND CHICAGO

The illustrations in this book appear courtesy of the Cleveland Press
Collection, Cleveland State University Library, Cleveland, Ohio.

Library of Congress Cataloging-in-Publication Data
Moore, Leonard N. (Leonard Nathaniel)
Carl B. Stokes and the rise of Black political power / Leonard N.
Moore.
p.   cm.
Includes bibliographical references and index.
ISBN 0-252-02760-4 (acid-free paper)
1. Stokes, Carl. 2. African American mayors—Ohio—Cleveland—
Biography. 3. Mayors—Ohio—Cleveland—Biography. 4. African
Americans—Ohio—Cleveland—Politics and government—20th
century. 5. Cleveland (Ohio)—Politics and government—20th century.
6. Cleveland (Ohio)—Race relations. I. Title.
F499.C653S866   2002
977.1'32043'092—dc21   2001007063

Contents

Acknowledgments

A COMMUNITY of people helped make this book possible. Denoral Davis, Sheila Moore, and the entire Department of History at Jackson State University laid the foundation for my career as a professional historian. James Borchert, Donald Ramos, Dillard Poole, and Joyce Thomas at Cleveland State University sharpened my skills and encouraged me to pursue a Ph.D. in history. Warren Van Tine, Marshall Stevenson, and William E. Nelson at The Ohio State University helped me become a better teacher, writer, and researcher.

My research was made easier with the assistance of Samuel Black of the Western Reserve Historical Society; the staff of the Cleveland Press Collection at Cleveland State University; an Ohio Bicentennial Legacy Dissertation Fellowship; and the LSU College of Arts and Sciences Manship Summer Fellowship. I am grateful to Louisiana State University, which gave me, a young black scholar, a place where I could truly be myself. I especially thank my history department colleagues Paul Paskoff, Gaines Foster, Charles Shindo, Tiwanna Simpson, and John Rodrigue for being supportive. Thanks also to my students for making my classes so popular.

I am indebted to the staff at the University of Illinois Press, especially Joan Catapano and Theresa L. Sears, and to my copy editor, Polly Kummel. Special thanks goes to Darlene Clark Hine, who encouraged me to submit the project to Illinois.

Finally, I want to thank my family: my boyz, who kept me focused and motivated, including Jason Chambers, Sherwin Bryant, Marcus Cox, Louis Harrison, Brandon Ledyard, Kadiri Adero, Carlos Thomas, Ronald Roberts, Ralph D. Moore, Ralph L. Moore, and Kevin D. Golden; my mother, Peggy

Sue Moore, who is the sustainer of the family; my sisters, Beverly and Sandra—I love both of you; and my loving wife, Thais, who married this project when she married me. I reserve my greatest thanks to my late father, Leonard R. Moore, who was not only the ultimate friend, father, provider, and role model but also my research assistant. Whenever I called Cleveland in need of an obscure article, book, or fact, he would always track it down and send it to me. It is truly his book as much as it is mine.

* * *

Portions of chapter 2 previously appeared as "The School Desegregation Crisis of Cleveland, Ohio, 1963–1964" in Journal of Urban History 28 (January 2002): 3–25. © 2002 by Sage Publications. Used by permission of the copyright holder.

Portions of chapter 5 previously appeared as "Class Conflicts over Residential Space in an African-American Community: Cleveland's Lee-Seville Public Housing Controversy" in *Ohio History* 111 (Winter–Spring 2002): 1–19. © 2002 by the Ohio Historical Society. Used by permission of the copyright holder.

Portions of several chapters previously appeared as "Carl Stokes: Mayor of Cleveland" in *African-American Mayors: Race, Politics, and the American City*, ed. David R. Colburn and Jeffrey S. Adler (Urbana: University of Illinois Press, 2001), 80–106. Used by permission of the University of Illinois Press.

Carl B. Stokes and the Rise of Black Political Power

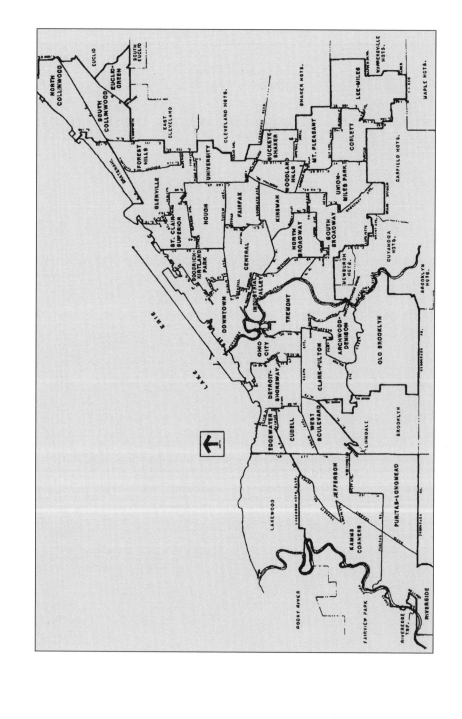

Introduction

BETWEEN 1967 and 1971 Cleveland mayor Carl B. Stokes transformed the energy of the civil rights movement into a local model of black political power. As the first black mayor of a major urban center, Stokes ushered in the next phase of the civil rights movement, political power. By linking the civil rights movement and black political electoral activism, Stokes occupied the key role in what was perhaps one of the greatest accomplishments of the black freedom struggle: the entry of African Americans into the political mainstream. This book is a biographical approach to examining the transformation from protest to black political power in a major northern city.[1]

While the passage of the Civil Rights Act of 1964 and the Voting Rights Act of 1965 represented major legislative victories for African Americans in the South, they had little effect on black people living in America's ghettos. The boycotts, sit-ins, marches, and mass campaigns brought Jim Crow to its knees, but they hardly touched the daily lives of millions of African Americans living in the urban North. Civil rights leaders ignored the problems of northern blacks largely because their problems seemed small in comparison to those of blacks in the South. Although black northerners could vote, use public accommodations, and attend integrated schools, if only in theory, they still suffered from an oppressive racial system.

The roots of black frustration in the North lie in the second great migration of African Americans from the South. Although the initial great migration during World War I was indeed a significant historical phenomenon, the mass influx of black migrants to the urban centers of America between 1940 and 1960 forever changed the face of urban America. Jim Crow, disfranchisement, the mechanization of southern agriculture, and the economic opportunities of the cities caused three million African Americans to leave for the North during those two decades. For many northern cities the resulting demographic changes were nothing less than cataclysmic.[2]

But although thousands of African Americans flocked to the cities in search of more opportunity, they faced tremendous obstacles once they arrived in the promised land. Perhaps the most critical issue for blacks in the urban North was housing, and their housing options were rather limited. They were forced into overcrowded all-black enclaves, paving the way for the construction of the second ghetto. The continued influx of black migrants placed a severe strain on the housing stock of urban America because no one had built new housing in the inner cities since before the depression. Consequently, much of the housing in all-black areas was either substandard or dilapidated, and it was certainly crowded. For instance, many black families unable to find conventional housing were forced to lodge in allies, cellars, attics, garages, basements, and abandoned warehouses. The redlining practices of banks, government policies, pandering politicians, and restrictive covenants by homeowners' associations all were important factors in the housing crisis because they effectively prevented working and middle-class African Americans from moving into all-white areas. As well, exclusionary zoning, the relegation of public housing to the inner city, and the outright intimidation of and violence against blacks seeking housing elsewhere in the city combined to keep the black population in the older areas of town. Inept urban renewal plans initiated in the 1950s to solve the housing problems of the city only exacerbated the problems. In theory, city agencies were to designate blighted areas, clear the land, and sell it to developers, who were supposed to build low- to moderate-income housing. Although many dwellings were razed, no new housing was ever built, and displaced residents were forced to settle into already overcrowded areas. Consequently, African Americans mockingly referred to urban renewal as "Negro Removal."[3]

Although many black migrants were lured north by industrial prosperity during World War II and the Korean War, they were confronted with employment discrimination as a fact of life. Many black workers complained about the unpredictability of the local labor markets. Some hired blacks, some did not. Many employers believed the racial stereotypes and thought that black workers would not make good employees because they were lazy, unproductive, unreliable, and prone to tardiness and high absenteeism. Further, many companies chose not to hire African Americans because they feared using the shop floor as an experiment in racial mixing. Employment agencies and local labor unions also represented a barrier to equal employment. Both public and private employment agencies allowed employers to specify racial preferences when registering job listings, while many locals of the American Federation of Labor went to went to great lengths to exclude black workers. Public employment, however, offered black workers a bit more opportunity. But even here they were still concentrated at the lower end of the occupational ladder. The majority of blacks who worked for the city were janitors, laborers, and sanitation workers.[4]

De facto school segregation also emerged as a principal source of racial conflict throughout the North. As the second great migration swelled urban America, many schools in predominantly black areas became severely overcrowded, and de facto school segregation became institutionalized. Consequently, black parents developed a long list of grievances: overcrowding, inferior teachers, low teacher expectations, high student-teacher ratios, outdated and Eurocentric curriculum materials, inadequate social services, and poor physical facilities. When school officials failed to respond to the concerns of black parents, those who had left the South for greater opportunities became even more angry and frustrated.[5]

The northern black poor were also frustrated by the nature of police-community relations. Residents of many black urban communities confronted the reality of police brutality and an unequal standard of law enforcement. Black residents had bitter complaints about a litany of issues: people killed and injured by police, harassment, insufficient police protection, lack of black officers on the force, few (if any) African Americans in high-ranking positions, discriminatory assignments, and segregated units. Many problems stemmed from the small percentage of black police officers in big-city departments.[6]

The passage of civil rights legislation did nothing to alleviate these problems. In fact, the civil rights impulse made black northerners more conscious of their oppression, and they saw little hope for change. White America and the civil rights movement paid little attention to the depth of black despair and frustration in the inner cities until Watts, a black ghetto in Los Angeles, exploded in the summer of 1965, leaving thirty-four people dead. Watts was not an anomaly; it was a predictor. Throughout the remainder of the decade virtually every major city in the United States would experience a serious racial disturbance. The riots that swept across the urban landscape throughout the mid-1960s finally drew attention to the problems of the black urban poor.

Watts caught civil rights leaders off guard. They were not prepared to take on the challenge of northern-style racism. They were accustomed to fighting the visible target of Jim Crow, not institutional or structural racism. After a failed 1966 effort by Martin Luther King Jr. and the Southern Christian Leadership Conference to tackle the issue with their Campaign to End Slums in Chicago, it was clear that nonviolent direct action would not work in the urban North. The problems of the black urban poor required a different set of strategies and tactics. But for activists trained in the tradition of love and nonviolence, that transition would prove difficult. Consequently, traditional civil rights leaders never found much of an audience in urban America. Although black urbanites supported and sympathized with the struggle against Jim Crow, they understood that sit-ins and marches were regionally specific.

Malcolm X became the spokesman for the millions of northern urban lower-income blacks. They flocked to hear the fiery orator who boldly shouted to the world what many blacks privately thought about white America. Also, his critique of the United States, his relentless emphasis on black self-determination, and his philosophy of self-defense captivated northern audiences. They embraced his indictment of the civil rights movement and its limited agenda.

Malcolm's philosophy was rooted in black nationalism, the belief that African Americans constitute a single body and have the right to determine their own destiny. As civil rights leaders stood at a crossroads in the aftermath of Watts, younger activists in the movement embraced Malcolm's ideas and rejected the integrationist thrust of the movement. They reveled in the slogan "Black Power," a rejection of integration, assimilation, nonviolence, passive resistance, and the entire civil rights movement. When the black urban poor also embraced the slogan, Black Power wrought a nearly overnight transformation of African American life and culture as black Americans sought to take control of their destiny.

A central component of black power was black political power. At a Cleveland rally by the Congress of Racial Equality (CORE) on the evening of April 3, 1964, Malcolm X delivered what was perhaps his most famous speech, "The Ballot or the Bullet." Before more than three thousand black Clevelanders engaged in a bitter school protest, Malcolm X was clear about what black power actually meant: "The political philosophy of black nationalism means that the black man should control the politics and politicians in his own community no more; the black man in the black community has to be re-educated into the science of politics so he will know what politics is supposed to bring him in return. Don't be throwing out any bullets. A ballot is like a bullet."[7]

Mainstream civil rights leaders such as Martin Luther King Jr. and Bayard Rustin borrowed many of Malcolm's ideas in their own writings concerning the future of the civil rights movement. In a 1965 article in *Commentary* entitled "From Protest to Politics," Rustin argued that political power was the next logical phase of the civil rights movement. Likewise, in *Where Do We Go from Here?* King suggested that African Americans needed to acquire some degree of electoral control.

Black Clevelanders were the first to implement Malcolm's ideas. After decades of employment discrimination, poor housing, unfair law enforcement, and segregated schooling, black Clevelanders understood the importance of controlling the city's political system. Although the city's African American community had actively participated in the voting process since the nineteenth century, white politicians had failed to reward them for their support. Consequently, the black community began a series of marches, sit-ins, and boycotts in an effort to bring about change. However, black Clevelanders soon realized that sporadic protest produced only temporary change; they needed a more permanent solution. And by the 1960s, thanks to the second great migration, they constituted the largest potential bloc of voters— 39 percent. Black leaders, recognizing that this voting base gave them a legitimate shot at electing a black mayor, began looking for a candidate in the early months of 1965. They had one main criterion: someone who would not sell out to the city's business and political elite. Carl Stokes emerged as the ideal candidate for several reasons. He was personally familiar with the problems of the ghetto, he was a veteran of the civil rights movement, and he exercised political independence. But more important, Stokes was serious about improving the lives of the city's black residents. Although he lost in the 1965 race, Stokes became mayor of the nation's eighth-largest city in 1967.

When Stokes became mayor, he was driven by three overlapping purposes: to improve the lives of the black poor, to give blacks a voice in municipal government, and to prove to the nation that an African American could govern.

This book is not a day-to-day account of the Stokes administration. Rather, its central focus is how Stokes used Cleveland City Hall as an extension of the civil rights movement and how he defined his agenda. More specifically, I discuss how Stokes used his power to address issues vital to black urban life: employment, housing, law enforcement, and social welfare. Several other themes emerge as well: ghettoization, black political mobilization, the development of an African American political culture, and black control of central cities.

The opening chapter sets the stage for Stokes's political career by looking at his life before politics. He grew up poor in the predominantly black East Side ghetto of Cleveland where poverty, poor housing, and high unemployment were facts of life. He dropped out of high school in 1944 but later earned his diploma after a short stint in the army. After earning his undergraduate degree and a law degree, he was attracted to politics by his growing disgust with the conservatism of local black politicians who placed self-interest ahead of community uplift.

Stokes's early political career can best be described as the "Making of a Mayor," which is the title of chapter 2. After two unsuccessful runs for the state legislature, Stokes in 1962 became the first black Democrat to serve in the Ohio House. Black voters soon realized that, unlike other local African American politicians, Stokes was sincere, honest, independent, and, most important, racially conscious; they rewarded him with three terms. Meanwhile, Cleveland's leaders were continuing to ignore the needs of the city's black community. When marches, rallies, and demonstrations failed to bring about meaningful change, the frustrated masses resorted to violence. In the summer of 1966 Hough, a poor black enclave on the city's East Side, saw five days of rioting. Four died, hundreds were wounded, and the city sustained more than $2 million in property damage. The basic cause of the riot was clear: black frustration. The uprising convinced the city's white establishment to end its philosophy of politics as usual. When Stokes made a second run for mayor in 1967, the city's business elite supported him in the belief that he represented the best safeguard against black unrest and that he could deter the development of a local militant movement. Although Stokes accepted the assistance of the business community, he made it clear that he was not going to be, as he put it, anyone's "house nigger."

Chapter 3 examines the first eight months of the Stokes administration. To the delight of the business community, in 1968 Stokes won restoration of the city's urban renewal dollars, which the federal government had cut off because of Cleveland's poor record of completing projects; Stokes also kept Cleveland free of racial violence after King's assassination that April. Weeks later Stokes capitalized on his cordial relationship with the corporate elite and began a broad-based $1.5 billion urban redevelopment program called Cleveland: Now!

Stokes's honeymoon came to an abrupt end on the evening of July 23, 1968, when local black nationalists engaged in a gun battle with police in the East Side community of Glenville (see chapter 4). The riot's toll was heavy: seven deaths, including those of three white police officers, hundreds of injuries and arrests, and more than $2.6 million in property damage. For Stokes the damage was much worse. It confirmed the predictions of his enemies: that a black mayor was no insurance against black unrest. Furthermore, the business community withdrew much of its support when it learned that Ahmed

Evans, the main figure in the shootings, had received a Cleveland: Now! grant to open a community center. Evans used the grant money to buy weapons for the riot.

Chapter 5 examines Stokes's efforts to place 274 single-family units of public housing in the black middle-class community of Lee-Seville. His idea was to begin a new era in low-income housing by building outside the city's rigidly segregated low-income areas. However, his efforts were blocked by two black city council members, whom he later labeled "black bigots."

Police reform and black economic power were central concerns for Stokes. The first half of chapter 6 looks at Stokes's efforts to place more blacks on the police force and to secure promotions for black officers already on the force. These efforts resulted in a testing scandal, which made it difficult for him to implement any major reforms in the negrophobic Cleveland Police Department. The latter part of the chapter looks at the McDonald's boycott and how Stokes used his power to facilitate the sale of several white-owned franchises to black community organizations.

Chapter 7 discusses Stokes's 1969 re-election campaign. Because of the scandals and controversies of his first term, Stokes faced an uphill battle for re-election. Civil rights was no longer in vogue; conservatism was now the order of the day. However, the Stokes team remobilized the black electorate and convinced white liberals that he deserved another two years in office.

Just weeks after his second inauguration, Stokes appointed the retired air force general Benjamin O. Davis Jr. to head city safety forces. Chapter 8 examines Davis's brief tenure in Cleveland. The mayor was confident that because of Davis's military background, he would have little trouble gaining control of the police and fire departments. However, when Davis arrived, he made several administrative moves that illustrated his desire to maintain the status quo. Davis resigned in July but only after telling reporters that Stokes was a foe of good law enforcement. The general's allegations gave credence to the charges that Stokes was a closet black nationalist.

Chapter 9, "Council Wars," discusses Stokes's bitter relationship with the Cleveland City Council. Throughout his four-year tenure he was unable to gain any degree of control over the thirty-three-member council, although twenty-seven were Democrats. The steady resistance from the city council eventually convinced Stokes not to seek a third term.

Chapter 10 explores Stokes's efforts to keep the mantle of power within the black community. Shortly after his re-election Stokes formed the all-black Twenty-first District Democratic Caucus in an effort to unify the city's African American politicians, compete with the Cuyahoga County Democrats, and institutionalize his power base. Within a year the caucus was one of the most powerful urban political machines in the country. The book's conclusion, "The Stokes Legacy," examines the successes and failures of the Stokes administration, compares Stokes's performance to that of other black mayors, and evaluates the broader significance of Carl Stokes's takeover of city hall.

1. Cleveland Boy

CARL BURTON STOKES was born in obscurity on June 21, 1927, in Cleveland, Ohio. He was the second son of Charles and Louise Stokes, both natives of Georgia, although they did not meet until after they arrived in Cleveland during the great migration to search for better social and economic opportunities. Louis Stokes was two years old when his little brother was born.

Louise Stone, born in Wrens, Georgia, had ten siblings. Her mother worked as a cook on the massive Olephant Plantation, and when her father was not sharecropping, he pursued his passion, which was preaching. As she entered adolescence, Louise was eager to leave Georgia. During the early years of World War I she moved with a sister to Jacksonville, Florida, and in 1918 came to Cleveland at the urging of another sister. That sister, Lillian, and her husband, Albert Simms, a steelworker, provided Louise with a support network as she made the adjustment from the rural South to the industrial North. Other members of the Stone family also came to Cleveland in later years.[1]

Upon arriving in Cleveland, Louise found work at the downtown Union Club, the social home of Cleveland's business and political establishment. Her duties: "cleaning out spittoons and sweeping up cigar butts." After earning a reputation as a faithful employee, she secured a better position at the Cleveland Hotel, then found work as a sleep-in domestic in the home of F. W. Ramsey, president of the Cleveland Stove Company. Although live-in domestics worked tirelessly, her decent salary served as a strong incentive.[2]

Although World War I opened up industrial opportunities for black men, Charles struggled to find work after he arrived from Cordele, Georgia. He worked as a laundryman two days per week. After Charles and Louise fell in love, they married on June 21, 1923, at the home of Rev. S. M. Robinson, pastor of Liberty Hill Baptist Church. According to their son Carl's memoir, the ceremony was simple; the bride and groom took their vows in "ordinary street clothes."[3]

The new couple lived on the predominantly black East Side, which was surrounded by pockets of Italian, Polish, Eastern European, and Irish Americans. The Cuyahoga River divided the city, and it represented a racial barrier as well: The West Side was virtually all white, whereas more than 99.9 percent of the city's African Americans lived east of the river. For the Stokes family and other depression-era black Clevelanders, poverty and poor housing were stark realities. Louis was born on February 23, 1925. As an adult, Carl often reflected on the early years of his parents' marriage, wondering what it was like to be in love yet utterly poor. Charles died in 1928 of acute peritonitis, leaving Carl with few memories of his father.[4]

The young widow was forced to raise her two boys in the downstairs unit of a rundown two-story house at 2234 East 69th Street. The lack of adequate heating made many of Cleveland's cold winter days brutal. As Carl recalled, "We covered the rat holes with the tops of tin cans. The front steps always needed fixing, one of them always seemed to be missing. The coal stove kept the living room warm; we used heated bricks and an old flatiron wrapped in flannel and together we would rub our collective feet against it" to keep warm. Louise and the boys shared one bed. No wonder Carl Stokes would later refer to his East 69th Street home as a "poor excuse for a shelter."[5]

He despised growing up poor, and as a politician he never forgot those cold nights on East 69th Street during the depression. Although Stokes acknowledged that he enjoyed his childhood, "you won't catch me being nostalgic about those times or recommending that it is good for a boy to grow up in such conditions."[6]

While they were in elementary school, Carl and Louis took odd jobs to help their mother meet expenses. They collected bottles to take to junk dealers, ran errands for prostitutes, and hassled fruit vendors for week-old produce. "A rotten peach for example could be cut in such a way as to provide a perfectly good half piece or quarter section," Stokes explained. They also ventured to the Works Progress Administration dispensary at East 79th and Quincy for rice, dried peas, flour, and powdered milk. Whatever they managed to procure on their adventures, they had to protect on the way home. They armed themselves "with iron pipes for protection against adults, who would hide in doorways and then pounce down mercilessly and steal" their food. When times got especially hard, they stole car batteries for fuel, tore down wood fences for firewood, and shoplifted from neighborhood stores.[7]

Carl was still young when he learned to appreciate his mother. He remembered accompanying her to work in Shaker Heights when he was five. After they got off the train, they walked "to a big house in an all white neighborhood." Custom prohibited her from approaching the front door; she was told, "You can come around back and change your clothes in the basement." Her reply was "yes, ma'am," or "yes, miss." But she merely played a role, similar to that "of what slaves used to do in the daytime while planning to cut their master's throats at night," Carl Stokes wrote. "There was nothing servile about my mother other than a one to one survival relationship. Whatever was necessary to take care of her children she was going to do it."[8]

Louise did not wear the mask of submissiveness twenty-four hours a day. Whenever the landlord and the social service worker came to visit, she could be tough. Her children meant everything, and she went to great lengths to protect their well-being. Carl found this to be a universal quality of black women. It was "the essential miracle of womanhood, this necessity of certain women to center their concern in the preservation of their children. It is a quality to be especially admired in Black women, who for years have done without the frills tagged onto the white world's idea of femininity in order to insure a future of their own."[9]

Carl's peer group reinforced the respect and fondness that he had for his mother. When Carl and his friends played the dozens, "a comment about another kid's mother would almost always end up in fight."[10] The Stokes boys were protective of their mother, and they made it clear that they would not tolerate any negative comments about their mom.

Louise stressed education. On one occasion she noted Carl's excitement when he saw how many toys the son of her employer possessed. "To say I was overwhelmed would be to express only a fraction of my amazement and my desire on that occasion, but I will never forget the way in which my mother punctured those feelings." Louise told him, "Carl, you see them toys? I can't afford those kinds of toys so don't ever ask me for what I can't give you, and while you're here in this house never touch any of these." She made one exception: "There ain't but one toy here that I'll let you play with," she told him as she grabbed a book from a nearby bookshelf. "You play with this and learn how to read it so when you get older you won't have to do the kind of work I'm doing."[11]

Carl grew increasingly rebellious and disobedient as he approached adolescence. Because his mother worked throughout the day, his grandmother, Fannie Stone, shouldered a good portion of the responsibility for raising him and Louis. She never hesitated to whip Carl, especially when he was disobedient or disrespectful. When his grandmother was unable to discipline him, she solicited the help of her son, Pughsley Stone, also known as "Dock," who

lived two doors down at 2230 East 69th. Although the proprietor of a notorious and illegal after-hours operation, he served as Carl's joint disciplinar-
ian and father figure. "If he caught me talking back to Fannie Stone, his
mother," Carl Stokes recalled, "he would whip me worse than she would. On
the street, outside, anywhere he would catch me, that's where he would whip
me." Although Carl did not appreciate this discipline, he nevertheless admired Dock because he lived in open defiance of the law. "He was a very
rough man and I was proud of him. In a community where people live in
despair and denial, the man who defies the rules and is able to make a living
becomes a hero. Dock was one of our heroes."[12]

In 1938 the Stokeses were one of the lucky families to move into the brand
new Outhwaite Estates on East 55th Street, the first federally funded housing
project in the nation. Carl was overcome with excitement when his mother
announced they would be moving. The new apartments contained "a sink with
hot and cold running water, a place where you could wash clothes with a wash-
ing machine," and an "actual refrigerator." For the first time the Stokeses had
two bedrooms and two beds. Carl was thrilled when he located the tenants-
only recreation center and swimming pool.[13]

As a student at the all-black Giddings Elementary School, Stokes was a
model student. "I sang in the school choir, acted the lead in most of our
Christmas and other pageants, was the top speller in the school and had the
second or third highest" intelligence score, he recalled. Louise was proud of
her younger son, but academic success brought him little respect from his
peers.[14]

When Carl entered Central Junior High, he maintained his standard of
academic excellence at first. But by the ninth grade school had become less
of a priority. "It was during this time that I had learned to gamble with cards,
dice, and play hooky." Parent-teacher conferences, school discipline, and his
mother's advice were seemingly meaningless, he recalled: "It was too late, my
values had shifted." With cutting class and playing hooky part of his daily
regimen, his grades rapidly declined.[15]

After a brief bout with pleurisy, Carl Stokes entered East Technical High
School, not far from Outhwaite at East 55th Street and Scovill. Despite its
location in the heart of the black community, the school was only 10 percent
black—white students were bused and driven in from all across the city.
(Years later Stokes was certain that many of these same white classmates probably resisted the idea of busing black students to white schools.) When he
entered East Tech, he noticed that white teachers didn't expect much from
the black students. He and others were discouraged from taking courses in
the skilled trades. The school's white guidance counselor once advised him

"to pursue a course in foundry rather than the mechanical course I really wanted." The counselor both accepted the myth of black inferiority and was convinced that local employers would not hire black men in the skilled trades. The counselor's rationale: "There was a small chance of a colored boy getting a job in the field of mechanical drawing." Many of Stokes's friends had similar encounters with other teachers and administrators. Black students were even discouraged from playing basketball and football, although East Tech was the alma mater of Olympic track stars Jesse Owens and, later, Harrison Dillard.[16]

The racial attitudes of white administrators, teachers, and students meant that black students were well aware of racial tensions. "Fights were frequent," Stokes recalled. "Racial epithets were common." There were few friendships and relationships between the races, and teachers often referred to Carl and other black students as "you people." He retaliated by fighting. "If I caught one [white] standing around by himself waiting for a bus, I would just run up and start hitting him." By Stokes's own account, "it was in East Tech that I first learned not to like white people."[17]

His bitterness increased when he realized that many of the white-owned businesses in his community refused to hire black workers. Stokes recalled that Kresge "hired no Negroes above stock boy," although the company served an all-black clientele. He noticed a similar pattern at the popular Farmers Market, where none of the fifty white merchants had black clerks.[18]

Although class divisions were nearly invisible in the lower-income neighborhood called Central, they became clear whenever Stokes traveled to community events. Like many Central area teenagers, he enjoyed the social functions at both the Cedar and Central YMCAs. But he soon noticed a disturbing pattern: Youngsters from the black middle class avoided any contact with him and his friends. "The middle-class girls would often dance only with boys from similar families." In 1940s Cleveland race discrimination against and class discrimination within the black community were stark realities.[19]

As he approached adulthood, he saw little advantage in continuing his education. Instead, he hung out with petty criminals, drug users, and con artists, even though he did not participate in their extralegal activities. While his friends took liberties with the law, Stokes took boxing lessons in an effort to hone his physical prowess.[20] He trained under the nationally known "Whiz-Bang" Carter, who held Stokes to a strict workout routine that included running, jumping rope, and hitting the punching bag. His confidence increased as his skills and strength did. During a light sparring session with a more experienced fighter, Stokes delivered a hard right. Seconds later his opponent knocked him unconsciousness. Stokes recalled that the blow taught him a lesson that he applied to his political career: He never challenged a pro until he knew he was ready. Stokes eventually posted fifty amateur wins during his four-year boxing career.[21]

Stokes disappointed his family and friends when he decided to drop out of high school. He later remembered that it was not a conscious or rational decision to quit but that he saw few alternatives. With no programs that would give him a leg up, Stokes pursued success on his own. He later acknowledged that at that point in his life, his heroes were "pimps, number-runners, gamblers," professions that required more street smarts than book learning.[22]

After leaving school, he worked at the Otis Steel Foundry shoveling salt out of a box car and later as a valve polisher at the Thompson Aircraft Company. He was at a crossroads: "I had felt inadequate in my life before, but not inferior. I had always known how to work at being the equal of anyone else, even if I did not succeed. But I did not know how to cope with race prejudice. I felt baffled, without direction, and had no ambition beyond the work I was doing and the life I had developed on the streets." Although these were decent-paying jobs, Stokes felt empty. He began to spend more and more of his time on the streets. "During the year between the time I dropped out of high school and the time I enlisted in the Army, I learned how to live on the street. I badly wanted to be successful, and I was. But I came to see that no matter how good I was a street hustler, it wasn't a way out. At some point I would wake up still tied to the old ways and still not secure against poverty."[23]

Stokes ended his misery on July 17, 1945, by enlisting in the army just after he turned eighteen. "This was not a moral decision," he recalled. "The war was over. I just wanted to get the hell out of a world I had had enough of." After a few days in Atterbury, Indiana, Stokes and his buddies boarded a train for Fort McClellan, Alabama. En route they made a dinner stop at a Birmingham restaurant. The black recruits were ushered to the back of the restaurant, where a waitress dumped their silverware on the table and yelled, "Help yourself, boys!" When Stokes demanded better treatment, she warned, "You may not know it, nigger, but you're in Alabama now." Stokes left the restaurant convinced that "in the South the white man could kill any black person he wanted to." He never forgot this incident. "The effect on me was so strong that in the thirteen weeks spent at Ft. McClellan I never left the camp. I was the only man there who did not go to town. I wanted the fun and the release as much as any man there, but I wasn't going to go looking for it at the cost of humiliation or bodily harm." After basic training, he was sent to Germany, with brief stops in New Jersey and France.[24]

At the end of his tour of duty eighteen months later, he returned home. "Almost immediately on arriving home, I was enveloped in everything op-

pressive about being poor and black and uneducated." He quickly concluded that without a high school diploma, he was going nowhere. He returned
to East Tech and graduated in 1947. This was the turning point in his life: "My
attitudes had been changed. The contact with educated black men in the
Army had made me see a new value in going to school."[25]

In 1947 he used the G.I. Bill to enroll at the historically black West Virginia
State College. The freshman from Cleveland soon established a relationship
with Professor Herman Canady, who chaired the Psychology Department. The
intellectually demanding professor was quite popular among students because
of his tireless dedication and commitment to teaching. In many ways Stokes
looked upon Canady as a mentor and father figure; Canady impressed upon
the young Stokes the importance of social activism. When Stokes transferred
to Western Reserve University (now Case Western Reserve University) at the
end of the year, he was determined to do something meaningful with his life.[26]

At Western Reserve the psychology-sociology major joined the Youth
Council of the National Association for the Advancement of Colored People and the Young Progressives, an organization affiliated with Henry Wallace's Progressive Party. Stokes recalled those days: "We'd go to all the political meetings, especially when a speaker for Wallace or for Harry Truman
would appear. We'd go to those meetings and harass the speakers for Truman and generally raise hell or get into intense discussion with the people
who were for Truman." Stokes became acquainted with Bert Washington, a
sometime labor leader who was rumored to be a communist and who later
introduced him to Paul Robeson. Stokes would later write that Robeson
"heavily influenced my style of government" by raising the younger man's
awareness of the inequities of wealth in the United States.[27]

Stokes took Robeson's philosophy and combined it with a practical approach to politics that he learned when he worked for the long-time civil
rights activist John O. Holly. Holly had gained national headlines in the 1930s
when he launched successful economic boycotts against white merchants. In
the summer of 1949 Stokes served as Holly's chauffeur as he organized black
Democrats across the state. Stokes, then twenty-two, got free lessons in electoral politics from a maestro. "We heard the details of how to put together a
local chapter of a campaign organization; who should go for the money; who
would see to it that they got a storefront for headquarters; whom you should
watch out for in town; who was for you and who only seemed to be and who
was working against you," Stokes recalled. More important, Holly taught him
the basics of political power: how to get it and how to keep it. Stokes was
inspired by the efforts of his childhood hero: "If he could do it . . . why can't
I?" he said. In essence, Holly gave Stokes the "desire to achieve, to be a lead-

er, have fame, respect and stature, to not be poor and faceless . . . in short, to be somebody."[28] At the end of the summer Holly rewarded Stokes with a patronage job in a state liquor store. Stokes was especially grateful because it paid more than the G.I. Bill and left him time for classes at Western Reserve. But Stokes soon grew tired of being a part-time clerk and part-time student. Holly then got him a full-time position as a state liquor agent.[29]

The young agent first went to Canton, Ohio, and when he tried to arrest a bartender for violating the state's liquor laws, trouble developed. "Mr., you're serving liquor here and that's against the law," Stokes said. "You have to go to jail." The bartender refused to be arrested. "At that point I took out the pistol they had told me I could wear and hit him on the head. Blood popped out all over, and he hit the floor. I was as scared then as I ever expect to be. I turned and, waving my gun at the crowd, said, 'Don't anybody move, please just don't move, I'm scared, I'm frightened, and if anybody moves around here I'm liable to shoot you.'" Stokes provoked another incident weeks later when he was refused a drink at a Jim Crow tavern in rural Ohio. "I asked for a drink and was told I had to go behind a pillar, all colored people had to get their drinks at the end of the bar." Stokes then decided to enforce a little-known ordinance requiring any liquor establishment to operate on an equal opportunity basis. "There were five bars on the main street of that town. Within a half-hour, I had cited all of them." The next morning his angry supervisor reminded Stokes of his jurisdiction: "You had no goddamn business down there trying to get served, you had an assignment to go down there into the bootleg joints in the Negro neighborhood." Stokes was immediately transferred to Dayton and later to Toledo.[30]

Toledo was the home of the noted black racketeer Jinx Green, and Stokes was eager to put him out of business. When Stokes and his partner raided one of Green's bars, things got ugly. "I wheeled around and shot Jinx twice, once in the stomach and once in the thigh, and he fell," Stokes recalled. This incident convinced him that it was time to pursue another line of work. "I wanted out of the enforcement job."[31]

Stokes then decided to follow his brother's example and become a lawyer, largely because they "were the only black men I could see who didn't have white masters." He took the advice of several friends and enrolled as an undergraduate at the University of Minnesota, where he supported himself by working as a dining-car waiter. When he was not studying, he participated in the political life of the community as a member of the Panel of Americas, which traveled throughout Minnesota and Wisconsin promoting civil rights causes. He also got involved in local politics by managing the campaigns of a black city council candidate and a white candidate for the state legislature.

Although neither of his candidates won, his experiences in Minnesota politics would aid him tremendously when he returned to Cleveland after receiving his bachelor's degree in 1954.[32]

Stokes worked as a probation officer during the day, while he pursued his law degree at night at Cleveland-Marshall Law School. His new job brought him into direct contact with the black urban poor. Late one evening the wife of one of his parolees called and said that rats had attacked their baby. When Stokes arrived at the filthy apartment, he noticed that the child's nose and upper lip had been completely gnawed away. This event convinced him that the black poor needed more than social workers: "They needed advocates at the highest levels of government." After graduating from law school in 1956 and passing the bar one year later, Stokes joined his brother's law practice.[33]

Like most brand new lawyers, Stokes focused on criminal law, real estate, and divorce cases. Although he was financially successful his first year, the desire to be a full-time politician was evident—he joined the Cleveland Urban League, the local NAACP chapter, the County Federated Democrats of Ohio, and the mostly white Young Democrats. To gain some a degree of recognition, Stokes volunteered at neighborhood and community events. Whenever "some small church group needed a speaker, I would accept, always without question." Stokes recognized the power of the black church, and he did not hesitate to tap into it: "There is no more effective political voice in the black community than the church. When you need zeal, when you need people out there working for you, having a hundred black preachers out there rallying them up for you is invaluable. So, during the years after I started the practice of law, I did anything I was asked to do in the community."[34]

As Stokes increased his visibility in the black community, he met Shirley Edwards, a graduate student at Case Western Reserve University. He soon fell in love with the Mississippi native, and they married in 1958. They had three children, Carl Jr., Cordi, and Cordell, before divorcing in 1973.

While Stokes and his new bride were adjusting to family life, Cleveland was in the midst of postwar change. Back in the late 1940s the local chamber of commerce had adopted the slogan "Cleveland, the best location in the nation" in an effort to capture the upbeat mood in Cleveland during the immediate postwar years. Because the city had produced more than $5 billion worth of defense goods, it did indeed have reason to be optimistic. In 1945 Cleveland ranked fifth in the nation in terms of industrial output; the employment rate rose, allowing the city to recapture some of its early twentieth-century prosperity. However, by the mid-1950s Cleveland's industries had exhausted their defense work, and the city entered a deep economic decline from which it has yet to recover.

In 1950 the census reported a total population of 918,808 for Cleveland, making it the eighth-largest city in the United States. In fact, that number would mark the city's peak population. That year 147,847 Clevelanders—16.2 percent of the population—were African American. Across the city's postwar landscape were pockets of virtually every European ethnic group—Irish, Germans, Italians, Hungarians, Russians, Poles, Slovaks, Slovenians, Ukrainians, Czechs, Serbs, Croatians, and Rumanians—people who had been drawn to Cleveland because of its industrial prosperity. Many of them found work in the more than three hundred iron, steel, and ore companies of various types in the Cleveland area during World War II and its aftermath.

But between 1953 and 1964 Cleveland lost roughly 80,000 blue-collar jobs, particularly in heavy industry, to the sunbelt. Meanwhile, the city's emerging service sector gained approximately 30,000 white-collar positions. The disappearance of jobs from the central city had a profound effect, considering that in 1946 most of the 560,000 people in Cuyahoga County's workforce were employed in four industrial categories: machinery, iron and steel, transportation equipment, and electrical machinery. Along with white commercial and industrial flight, the city experienced disinvestment. Of the approximately $1.7 billion that the area's industries spent on postwar industrial expansion, they spent only $700,000 in the central city. Likewise, of the 170,000 new jobs created in the metropolitan area, 100,000 were in the suburbs. Last, new home construction in the city came to a virtual halt, while the suburbs boomed. Consequently, Cleveland was on the steep slope of deindustrialization, disinvestment, and unemployment.[35]

Aided by freeway construction and generous federal loan programs, white residents fled the central city for the suburbs. Their departure had a dramatic effect on the Cleveland economy. Despite the influx of southern blacks and Appalachian whites during the second great migration, Cleveland's population declined by 104,000 during the fifteen years from 1945 to 1960. Most of those who left were working- and middle-class whites who flocked to the eastern suburbs of Shaker Heights, Cleveland Heights, Garfield Heights, Mayfield, Lyndhurst, and Bedford. The western suburbs of Lakewood, Parma, Rocky River, Bay Village, and North Olmsted all experienced significant population increases as well. Unlike the city's streetcar suburbs, which catered to the white middle class, these postwar suburbs provided homes for industrial workers. In 1950 roughly 60 percent of all white residents in Cuyahoga County lived in the inner city. Ten years later fewer than 50 percent of whites in the county lived in the city; for the first time, more of the county's white population lived in the suburbs than in the city. White flight also left the city's business and political leaders struggling to deal with the consequences: declining tax revenues, more unskilled and poor people, growing welfare rolls, and the massive loss of jobs. And Cleveland's business leaders were neither enlightened nor progressive enough to offer workable solutions.

Locals referred to the whites who remained in the central city as "ethnics," or "cosmos" (short for cosmopolitans)—foreign-born or first-generation European immigrants. As white ethnics collectively became a larger part of the city population, they took control of the city's political structure with little interference from the industrialists who controlled the city's iron and steel interests. In many ways it was a forced compromise: The economic elite was largely unable to exercise any control over the newly arrived European immigrant, and the immigrant had no interest in the conservative reform impulse of big business. By the 1930s Cleveland was a city that clearly had separate spheres of influence. The industrialists allowed working-class immigrants to run local government so long as they kept taxes low to attract investment, maintained services for businesses, and deferred to the wisdom of the business elite in reaching economic decisions. In return, the working-class immigrant gained prestige and controlled the patronage of municipal government.[36]

The city's business community accepted this arrangement because of its conservatism. Unlike the industrialists of the East Coast, Cleveland's economic elite occupied the far right wing of the Republican party. The industrialists did not look to the public sector for long-term solutions, nor did they need any new infrastructural initiatives from city hall because those had been made in the early twentieth century. This "conservative social contract" between white ethnics and local industrialists would not be broken until Stokes entered city hall in 1967.[37]

Although white ethnics were active in local politics at the ward level, an ethnic did not become mayor of Cleveland until 1941 with the election of Frank J. Lausche, one of the first ethnic mayors of a major U.S. city. The ethnics' rise to power ushered in a period of governance that catered to the immigrants' mistrust of politics: limited government, low taxes, and few services. White ethnic domination of city hall and the city council continued for three decades. Lausche was succeeded by Thomas Burke, an Irish Roman Catholic who served from 1945 to 1951, and Anthony J. Celebrezze, an Italian American who governed the city from 1953 to 1961, when he joined the cabinet of John F. Kennedy. Ralph Locher, the city's law director (city attorney), succeeded Celebrezze. The Lithuanian would serve as mayor until 1967. Although black Clevelanders had benefited under earlier Republican mayoral administrations, in the Lausche era the official policy of city officials toward the concerns of black Clevelanders was neglect. In sum, throughout the 1940s,

1950s, and 1960s Cleveland had "a caretaker type of government that never really appreciated the tremendous changes taking place in the city and never moved to really respond to them." African Americans, more than any other group in the city, would be hurt by this political inaction.[38]

Between 1950 and 1965 Cleveland's black population grew from 147,847 to 279,352, while its overall population shrank from its all-time high of 914,808 to 810,858. In 1950 black residents represented only 16.2 percent of the population, but by 1965 they accounted for 34.4 percent, and more than 99.9 percent of them lived in the rigidly segregated corridor on the East Side. In all, the city of Cleveland had lost approximately 242,000 white people while gaining roughly 128,000 African Americans in just fifteen years. The majority of black migrants who settled in Cleveland after 1945 were attracted by the prosperity brought by World War II and the Korean War. In fact, the majority of black migrants arrived between 1952 and 1958, when local industrial firms recruited actively in the South to solve the city's labor shortage. By 1960 more than 50 percent of the city's black population had been born in the South, a higher proportion than in any other northern city with a large black population.[39]

But as the number of black Clevelanders increased, racial turmoil developed around four main issues: housing, employment, education, and police brutality. Because hardly any new homes had been built in Cleveland's inner city since the depression, the arrival of black migrants brought a severe housing crisis. The majority settled into one of five neighborhoods on the city's East Side. The black poor and working class settled in Central, Hough, and Glenville, while the small black middle class planted its roots in Mt. Pleasant, Lee-Harvard, and Kinsman. The influx of thousands of black migrants into the Central/Hough area made the housing situation worse: By 1960, 28.2 percent of all black-occupied housing was either substandard or dilapidated. But because of the severity of the housing shortage, some families had to rely upon unconventional and unsanitary housing. For instance, it was not uncommon to find black families living in garages, alleys, sheds, attics, cellars, and basements. Although home construction in the suburbs peaked in the 1950s, these developments were off limits to middle-class blacks either through banking discrimination, restrictive covenants, exclusionary zoning laws, or outright intimidation and violence. Because the black middle class was unable to move outside the city, the black poor and working class had to squeeze into the city's traditional slum areas.[40]

Black workers had similar difficulties finding employment. Although many black southerners had come to Cleveland for the economic opportunities, they found racial discrimination in every sector of the job market. Black

Clevelanders represented only 10.5 percent of the metropolitan labor force in 1960 but 31.5 percent of the unemployed. Further, in predominantly black areas the unemployment rate for men was 11.3 percent and 10.1 percent for women, whereas the citywide unemployment rate was 7.5 percent. Among those black residents who had jobs, the majority were confined to the low-est-paid and most menial jobs, both in the public sector and private indus-try. For instance, in the manufacturing trades the majority of black workers served as laborers, while in municipal employment the overwhelming ma-jority of African Americans worked in the service department (public works). One main barrier to equal employment in Cleveland was local labor unions, which openly barred black membership or made it very difficult for African Americans to join.[41]

One obvious consequence of the black employment situation was that the African American family had substantially less income than its white coun-terpart. For example, in 1959 the median family income for a white family was $7,350, compared to $4,768 for African Americans, a difference of $2,582. As a result many black families had to rely upon Aid to Dependent Children (ADC) and general welfare to survive. In fact, in 1962 more than 84 percent of all recipients of ADC and 72 percent of all recipients of general welfare lived in predominantly black areas.[42]

The enlarged black population and its shift into new areas of the city cre-ated new opportunities for black politicians. In 1955 Alexander H. Martin Jr. made history as the first African American to run for mayor of Cleveland. Martin was virtually an unknown in local political circles, but he waged a strong campaign. His platform called for improving public transportation, developing the lakefront for public use, removing racial housing barriers, and kick starting new home construction within the city. Because Martin did not have a strong base of support, he was forced to make boastful comments about himself and derogatory comments about his opponents. When a voter asked about his qualifications, Martin often bragged about his law degree and his twenty-eight-month tour of duty in World War II. Martin also stressed the "independence" of his own campaign by accusing Mayor Celebrezze of be-ing a "bossed" politician, who lacked initiative and leadership and whose political agenda was set by newspaper editors and former mayors. Martin later characterized the Celebrezze administration as "hollow-chested," and "stoop shouldered."[43]

But many citizens, both black and white, did not take the Martin candi-dacy seriously. Critics suggested that he was merely a "guinea pig" in an ex-periment to test the strength of the black vote. Others argued that his real intent was to steal black voters from Celebrezze, an independent Democrat, and help elect the Democratic organization's candidate, Joseph Bartunek. Martin turned both suggestions aside, claiming that he was "in this contest to win."[44]

Martin's candidacy left black politicians and ward leaders in a precarious situation. While the Republican Party supported Kermit Neely, three African American Republicans—John Kellogg, a city council member, and William O. Walker and Lawrence Payne, both ward leaders—withheld their support for Neely because Martin was in the race. Their decision was revolutionary because party members generally endorsed the party's candidate. Because the situation was so unusual, A. L. DeMairolus, the local GOP chairman, excused black ward leaders from making an official endorsement. Two other black ward leaders were up-front, albeit anonymously so, in discussing their reluctance to endorse Neely. One told a local paper, "I'm not going to be caught out on a limb on this Martin thing." Another remarked, "There's no sense taking a chance when there's so much support for Martin in my ward."[45]

On election day Martin took only 10,000 votes. But the importance of his candidacy had nothing to do with the number of ballots cast for him. Martin's campaign signaled to political observers that as the black population grew, black voters would play an important role in local political affairs.

The 1957 council elections were a turning point in the political history of the city—blacks picked up three additional seats on the thirty-three-seat city council; Cleveland would have seven black council members in all, the most of any city in the country. The groundwork for this political takeover was laid in the fall of 1956 as Charles Loeb, a reporter for the *Call and Post*, the city's black newspaper, and Rev. Wade H. McKinney, pastor of Antioch Baptist Church, spearheaded a massive registration campaign that enrolled more than fifty thousand new black voters.[46]

Stokes played an integral role in the 1957 elections as manager of Lowell Henry's successful city council campaign. "It was an easy campaign, pure majority politics," Stokes recalled. For Stokes this election was significant for two reasons. It signaled his entrée into local politics, and black Clevelanders had significantly increased their representation on the city council. In the aftermath of this election Stokes and other community leaders were optimistic that the seven African American council members would act collectively to alleviate some of the problems in the black community. William O. Walker, editor of the *Call and Post*, warned the "lucky seven" not to follow in the footsteps of their predecessors: "Negro councilmen over the years have not compiled any extraordinary records for zealousness in pursuit of their constituents, nor have they always been the most reliable to what is best . . . for black citizens."[47]

However, Charlie Carr, an African American council member, asked black voters to temper some of their enthusiasm. "Although there are seven Negroes [on the city council] we are still but a minority, it takes seventeen votes to adopt legislation and in some circumstances twenty-two votes." Carr's admonition aside, black voters saw seven black faces on the city council, and they were expecting race-based legislation, reinforced by bloc voting, across party lines.[48]

The council member of the late 1950s who was most popular with the black community was Leo Jackson of Ward 24. In the first three months of his first term, Jackson was extremely vocal about the poor conditions of the predominantly black wards, and he publicly held the white community responsible. At a town hall meeting in January 1958 Jackson argued that conditions in the black wards would not improve until real estate agents "stopped creating slums." Likewise, the new council member was upset that bars in black wards were owned by white suburbanites, who also owned many of the overcrowded and subdivided apartment buildings there. To address these concerns Jackson sponsored legislation providing for stiff penalties for slumlords, and he made a strong effort to place a ban on new liquor permits in black areas as well. Jackson was also outspoken about the Cleveland Police Department, which, he argued, allowed vice and crime to flourish in many black communities while vigorously enforcing the law in white areas. In essence, Jackson believed that the white community was ultimately responsible for the problems of black Cleveland. "Crime, slums, enforced idleness, poverty, and other such problems are beyond effective control by the Negro," he stated at a banquet at Antioch Baptist Church in 1959. "If any segment of the black community can be said to have a greater responsibility for these problems," he continued, it belongs to those "who control the conditions which cause and promote them." Unfortunately, other council members placed personal and party interests ahead of the needs of their constituents and rarely matched Jackson's outspokenness. Instead, the other main voice of black protest during the 1950s came from Rev. Wade H. McKinney.[49]

As pastor of the influential Antioch Baptist Church, McKinney occupied a central position in the city's black leadership structure. While many black preachers throughout the city accommodated themselves and their congregations to northern-style racism by remaining on the sidelines in the nascent civil rights movement, McKinney became an outspoken leader on issues affecting the black community. During his thirty-four-year tenure at Antioch (1928–62), the native of Wahoo, Georgia, and alumnus of Morehouse College increased the size of his congregation from seven hundred to more than three thousand. As his congregation grew, so did his visibility in the black community. He served as president of the Cleveland Baptist Association and the Cuyahoga Interdenominational Ministerial Alliance, and in 1951 he became the first black foreman of the Cuyahoga County Grand Jury. Despite his accomplishments and the largely middle-class nature of his congregation, McKinney had a strong identification with working-class and poor black people. For instance, he was instrumental in the founding of Forest City Hospital, an all-black hospital formed because of discrimination in Cleveland's health care system, and he was persistent in his belief that the city's white power structure was the source of the black community's problems. Further, as black migrants continued to enlarge the city's black population throughout the 1950s, he organized several voter registration campaigns in an effort to boost black political power.

As Stokes and other local African American leaders looked at the changing demographics in the city, they realized that they made up the largest potential bloc of voters. When the local white power holders realized that a black political takeover was indeed a possibility, in 1959 they proposed the formation of a metropolitan form of government. Because this proposal was designed to sap black political strength, black voters soundly defeated the measure. Since then, no one has tried to create a county or metropolitan form of government.[50]

Despite the multitude of issues that affected Cleveland's African American community during the second great migration, middle-class black Clevelanders, represented by the local NAACP and Urban League chapters, failed to address the situation aggressively. As the saying went, they considered Cleveland the "best location in the nation for Negroes," largely because throughout its history the city had avoided a major racial confrontation. Further, they often pointed out that Cleveland had the highest number of black judges and city council members of any U.S. city and that the Cleveland Browns and Cleveland Indians were among the first professional sports franchises to integrate their teams. The attitude of the black middle class contributed to the conventional wisdom among whites that black Clevelanders had few, if any, grievances. Further, the conservatism of the black middle class created a leadership vacuum in the city, causing U.S. Rep. Adam Clayton Powell of New York to characterize Cleveland as a "city with no real black leadership."[51]

Local NAACP officials took issue with Powell's characterization. As one of the largest chapters in the country in the 1950s with more than ten thousand members, the local branch was perhaps more active than any other branch in addressing local issues. Founded in 1912 by a group of thirteen black postal workers, the Cleveland NAACP appealed to the city's black middle class while claiming to represent the interests of the black poor and working class.

Throughout the first few decades of its existence the NAACP followed the organization's national policy of quietly challenging discrimination through legal channels. By the mid-1930s the Cleveland chapter had assisted the national NAACP in its fight against lynching and segregated schools and to secure voting rights. But in response to the second great migration, the local branch placed a tremendous emphasis on local issues. Throughout the late 1950s and early 1960s the local NAACP set up picket lines and spearheaded boycotts to obtain equal employment opportunities; it also was behind attacks on the discriminatory policies of the local schools; and the chapter made a determined effort to end all vestiges of northern-style Jim Crow laws. But despite these efforts the local NAACP was still considered somewhat elitist and out of touch with the larger black population.

The Cleveland Urban League encountered similar criticism. Initially established as the Negro Welfare Association of Cleveland in 1917, the Urban League, whose membership ran strongly to black professionals, was formed to confront discrimination in employment and to assist black migrants from the South in making the transition to the city and the factory. During World War II the league obtained jobs for skilled black Clevelanders by negotiating with local employers, and in the immediate postwar period the organization focused on vocational opportunities for black youth. As black frustration grew throughout the city, the Urban League came under intense pressure from the black working class to be more visible in the civil rights arena. However, the officers and members of the league were somewhat reluctant to participate because they did not want to jeopardize the financial support that the league received from the white business community.

Although the city's traditional black leadership class was a bit conservative in addressing the needs of the city's poor and working class, it actively supported the emerging civil rights movement through fund-raising and sympathy protests and by bringing national civil rights leaders such as Martin Luther King Jr. to the city. Because the majority of Cleveland's black migrants were from Alabama, the Montgomery bus boycott, and the later civil rights campaigns in Birmingham and Selma, captured the attention of the city's black community. Further, the *Call and Post,* one of the most popular black weeklies in the country, provided strong coverage of civil rights activity throughout the country, thereby raising the racial consciousness of Cleveland's black population.

2. The Making of a Mayor

AFTER ENTERING politics as a successful campaign manager, Stokes was determined to pursue it as a vocation. In 1958 he took a leave of absence from practicing law to work as an assistant police prosecutor (assistant district attorney). While working under Law Director Ralph Locher, Stokes was amazed at the level of corruption within the Cuyahoga County judicial system. This convinced him that the entire criminal justice system was flawed and that for black people it was a joke. "The people who have, get more, and the people who have not, get more trouble."[1] The city's political community was shocked that same year when Stokes announced his candidacy for the Ohio State Senate. Although he knew he had little chance of winning the countywide position, he entered the race primarily to gauge his support for future elections. "The seriousness of my effort lay in finding out how many people would vote for Carl Stokes just on the pull of the name alone," he wrote. His confidence in his name recognition sprang from his management of the Lowell Henry campaign and his wide involvement in the community. Nonetheless, Stokes went down to defeat with only 5,000 votes.[2]

Two years later he ran for a seat in the Ohio House of Representatives on issues vital to black life: civil rights, housing, welfare, and education. Fellow black Democrats had discouraged him from entering the race because a black Democrat had never been elected to a countywide office. After studying and analyzing voting data, Stokes was convinced that he had a legitimate chance of winning the election. He rented a campaign office at the downtown Hollenden Hotel, hired a campaign manager, and distributed campaign literature. Al Sweeney, city editor of the *Call and Post,* took note: "If effort pays off, Stokes should win handily. He is pulling out all the stops with a headquarters, an aggressive organization, billboard signs, et al." Stokes soon received the influential endorsement of the city's major papers, the *Cleveland Press* and the *Plain Dealer*. His most powerful endorsement, however, came from the Cuyahoga County Democratic Party.[3]

Stokes realized that his biggest challenge was to attract white support. Although black politicians preferred to keep their faces hidden from white voters, Stokes adopted the opposite strategy. "It seemed clear to me," he explained, "that other than those with politically popular names, people vote for you because they know you; if you don't let them know who you are, there is no way in hell they are ever going to vote for you." Stokes recalled that campaigning in white areas was a "marvelous experience." Whenever he entered a room, "there was a chill," and once he opened his mouth, "I had an advantage over the other candidates. I was the alien, the exotic, and I knew I could count on their complete attention." Whites were even shocked that he spoke English; Stokes was certain that the first word they were expecting to hear from him was *motherfucker*.[4]

Stokes was able to capture their attention because he did not fit their stereotypical image of a black man. He was good looking, charming, personable, and articulate. During many of his campaign stops in white areas, he "could feel them melt." Many whites who "disliked Negroes," Stokes believed, "didn't dislike Carl Stokes." Nonetheless, he failed to qualify for the general election, even after a lengthy and controversial recount in the Democratic primary. His narrow defeat—8 votes—largely resulted from his failure to capture white votes. Even so, his campaign for the state house signaled a new era of black political participation in Cleveland. While other aspiring officeholders were content to seek city council seats, Stokes battled the old defeatist attitude that white voters would not support black candidates. Further, as African Americans continued to represent a larger proportion of the city's inhabitants, Stokes was eager to test the limits of the city's black political base.[5]

In 1962 he resigned from the prosecutor's office to focus on building a black power base for another run at the state House. In the interim he had remained visible in the black community through his participation in a number of community and civic organizations. Black residents saw that he represented a different style of politician, that he spoke the language of political power, not just political access. Stokes capitalized on his political distinctiveness in November 1962 when he became the first black Democrat to sit in the Ohio legislature.

He made black issues a priority. During his first term his fair housing bill, which would have outlawed discrimination in housing and real estate, was postponed indefinitely, but he had more success with other legislation.[6]

One successful bill required police officers to take inventory when execut-
ing search warrants; another gave prisoners the right to see an attorney
within seventy-two hours of arrest; and a third increased state support for
children on Aid to Dependent Children (ADC) lists. By representing the
interests of his largely black constituency, Stokes quickly won the respect
and admiration of both party leaders and colleagues, who applauded him
for getting a traditionally conservative legislature to enact liberal measures.
At the end of the 1963 session Stokes was nominated for Freshman of the
Year, and both Republicans and Democrats alike labeled him "a tribute to
the state house."[7]

When he returned to Cleveland at the end of the legislative season in the
spring of 1963, he was considered the "newest member of the Negro power
structure" and was in demand as a public speaker. He used his new platform
wisely. In a speech before the delegates of the National Dental Association,
Stokes urged black dentists and other "professional Negroes" to take a more
active role in the local civil rights struggle. He argued that the black upper
class was "enjoying the fruits of the struggle without getting involved." By
virtue of their absence from picket lines or "in groups which go to see the
Mayor to present grievances," they indirectly supported oppression. Stokes
closed by asking the dentists to become more involved in the "community
struggle for equal rights."[8]

That winter he summoned five friends to his apartment to tell them that
because of the changing racial dynamics in Cleveland, "one of us could be
mayor of this city." According to 1963 U.S. Census figures, the city's 277,600
black inhabitants represented 32 percent of the city's overall population of
858,648. With the continuing influx of black migrants from the South and
white flight to the suburbs, Stokes was certain that a black political takeover
was only a few years away. Although he did not acknowledge it to his close
friends that evening, he concluded that if his predictions were accurate, he
might be able to become mayor.[9]

Meanwhile, a new breed of black leadership was developing alongside an
escalating school crisis in Cleveland. As the second great migration enlarged
the city's African American population, it also caused the school population
to rise from approximately 98,000 students to 149,655 between 1950 and 1965,
with African Americans representing about 54 percent of the district's total
student body. Because the district assigned all students to schools in their
immediate neighborhood, segregation and overcrowding became more intense on the predominantly black East Side. Black parents, including the
Stokeses, developed a long list of grievances: inferior teachers, teacher segre-

gation, a lack of remedial teachers, low teacher expectations, few blacks in administrative positions, high student/teacher ratio, poor physical plant, inadequate social services, and a severe lack of vocational courses. In comparison, schools on the all-white West Side had the most experienced teachers, the best services, the most attractive buildings, and a low student/teacher ratio. Black parents expressed tremendous concern about the school district's apparent discrimination, but school overcrowding became the principal source of their frustration.[10]

Although schools at all levels experienced some congestion, the problem was most apparent at the elementary school level. Between 1952 and 1963 the total enrollment of the city's elementary schools rose from 66,798 students to 92,395, with the second great migration responsible for much of the growth. Because the school board had failed to adequately plan for the massive influx of black children, school administrators used libraries, gyms, storerooms, playrooms, dispensaries, basements, attics, and portables as classroom space. Further, some elementary school students took classes at nearby libraries, churches, community centers, and at the former stadium of the local Negro League baseball team. Despite these emergency measures, thousands of kindergarten students were on waiting lists to begin school during the mid-1950s. In 1956, for example, 1,465 children could not enter kindergarten because the school system had no space for them.[11]

In response to the issue of overcrowding, school officials launched a controversial "relay" program in 1957. With the permission of the Ohio State Board of Education, elementary students at congested schools attended class in double sessions. Half the student body attended school in the morning, the other half in the afternoon. By 1961, 130 classes were operating on double sessions. However, at least seventeen hundred kindergarteners were still on waiting lists that same year.[12]

In response to the board's controversial decision to implement double sessions, black parents demanded that school officials bus black students to half-empty schools on the all-white West Side. When school personnel ignored their demands, concerned parents formed the Relay Parents March to Fill Empty Classrooms and picketed the school board's headquarters.[13]

Once it became clear that the school board would not bus black students to white schools, the Relay Parents continued picketing at school board headquarters throughout September and October 1961. The demonstrations attracted much publicity, and they produced results: The school board agreed to provide transportation from crowded schools to those with space. The Relay Parents had broken the city's pattern for resolving racial conflict, which primarily had been negotiation since the 1930s. But the Relay Parents, inspired to a great extent by the emerging civil rights protests in the South, knew that direct action would attract media attention to the plight of their children and to the discriminatory policies of the school board. The appearance of protesters at the school board building came as a shock to the city's white residents because Cleveland's black leadership class had preferred to quietly negotiate behind the scenes. However, the Relay Parents were outside the black leadership clique. Many were college-educated southerners who had moved to the Glenville area in search of better living conditions for their families and better educational opportunities for their children. When the school board gave in to their demands, the entire city—especially Stokes and other young black politicians—took note, and the atmosphere became conducive to change.

Although the receiving schools appeared to an outsider to be integrated, the bused students were treated, in the words of one observer, "like a containerized shipment of cattle." For instance, once the students arrived at the receiving school with their teacher, they had to remain in their classroom for the entire day. Further, the students could not eat their lunch in the cafeteria, were banned from assemblies, could not take physical education classes, and were barred from schoolwide extracurricular activities. Finally, black students had access to the school restroom at only one designated time per day and were not allowed to see the in-school nurse.[14]

School officials deliberately segregated the bused students because they did not want to antagonize white parents by integrating the schools. Before putting the controversial plan into practice, school administrators explicitly told white parents that busing was only to relieve overcrowding until they could build new schools. The president of the school board was thirty-five-year-old Ralph McCallister. Although he often espoused the rhetoric of a liberal, his leadership during the school crisis convinced African Americans that he had little concern for civil rights issues or black people in general.[15]

McCallister's base of support was white ethnics, the Italian, Polish, Eastern European, and Irish Americans who lived in pockets on the predominantly black East Side. The white ethnics' children, who attended predominantly white schools within their neighborhoods, would be directly affected by any change in school policy. Groups such as the Collinwood Improvement Association and the North American Alliance for White People were at the forefront of the resistance effort. Like their white counterparts in the South, these organizations represented parents who wanted the schools to remain segregated and for there to be no change in race relations in general. They viewed black youngsters as socially pathological and intellectually inferior to their own, and they feared miscegenation. Although not all white politicians were this extreme in their views toward black people, the white ethnic voting bloc was large, and many politicians, including McCallister, were unwilling to antagonize those voters. Appeasing these white parents was why McCallister segregated the bused students, but in the process he angered the Relay Parents, who had now taken on the name of the Hazeldell Parents Association.

When the parents of the bused students discovered the discriminatory treatment at the receiving schools, they received support from the newly formed United Freedom Movement, a civil rights coalition organized to coordinate all of the city's civil rights activity. The formation of the organization was historic in that it represented the first time that the city's black community presented a united front to white civic leaders. Before its formation the black community was deeply divided by class and ideology. The traditional black leadership class, which was represented by ministers, politicians, and the middle class–oriented NAACP and Urban League, often preferred to work behind the scenes to bring about change. They kept the visibility of black frustration low while focusing on symbolic issues. In the eyes of the city's white power structure, the NAACP represented the responsible leaders of the black community, because they did not expect too much, too soon in the area of racial justice. Although the city's middle class supported the NAACP's gradualist approach to race advancement, the city's black poor looked to the Cleveland chapter of the Congress of Racial Equality (CORE) for support.[16]

Young and militant, Cleveland CORE gave voice to Stokes's constituency: the black poor and working class, particularly many southern migrants who had come North in search of the promised land, only to be disappointed. Unlike the NAACP, CORE defined the problems of the city's African American community in terms of housing, jobs, and schools, concerns that the black middle class rarely addressed as it celebrated individual success. For CORE individual success was irrelevant; what mattered was the collective nature of black life in Cleveland, and with support of black southern migrants CORE leaders used aggressive direct-action techniques in an effort to bring about change. Although the NAACP was somewhat uncertain about forming an alliance with CORE and other more militant groups, its survival as an effective civil rights organization required it. Also, discrimination in the schools was an issue that cut across class lines. It affected nearly every black family in the city.[17]

After four weeks of fruitless negotiations with the school board, the United Freedom Movement issued an ultimatum: Fully integrate students into the receiving schools by September 23, 1963, or the public protests would start. The school board ignored it.[18] The move was in keeping with a larger civic tradition in Cleveland that was supported by city hall, the city council, big business interests, newspaper editors, and white ethnic voters. Throughout the city's history the political and economic elite had neglected the serious issues of the city—housing, health and welfare, education, and unemployment—while trumpeting its low taxes and small government. Moreover, the white community had a history of ignoring black grievances, confident that whatever protest African Americans launched would be sporadic, short lived, individualistic—and resolved behind closed doors. But this time the city experienced its first major racial confrontation.[19]

On the morning of September 25, 1963, the United Freedom Movement picketed the Cleveland school board and demanded an end to de facto segregated schools and other discriminatory practices. Protesters toted signs that read "Ghetto Schools Must Go" and "McCallister Is Stalling." Picketing continued throughout the week with the hope that by the following Monday the school board would respond at its next meeting (it met twice a month).[20] It did. The school board agreed to integrate some bused students immediately and all of them by the beginning of the second semester, January 15, 1964, as long as the decision met "sound educational principles," a deliberately vague criterion. The school board also agreed to appoint a human relations committee to develop plans for systemwide integration. In light of the board's concession the United Freedom Movement decided to cease picketing, given that the bused pupils would be fully integrated in less than five months.[21]

As the second semester began in January 1964, United Freedom Movement officials eagerly awaited the board's plan for integrating the 940 bused students. They soon learned that school officials had no intention of honoring the September 1963 agreement. Rather, the school board had decided to implement a "diffusion" plan, which called for mixing about 20 percent of the bused students for a forty-minute period each day. The bused students were to remain separate at all other times.[22]

On Sunday, January 26, the United Freedom Movement staged protests at the receiving schools to publicize what was happening to their children. Its first mass protest was held at Brett Elementary School in the white working-class enclave of Collinwood on Wednesday, January 29. As the Hazeldell parents marched along the sidewalk with placards reading "Down with McCallister" and "We Are Americans, Too," they were met by white hecklers. Tensions quickly developed as whites repeatedly referred to the demonstrators as "dirty niggers." The harassment turned physical when an angry white resident knocked a picketer off the sidewalk. At the other end of the picket line, white hecklers appeared with dogs. According to one journalist, "They tried to make the dogs attack the pickets. The hecklers marched through the line saying 'sic-em, sic-em.'" Although the demonstrators were being harassed, white police officers failed to protect them. Luckily, the protest ended without any injuries. While some were picketing at Brett, other members of the United Freedom Movement staged a sit-in at the board of education as they waited for Superintendent William Levenson to report for work. He never did.[23]

On Thursday the protest spread to Memorial Elementary in Little Italy. The pickets arrived to face a mob of fourteen hundred white people, who attacked the protesters with bricks, guns, knives, and clubs. Some black residents were caught up in the riot, although they were not part of the protest, including a couple whose car windows were broken by baseball bat–wielding whites. Another vehicle occupied by blacks was riddled with bullets as it passed through the same intersection. The mob also attacked reporters Allen Howard and Kenneth Temple of the *Call and Post*. Howard recalled the tense moments as he and Temple arrived at the scene: "I don't know about Ken but I suddenly felt like Daniel in the lion's den. Frightened and speechless, we realized that we were trapped. There we stood with about 200 red-blooded American mobsters staring us right in the eyes. Hate and prejudice dripping from the eyes like blazes of fire." The brutality began. "And then there was a kick, which fortunately landed short of the mark. Then the whole pack rushed forward." Howard managed to stumble toward a police officer and related what had happened. The officer's response: "You went in there and started something. You incited a riot. Don't start anything. Get out of here." In fact, the police did not arrest a single rioter. But the failure of the police to stop the riot and make arrests did not go unnoticed. Temple reported, "Police were present in large numbers and saw repeated examples of violence and lawlessness; yet, not one person was taken to jail, booked, or held for court." When United Freedom Movement officials presented Ralph Locher (who had been mayor since January) with evidence of police neglect, he said, "There comes a time when no matter how many police you have, it is impossible to prevent violence."[24]

The appearance of white counterprotesters was a clear sign that the school crisis, which had begun as a battle between black residents and the school board, had become a struggle over board policy between black and white residents. In many ways the violence at the schools took the focus off the school board's discriminatory policies and turned it on angry parents and protesters. Ralph McCallister had skillfully played black and white residents against each other to deflect attention from the school board.

On Tuesday, February 4, the demonstration spread to the board of education, where the United Freedom Movement staged a sit-in. Tempers flared as white police officers forcibly removed the demonstrators. During the disturbance several protesters were dragged down three flights of concrete stairs. Among them were Hazel Little and May Myrick, both in their fifties. Little told a reporter about the brutality: "I was dragged down three flights of stairs by the police, and when they got me to the bottom of the stairs they threw me into a corner." Although she pleaded with police officers to take her to the hospital, they first took her to jail, along with twenty other protesters, and charged her with obstructing justice and assaulting a police officer. Myrick recalled that the harassment and brutality continued inside the jail: "While in the cell, I was treated horribly, the matrons wanted me to remove my clothing so that they could examine me while policemen and other males were present." Despite the unlawful arrests and brutality, upon their release the protesters staged an impromptu picket line in front of police headquarters.[25]

Stokes and other black community leaders noticed that Mayor Locher and other white politicians were unusually quiet throughout the weeklong disturbance. Although the mayor had no control over the school system, blacks were outraged that Locher refused to mediate the dispute and that he would not protect black protesters from white attacks. When the United Freedom Movement demanded a public investigation into the conduct of police officers in Little Italy, Locher rejected the request, saying it was the United Freedom Movement that had triggered the violence. Despite community outrage, the mayor refused to get involved. Instead, he made a plea "to let law and order prevail in this city."[26]

However, the disturbances did not sit well with the city's business community, which understood that racial violence did not make for a good business climate. Consequently, the business community convinced Locher to negotiate an agreement that called for the immediate integration of the bused pupils into the receiving schools on March 9 and the building of new schools to relieve overcrowding. Days later the school board announced the construction of three elementary schools in the all-black Hazeldell neighborhood to relieve overcrowding at Hazeldell Elementary. However, the United Freedom Movement did not interpret the board's construction plans as an attempt to relieve overcrowding but as a shrewd way of extending the school district's historic pattern of segregation. The board's actions led protesters to shift their focus from the treatment of the bused students to the board's construction plans and an all-out attack on the board policy of neighborhood schools.[27]

The school construction plans were the school board's way of appeasing white parents. School officials sold white parents on the idea of integration by informing them that it was only to be a temporary arrangement until new schools were built. Upon completion of the new schools, the bused students would be resegregated in their neighborhood schools. McCallister understood that this was his only way out of a precarious situation and he used it. Although the school board president had satisfied the concerns of white parents, he would soon come face to face with a unified black community.

When the board announced its construction plans, the United Freedom Movement immediately called for a moratorium on all school construction. School officials rejected it. "Who appointed it [the United Freedom Movement] dictator of policy for the people of Cleveland?" McCallister asked reporters. "We have purchased land and retained architects, and advertising for bids is underway. How far can we go before turning back just because one group wants to select second sites and set school policy?" The school board also refused to discuss plans for the full integration of all students in the district. In response, the United Freedom Movement's school committee announced its own plan for systemwide integration. That proposal called for the elimination of neighborhood schools in favor of centralization, the building of new schools in fringe areas, and expansion of the busing program to alleviate overcrowding instead of building new schools. At the next school board meeting William F. Boyd, the only African American on the board, asked his colleagues to consider hiring William Briggs of the Ohio Civil Rights Commission as a consultant to help the board handle the crisis. "The other board members made no response to Boyd's suggestion," said one observer. A dejected Boyd said, "They just don't recognize the scope of the problem and they just keep opening themselves to further badgering."[28]

In mid-March construction crews arrived at the school sites to prepare the property for excavation. When United Freedom Movement officials learned that construction was under way, they announced that they would picket and maybe even stage a school boycott. "We have to do something to stop the building of these schools and stop our children from being resegregated," said Eddie Gill, the president of the Hazeldell Parents Association.[29]

In an effort to attract additional support for the school protest, CORE held a massive rally with Malcolm X and Louis Lomax, author of *The Negro Revolt*, as principal speakers on Friday, April 3. During his speech Malcolm X made it clear that although he did not believe in integration, he would gladly assist black Clevelanders in their efforts to desegregate the Cleveland public schools: "We will work with you on the school boycotts because we're against a segregated school system. A segregated school system produces children who, when they graduate, graduate with crippled minds. But this does not mean that a school is segregated because it's all black. A segregated school means a school that is controlled by people who have no real interest in it whatsoever."[30]

After fruitless negotiations with the school board, the United Freedom Movement decided to picket at school construction sites to express displeasure with the board's plans. Approximately fifty demonstrators arrived at the Lakeview property on Monday, April 6. As some set up a picket line on the sidewalk, several other protesters decided to form human barricades in an attempt to stop construction. Thirty-year-old Booker T. Eddy shocked other protesters when he crawled beneath a slow-moving truck as it headed onto the construction site. "Eddy had to be dragged from underneath the truck by several policemen," the *Call and Post* reported. After the protesters ignored police requests to get out of the ditch, the police forcibly removed them. Police lifted the female demonstrators out of the ditch, while the men "were simply thrown out." Mounted police quickly grew impatient with the demonstrators and hundreds of onlookers and disbursed the crowd by pushing, shoving, and making arrests. Several spectators had to be restrained from attacking the police. At the end of the afternoon twenty protesters had been arrested.[31]

Protesters used similar techniques the next day as picketing continued at the Lakeview construction site. It quickly turned deadly when Rev. Bruce Klunder, a twenty-seven-year-old white minister and CORE activist, was crushed to death by a bulldozer while he was lying in a ditch. Although the operator of the tractor tried to stop, "his reaction was too slow," said one eyewitness. Klunder died instantly. Within seconds one spectator attacked the operator, and another tried to commander the bulldozer. Minutes after the tragedy police in riot gear arrived to disperse the crowd. Despite the tragedy construction crews resumed work later that day, and that evening angry black youth expressed their ire at Klunder's death by throwing rocks and stones at police cruisers and looting several white-owned stores in the area.[32]

The following night Locher secured an injunction forbidding interference with construction crews and limiting picketing to ten people at a time. The mayor also negotiated an agreement between the United Freedom Movement and the school board that called for a two-week truce on demonstrations while the board restudied its construction plans. The board agreed to stop construction until a panel of experts examined the entire "school segregation problem." The truce was short lived, however. The next day McCallister shocked United Freedom Movement officials by announcing that he would not honor the agreement and that the school board would proceed with its construction plans. United Freedom Movement demonstrators then staged a series of sit-ins at board headquarters over the weekend before Common

Pleas Court Judge John V. Corrigan issued a temporary restraining order against further demonstrations at school headquarters. The United Freedom Movement responded by calling for a one-day boycott of the schools.[33]

The boycott on Monday, April 20, 1964, was a success. More than 92 percent of all black students shunned their public schools that day and attended instead the more than eighty "freedom schools" set up throughout the city. The day's curriculum centered on African and African American life, history, and culture. Also, members of both the CORE and NAACP youth councils spoke to students about their role in the civil rights movement "so that the next generation might enjoy freedom."[34]

According to several observers, the Afrocentric curriculum appealed to the students. Most appeared genuinely interested in learning about their history. At the end of the day each student received a "freedom diploma" stating that she or he had participated in the "stayout" for freedom and completed the requirements for the experiment in "democratic education." The only casualty of the boycott was five-year-old Randy Adkins, who was killed in a traffic accident on her way home from a freedom school. Her grieving parents told reporters that they hoped the tragedy would remind the public of the school board's resistance to school integration.[35]

Although the boycott was a victory for the black community, which interpreted it as a mandate to change the board policy of neighborhood schools, the school board continued with its school construction plans. Because the injunction had discouraged the continuation of disruptive tactics, United Freedom used the courts to try to stop construction and to change the systemwide pattern of segregation. The first battle, in April, was an appeal of the court order limiting the number of pickets at the school sites. Judge John J. Corrigan quickly rejected the appeal in the name of public safety. United Freedom Movement lawyers then filed a $1 million taxpayers' suit in April challenging the awarding of construction contracts and attacking the construction plans as inadequate. The suit was soon dropped. In May the NAACP filed a suit on behalf of Charles Craggett and twenty schoolchildren, charging the school board with fostering school segregation. The NAACP was hoping to suspend school construction until the suit was resolved. But when a federal judge refused to suspend construction, the suit became entangled in the legal system and was eventually dropped.[36]

While the yearlong protest failed to desegregate the schools, it was a victory in several respects because it unified the city's black community to an unprecedented degree. Although the broader black community and the United Freedom Movement continued to have ideological differences, members of the United Freedom Movement played them down. Because school segregation and discrimination affected nearly every black family in the city, the entire community understood the importance of racial unity as it confronted the city's white power structure. The *Call and Post* writer Charles Loeb celebrated the school boycott as a historic display of unity: "Last week was really 'The Week That Was.' Cleveland's Negro Citizens wrote for the record an epic of racial solidarity that will not soon be forgotten by the Cleveland power structure."[37]

The failed school protest also helped black Clevelanders understand the limitations of negotiation, direct action, boycotts, and using the legal system in bringing about permanent change. They turned to politics. By late 1964 it was clear not only that Locher would seek re-election but that he was the heavy favorite. Black residents knew that they could not stand another two years of Locher's rule.

Stokes was active in the school demonstrations, but he did not play an active leadership role. As a young politician Stokes had no desire to upstage the grassroots leadership of the United Freedom Movement for headlines. His willingness to participate in the school protests illustrated to many of his constituents that he was not concerned about repercussions from the white power structure. Further, his visible presence during the nine-month crisis convinced the black poor and working class that he identified with their struggle, and it further strengthened their confidence in him as a man of the people.

As Stokes geared up for a relatively easy re-election bid, it became clear that his presence during the school crisis had not gone unnoticed. On one of his campaign billboards, someone crossed out his name and wrote: "Professional Agitator for Civil Rights Demonstrations." Although Stokes did not appreciate their actions, the vandals told Stokes two things: that he was gaining a reputation as a black power politician, and that although West Side whites probably didn't like him, they at least knew who he was. Stokes easily won re-election to the Ohio House in the fall of 1964.[38]

Shortly after returning to Columbus, Stokes became embroiled in a redistricting dispute. When Republican governor James Rhodes drafted a plan that favored the state's rural areas, urban Democrats labeled it discriminatory. Stokes, however, supported the governor's proposal because it meant that Cuyahoga County probably would elect three black state representatives. Although the chairman of the county Democratic Party pressured Stokes to vote against the bill, he stood firm, and the Republican plan narrowly passed.[39]

Stokes broke party ranks again during the heated debates about congressional redistricting. In 1964 the U.S. Supreme Court ruled that Ohio's congressional district had to be redrawn. Cuyahoga County had four congressional districts, with black voters solidly lumped in the Twenty-first. Albert

Porter, the chairman of the county Democratic Party, then drafted a proposal to place 50 percent of the black vote in another district in an effort to give his party more leverage in Republican-dominated areas. Stokes was livid, because Porter's plan also was a deliberate attempt by the county Democrats to nullify any possibility of black representation in Congress. Other black leaders, including Harold Williams of the NAACP, supported Stokes. Williams submitted an alternate proposal that made the Twenty-first Congressional District a majority-black district, and Stokes and other African American leaders made no secret of their motives. "We'll be frank with you," Stokes said. "We hope to someday elect a Negro Congressman from the Twenty-First district." John Kellogg, a black member of the city council, saw the measure in more psychological terms, arguing that the possibility of aspiring to Congress would give "the young Negro in politics some hope. We can get better candidates if there is hope that he can rise from a precinct committeeman to U.S. Congress." Despite the black community's opposition, the legislature narrowly approved the Democrat-sponsored plan. Early the next year Stokes assembled a group of NAACP lawyers, who filed suit in federal court charging that the newly implemented redistricting plan violated the principle of one man, one vote. Three years later the Supreme Court rejected the plan. And in 1968 Louis Stokes, Carl's older brother, became the first member of Congress from the predominantly black Twenty-first Congressional District.[40]

County Democrats were shocked that Carl Stokes had crossed party lines in an effort to boost black political power. They were accustomed to dealing with black officials whose goals were limited to receiving patronage. In many ways the Democratic officials felt they had been double-crossed, because they had endorsed Stokes in 1962. Stokes was well aware that since the 1930s black voters had been an essential base of support for the party, only to be ignored after election day. Although he was a registered Democrat, his actions signaled to the county organization that he placed racial allegiance in front of party loyalty.

As his popularity and visibility in the black community increased, he set his sights on city hall. "By the Spring of 1965, I had begun to see that I had a fighting chance to run for mayor." That February Jean Murrell Capers, a former council member, and Geraldine Williams, a community activist, had approached Stokes about running for mayor. Stokes told them that if they collected at least twenty thousand signatures, he would enter the race. While they were gathering signatures, Stokes privately decided to enter the race; he and Al Sweeney, political editor of the *Call and Post,* had analyzed voter registration and concluded that Stokes had a legitimate chance of winning because blacks now accounted for 39 percent of the city's voters.[41]

Rumors quickly spread throughout the region that Stokes was considering a run for city hall. He was speaking across the state on behalf of his fair housing proposal, now out of committee, and reporters frequently asked him to comment on his political future. He said that he was still undecided, but he made it clear that he did not believe the conventional wisdom, that a black man could not become mayor of Cleveland. "I think the time has come for Negroes, especially, to unshackle their political thinking. To take the defeatist line that a Negro can't win. That is a form of psychological slavery," he told reporters. He then told them that he would base his decision on several factors, including the city's economic condition, his ability to secure financial support, and his potential opponents.[42]

Stokes was fully aware that he had the right résumé to capture city hall: He was personally familiar with the harsh realities of urban poverty, he was a veteran of the civil rights movement, and he had a track record of political independence. Thus racially conscious black voters would believe that he would not sell out to the city's white establishment. Moreover, Stokes had the all-important intangibles: intellect, good looks, charisma, and personality.[43]

There were of course other, more established black politicians throughout the city, but Stokes was by far the best prospect for several reasons. Most important, Stokes had proved that he could capture biracial support because he had been elected to the state legislature two times from an at-large district in Cuyahoga County. Although the city council now had ten black members, all ten came from solidly black wards. Moreover, Stokes represented something many of the other black politicians did not: independence and sincerity. For example, half of the black council members—Charie Carr, George Forbes, Clarence Gaines, Leo Jackson, and John Armstrong—had filibustered Kellogg's March 1965 proposal to commemorate Martin King's Nobel Peace Prize by proclaiming Martin Luther King Day. Further, because the city's congressional districts favored white voters, no black member of Congress stood in Stokes's way, and black judges in the city had a relatively low level of popularity.[44]

To the disappointment of county Democrats, Stokes entered the race as an independent to force a four-way contest. The other candidates were Locher, running as a Democrat, Republican Ralph Perk, and Ralph McCallister, the school board president, who also filed as an independent. On the day he announced his candidacy, Stokes warned his supporters to close ranks for the upcoming campaign. "I will not become embroiled in ward fights or councilmanic races . . . we cannot afford to become divisive . . . our objective is City Hall."[45]

At a campaign meeting in late May, Stokes told his supporters that "issues, and not race" would be the focus of his campaign. "We have too many issues to discuss rather than race," he said in an emotional tone. "It is on the issues that I will wage my campaign. I feel that if the voters will permit me to discuss my grasp of them with the other candidates in a debate, I am quite certain how they will vote." Consequently, he did not want "anyone to judge me as Carl Stokes, the Negro, but as Carl Stokes, the candidate." It is "obvious that I am a Negro," he said. He later appointed two prominent African Americans to direct his campaign: Dr. Kenneth Clement, a local surgeon, would help him capture white support, and William O. Walker, editor and publisher of the *Call and Post,* would shape public opinion through his widely read newspaper. Their involvement gave his campaign instant credibility.[46]

The *Cleveland Press* and *Plain Dealer* ignored Stokes as he assembled his power base. Denied an opportunity for free publicity, Stokes took his message of reform directly to the people, speaking in churches, community centers, parks, hospitals, and homes, where he encountered little criticism because these voters were largely familiar with his strong record as a legislator.[47]

Throughout the summer of 1965 Stokes spent the majority of his time solidifying his power base on the black East Side by stressing his campaign themes: employment, health care, urban renewal, housing, crime, recreation, mass transit, and race relations. His campaign received a tremendous boost when Martin Luther King Jr. and the Special Project Committee for Voter Registration and Citizenship launched a campaign to register 40,000 black voters. Thousands of eligible voters responded, particularly those who had migrated from the South after World War II.[48]

As an independent, Stokes did not have to run in the October primary. And because the general election was scheduled for November 2, Stokes did not actively campaign until late September. On September 25 Stokes issued a written broadside against Mayor Locher concerning the city's discriminatory hiring practices. Stokes called the failure of Locher to appoint a black cabinet member, a black department head, or a black commissioner "inexcusable" in a city that was 37 percent black. It meant that one-third of the city's population had no voice in the day-to-day policy decisions at city hall. Stokes also argued that the city's failure to promote black police officers was equally shameful and that Locher was the reason for the city's current racial crisis because of his failure to adequately address the city's urban renewal problems and his silence during the school controversy.[49]

As the Stokes campaign gained momentum, the county Democratic leader Albert Porter and James Stanton, the city council president, went to great lengths to keep Stokes from becoming mayor. During the first week of October, Stanton called a meeting with the city's black Democratic council members to remind them that as Democrats they were to obligated to support Locher. After the meeting several black council members refused to confirm or deny reports that they were supporting Locher. Their actions did not surprise Stokes: "They always ran scared, staying safely within the fold of party dominance. They had a persistent and debilitating lack of faith in or understanding of the black community. They were as certain as Bert Porter that I would lose, and they were not about to jeopardize their standing with the mayor and the party by supporting me." Likewise, Porter specifically told African American city employees that if they failed to support Locher, they would lose their jobs. Thus it was common to see black city employees wearing or distributing "Locher for Mayor" campaign literature.[50]

Throughout the campaign many black council members refused to support Stokes. The only two who endorsed him were John Armstrong and George White. Other black council members, such as Clarence Gaines and Warren Gilliam, actively campaigned for Locher in their wards. Although seven of the nine black Democrats on the council did not support Stokes, many African American ward committee members and precinct workers campaigned actively for him.[51]

Stokes had alienated the city's black council members in mid-June when he moderated a community bloodletting symposium concerning their ineffectiveness as politicians. Sponsored by the Men Associated for Progress, 250 concerned citizens heard community leaders verbally assault the city's ten black council members. Although all ten council members were invited to the affair, only one, John Kellogg, a Republican, accepted the invitation. Although the other nine council members were not there to defend themselves, community leaders used the forum as an opportunity to express their disgust with their representatives' conservatism. "These councilmen should be made to realize that there is nothing wrong with speaking up for the people who put them in office," said Stanley Tolliver, a lawyer. Further, he remarked that the council members were losing respect from the "white man" by being silent on important issues. "The trouble is they haven't shown themselves as men," he concluded. Next, Richard Gunn, another lawyer, reminded the all-black audience that black council members were noticeably absent whenever racial strife occurred in the city. Gunn, who had been arrested just the week before while sitting in the mayor's office, told the crowd that while he and other United Freedom members were trying to meet with the mayor, several black council members were "busy circulating petitions for Mayor Locher." But Gunn placed much of the blame on black voters who failed to hold them accountable. When Stokes was asked whether an open forum was the best vehicle for such a discussion he answered in the affirmative.[52]

The Stokes campaign had a shoestring budget of $44,000, raised largely through individual and private contributions. The limited funding negated any possibility of running a highly professional campaign. It was strictly grassroots, door-to-door campaigning. This strategy worked well in black wards. But Porter had barred Stokes from speaking at any Democratic ward meetings, which hindered his entrée to white voters.[53]

Stokes tried to campaign two days per week on the West Side, where he made an attempt to allay white fears about black governance. "I want to get the Negro question out of the way; then we can talk about the issues. My election would not mean a Negro takeover, it would not mean the establishment of a Negro cabinet. My election would mean the mayor just happened to come from the Negro group," he would say. At the City Club Forum on October 22 Stokes used the same strategy, telling the crowd that he was not running as a Negro but as a lifelong Clevelander.[54]

The *Call and Post* called for black voters to unite behind Stokes on the eve of the election. In a dramatic front-page appeal Walker placed Stokes's destiny in the hands of black voters: "Will the Negro voters give him the support that he so well deserves?" Walker asked. In Walker's eyes black Clevelanders were going to be judged for years to come on whether they supported Carl Stokes. The publisher believed that this election was an opportunity for black Clevelanders to be "participants in a historic decision." Walker ended his editorial by making a strong appeal to race pride: "The Negro who votes against Stokes is a traitor; the Negro who cowardly stays home to keep from voting is worse. When the polls open on Tuesday the Negro race, not Carl Stokes, will be on trial."[55]

On election day Locher beat Stokes by 2,142 votes, 87,858 to 85,716. Although Stokes collected a record-high 85.4 percent of the black vote, only 3 percent of his votes came from predominantly white areas. Although he accepted defeat, his supporters urged him to ask for a recount when they heard rumors of voter fraud in predominantly white precincts. "It should be determined for the benefit of all the people of Cleveland, just who did win the November 2 election. We should know what the voters really intended," Stokes proclaimed. Many of his supporters concluded that white voting registrars stole the election. Their suspicions were confirmed when it was learned that a white police officer had been dispatched to bring in "a bag of missing votes" two hours after the polls closed. Stokes solicited $11,000 from supporters and paid for the recount, but Locher was ruled the winner. Although Stokes was disappointed in his defeat, he still considered it a moral victory:

"We had taken on an incumbent who had the support of the two newspapers, the local Democratic party, organized labor and his twelve thousand city employees and we had come within one percent of beating him. As far as I was concerned, we had beaten not only Locher but the whole traditional establishment of political power, in two years we would take it for good."[56]

Five months later local events propelled Stokes into the national spotlight. In April 1966 the U.S. Commission on Civil Rights held hearings in Cleveland to determine the extent of the city's racial problems. Many members of the black community saw the locally televised hearings as a wonderful opportunity to air their grievances against Locher and his administration. Locher and his lieutenants feared a public relations disaster for a city that had so far avoided a large-scale race riot. During the next seven days black citizens told of inadequate housing, segregation, job discrimination, and police brutality, which was by far the most explosive issue during the hearings.[57]

Throughout the Civil Rights Commission's session on police-community relations, black witnesses aired their grievances against the Cleveland Police Department. Their complaints centered on a host of problems: police brutality; insufficient police protection; police harassment; dual systems of law enforcement that meant slow response time in black areas; the lack of black officers on the force; and the discriminatory nature of police personnel assignments. While the majority of the problems within the department stemmed from its negrophobia, some of these concerns were directly related to the lack of black officers on the force. For instance, in 1965 only 133 of Cleveland's 2,021-member police force were African Americans. Further, of this group only two were above the rank of patrolman, and both were sergeants. In 1961 the local NAACP had demanded a set of initiatives in an effort to improve police-community relations, primarily a police review board to hear citizen complaints, a thorough recruiting program aimed at African Americans, and a community relations program. The mayor and police officials ignored all these suggestions.[58]

At the end of the hearings Stokes was one of several community leaders who made extended remarks. He blamed the city's racial tensions on Locher and other local officials who fostered discrimination in employment, housing, and urban renewal. He concluded by pleading for officials from the U.S. Department of Housing and Urban Development (HUD) to freeze urban renewal grants to Cleveland until these problems were addressed. The weeklong hearings showed the city's white community how bad things really were in Cleveland, and it validated many of the complaints that black Clevelanders had made for years. If nothing else, the hearings revealed that the city's racial powder keg was about to explode.[59]

If black frustration was high throughout the city, it was reaching a boiling point in Hough, an all-black ghetto that stretched for two miles from East 55th Street to University Circle on the East Side. Hough was filled with rows of dilapidated houses, empty lots, taverns, and store-front churches. Although Hough had been solidly white working class in the 1940s and early 1950s, the second great migration and the city's poorly planned urban renewal programs combined to turn it into an all-black slum overnight. Beginning in the mid-1950s with the Longwood, Garden Valley, and St. Vincent Projects, Cleveland's urban renewal program displaced several thousand residents and offered very little relocation assistance.

In the 1960s the Urban Renewal Department initiated several more disastrous projects, most notably Erieview and University-Euclid. Erieview was designed in 1961 with the hope of creating 4.7 million square feet of new office space and fifty-five hundred luxury apartments downtown. Once the land was cleared, however, developers could not attract investors. Instead, the Erieview project became nothing more than a "wasteland of parking lots." The city's most ambitious project was University-Euclid. The project stretched about three miles, from the eastern end of Hough to the University area, and included plans to rehabilitate more than four thousand units in 1961 alone. Five years later the department had exhausted its budget, having rehabilitated only six hundred units. Other reasons for the failure of the city's urban renewal program were inadequate planning, slow execution of plans, poor relocation assistance, and lax enforcement of housing codes. In fact, the city's urban renewal commissioner, James Friedman, testified before the U.S. Civil Rights Commission in 1966 that the department's policy was to allow housing in urban renewal areas to deteriorate so the land would be less expensive to buy and clear. However, no new housing was ever built, and the families that moved out rarely received relocation assistance. Forty million dollars and six thousand acres later, the nation's most ambitious urban renewal program had nothing to show for its efforts. By the mid-1960s the city had displaced thousands of poor families, who in turn had crowded into Hough.[60]

By 1965 Hough was 87.9 percent black and home to the city's poorest residents. The median income throughout the city was $6,985, but in Hough it was only $4,050. Contributing to the problem of low wages was a high level of unemployment and underemployment. The unemployment rate for Hough residents was much higher than in any other area of the city. For black men the unemployment rate was a whopping 14.3 percent, and it was 19.1 percent for black women. Consequently, although Hough represented only 7.3 percent of the city's overall population, it contained 19 percent of all the welfare cases in Cleveland. Likewise, more than one-third of the 1,372 children born in the

Hough area in 1966 had single mothers, and more than half were born to teenagers. The infant mortality rate in Hough was twice that in the rest of the city, and Hough had twice as many residents on Aid to Dependent Children. Hough was also an unsafe place to live. In 1965 roughly 20 percent of all major crimes in the city were committed in Hough. Adding to the frustration of Hough residents was that whites owned virtually all of the area's businesses, and absentee white landlords owned many of the homes. All these factors, coupled with inadequate city services, gave residents little incentive to take care of their community.[61]

As expected, racial hostilities between blacks and whites were high in the spring of 1966. Several racial skirmishes occurred along the northern border of Hough, which was surrounded on both sides by poverty-stricken blacks and lower-income white ethnics. This community, more commonly referred to as Sowinski, had historically been known for its hostility to African Americans. The recent tensions had begun in January 1966 when a group of Hough youngsters assaulted a white father and his son. As the weather warmed up, interracial fighting increased, but this time many attacks were by white youths on black youngsters. Much of the interracial tension in Sowinski occurred because black residents had to travel through the neighborhood to get to Sowinski Park, a popular hangout for black youth. By late May and early June the attacks had become more violent as white gangs beat and robbed several groups of black teenagers. To make matters worse, when community leaders approached the police to secure better police protection, the police consented only to monitor the situation. But they did not. When black youth would approach white officers about being attacked, the police would not even take their report, exacerbating tensions.[62]

On June 22, with tensions already high, two black youths were brutally attacked in Sowinski. A crowd gathered afterward and confronted police with evidence, including a description of the assailants and their automobile. However, the police refused to investigate or pursue the attackers. Soon after, black youths began protesting by throwing rocks and bottles at police cars on Superior Avenue. On the following day Hough area residents met with city and police officials three times, but the city took little action to resolve their complaints. That night, fueled by the frustration and anger of black ghetto life, groups of young people from Hough and Superior destroyed property in those neighborhoods and continued throwing rocks at white motorists. In the course of the rock throwing, a white man whose car had been struck by a rock shot a ten-year-old boy. When the youths linked the car to the owner of a community grocery store, Gale's Supermarket, they immediately gutted the store with firebombs, causing $45,000 worth of damage. Several other white-owned businesses were vandalized as well, but none as extensively as Gale's. Window breaking and rock throwing continued throughout the next day, but by Saturday night all was calm; the Cleveland Police Department had dispatched two hundred officers, most of them white, to the area. The officers showed unusual restraint in dealing with the rioters, and many members of the black community commended them for their actions. No one reported incidents of police brutality or misconduct toward the rioters. On Saturday, June 25, at a meeting between community leaders and Locher, black residents aired grievances and made specific recommendations concerning police-community relations and urban renewal.[63]

Since Wednesday the Locher administration had tried to use a Band-Aid to close the gaping wound in the community. At Locher's urging the Greater Cleveland Office of Economic Opportunity (GCOEO) announced a series of employment and recreational programs designed to keep idle and riot-prone youth busy through the summer. The city announced that it was prepared to spend $1.5 million on programs (including those offered by the GCOEO) to keep inner-city youth off the street. Although the black community expressed joy at this announcement, many concerned citizens wondered why the city had not established these programs sooner.[64]

Fifty black leaders placed these and other concerns on the table when they met with city officials on July 5 at a gathering that was broadly designed to ease racial tensions. The black leaders presented Locher with an eight-point program aimed at reducing tensions between the races and ameliorating the problems in the black community. Several recommendations dealt specifically with the police. The group asked that the police be instructed to treat all people with respect upon arrest, that "specially trained" police be sent into hostile areas until order had been restored, and that the shooting of the ten-year-old be fully investigated. The leaders also asked that the mayor appoint a special committee to make further recommendations to ease the tensions. They ended with a wide appeal for racial harmony. Locher and John McCormick, the safety director (to whom both the police and fire chiefs reported), agreed to the program.[65]

The eight-point peace pact was historic because it was one of the few times that Locher had made any effort to improve race relations, but it was too late. A symbolic, though well-intended, peace treaty could not remedy years of frustration about poor housing, police brutality, job discrimination, and unequal schooling. Many black residents were simply too angry by then to walk away.

On the evening of Monday, July 18, 1966, a sign appeared on the door of the popular white-owned 79ers Café in Hough: "No water for niggers." When he noticed that a large crowd of angry black youths had gathered outside his tavern, the frightened owner called police. Rioting began within minutes. When the police arrived, the crowd objected to their presence. As the crowd moved toward East 79th Street, rocks, bricks, and bottles began to fly. Soon, three chain grocery stores, a drugstore, and a clothing store were on fire as the crowd chanted, "Burn, baby, burn." The violence continued until 4 A.M., then resumed and continued throughout Tuesday.[66] Looting began early in the day, and as night fell, rioters and police exchanged gunfire. Realizing that his safety forces were no match for angry black youth, Locher summoned the national guard.[67] Guardsmen sealed off the riot-torn area, but sporadic looting and firebombing continued throughout Wednesday. By Thursday morning the riot had spread beyond Hough into Central and farther east toward the working-class suburb of East Cleveland. Things turned peaceful over the weekend, and by Monday, one full week since the start of the uprising, all was back to normal.[68]

The toll was high. Four black civilians were killed, police and civilian injuries numbered in the hundreds, police had made endless arrests, and property damage was estimated at $1 million to $2 million. After it was over, members of the white establishment were eager to know why the riot had occurred. For African Americans the answer was clear: the failure of city leaders to address the problems in the black community.[69]

White leaders asked Judge Thomas Parino of the Common Pleas Criminal Court to convene a special session of the county grand jury to make an "official" determination of the reasons for the unrest. After hearing a week of testimony, the grand jury presented its findings. The first section of the report concluded that the riot was "organized, precipitated, and exploited" by a relatively small group of "disciplined professionals" who had communist leanings. It named Lewis Robinson and Harllel Jones as principal agitators. The report described Robinson as a violent black nationalist and Jones as a "black power apostle" with active memberships in the Revolutionary Action Movement and the Deacons for Defense, both of which espoused the rhetoric of self-defense and rejected King's principle of nonviolence. The grand jury report also commended local police "for their efforts to maintain law and order in the face of great personal danger." The first section concluded with suggestions for tougher legislation against rioters, such as a one- to twenty-year prison term for anyone instigating a riot or for anyone assaulting a police officer or fire fighter who was on duty. The second section of the report examined the underlying socioeconomic conditions in Hough. The grand jury found that "poverty and frustration, crowded by organized agitators, served as the uneasy backdrop for the Cleveland riots." The report listed several inequities that contributed to the riot, most notably substandard housing, "woefully inadequate recreational facilities," "sub-standard educational facilities," and the "denial of economic opportunities." The grand jury did not mention police brutality.[70]

Mayor Locher and other white city leaders were pleased with the grand jury's findings. Locher seemed to take pride in the finding that communist agitators had caused the turmoil: "This Grand Jury had the guts to fix the approximate cause—which had been hinted at for a long time, that subversive and Communist elements in our community were behind the rioting." In contrast, Stokes and other black leaders labeled the report a whitewash, because the grand jury had gone to great lengths to remove "the liability of the city administration as the immediate precipitating causes of the riot." In Stokes's opinion grand jurors were acting "in the old Cleveland style of sweeping the city's mistakes under the rug." Stokes then wrote a three-page letter to U.S. Attorney Merle McCurdy requesting that he convene a federal grand jury to investigate the county grand jury's findings. In his letter Stokes questioned why Robinson and Jones had been singled out and noted that the grand jury had been unable to find any law under which to indict them. Stokes also pointed out that two undercover Cleveland police officers had spent a year in the Hough area infiltrating so-called nationalist and communist organizations, yet in their report they stated that they had no knowledge of "pre-riot planning" by Robinson, Jones, or communists. In addition, Stokes condemned the grand jury's failure to investigate police misconduct, which was widespread during the weeklong riot.[71]

In response to the controversial grand jury report, the black community decided to hold its own week of hearings, which were run by Baxter Hill, director of Cleveland CORE, and sponsored by the Cleveland Citizens Committee, an ad hoc citizens group. Testifying before a citizens' panel of ministers, teachers, social workers, and blue-collar workers, scores of witnesses told of inferior housing conditions, poor city services, job discrimination, and woeful merchant-customer relations. But the most common theme was police brutality during the riot, a side of the story that had gone untold.

One of the first witnesses was Diana Townes, who, along with her toddler son, had been severely wounded by police bullets in an altercation on the fourth night of the disturbance. Her husband, Henry, testified that as he and his wife and child tried to leave the burning area, a police cruiser had blocked their driveway. As he cut across the grass, several officers told him to stop the car and get out, but he would not; police and guardsmen began pulling his wife's hair. Someone wielding a billy club knocked Henry to the floor of the car; as his foot slipped off the brake, the car lunged forward, and the police started shooting. As Henry put his hand on the brake, they continued to shoot until someone yelled, "They're not going anywhere! Stop shooting." But by then both Diana and their three-year-old son were critically injured. The boy sustained extensive brain damage, as did she; she eventually lost her right eye. The officers in question were never charged with a crime. Henry Townes was arrested for aggravated assault.[72]

Testimony also shed light on the death of Percy Giles. A Mr. Lewis related that he had been walking toward the corner of East 86th and Hough when rioters started throwing bottles at police. The "policemen jumped out and started firing in the air," telling everyone to disperse. While the police were breaking up the crowd, someone threw a bottle that nearly hit a cop. "This time there was shooting, one policemen was taking a dead aim with a shotgun . . . and I saw his hand shake . . . and seen smoke from the gun and this fellow next to me [Giles] hit the ground." When another resident tried to help Giles, a police officer commanded, "Don't touch him." Lewis considered the Giles shooting a "cold-blooded murder." The shooter wore a Cleveland Police Department uniform and was never identified.[73]

What happened to the Townes family and Percy Giles were two of the more spectacular episodes of alleged police misconduct. Much more common was police intrusion into private homes. Edward Adams of 7401 Elk Avenue told the panel that he was watching the action from his front porch, when the police drifted toward his apartment. As the police shouted, threw tear gas, and fired their weapons, the Adamses ran to their bedrooms. Next, the police shot down the front door to the apartment and forced everyone onto the floor at gunpoint. The shooting particularly enraged the Adamses because no one was shooting at the officers. But police would later use the familiar refrain that they were looking for snipers. Adams further testified that many of his neighbors were subjected to the same treatment. Bertha Pollard said police kicked their way into her home and forced her outside at gunpoint to stand in the rain in her pajamas. As she attempted to find shelter under a tree, police told her: "Goddammit, get out from under the tree, get in the rain." Pollard was later charged with disturbing the peace.

Geneva Burns was arrested too, and her home ransacked, after her son observed police officers setting a fire to a home. Wallace Kelley was shot in the neck by police as he stood in his living room. He remembered the scene vividly: "I was in the living room, my sister was in the bedroom . . . and when I faced the screen door, and I seen a great big ball of fire . . . and it hit me." His family tried to take him to the hospital, but they were confronted by eight or nine officers with guns drawn. The police volunteered to take him to the hospital. He nearly died during his weeklong hospital stay, but he eventually recovered from all his injuries. Kelley was never charged with a crime; neither was the officer who shot him.[74]

To many Hough residents, the police brutality seemed planned because, many testified, they did not recall seeing police who were wearing their badges once the national guard arrived. Harllel Jones reported, "I said Officer, how come none of y'awl got on your badges? He told me that 'we have to buy these shirts . . . when a riot occurs, you know people get funny and they grab you and they will grab that badge and it will tear shirts and we don't want to pay for it.'" Asked her recollection by a panel member, Bertha Pollard said bluntly, "They didn't have no badges on them."[75]

The panel's published report said that the purpose for holding the hearings was that the grand jury had failed to give adequate emphasis to the underlying causes of the riot. "Further," it read, "there seems to be some unwillingness on the part of city officials and law enforcement agencies to deal with these acts of violence and humiliation against the black community despite the fact that first hand witnesses and ample evidence is available." The final report also stated that for the black community to allow the grand jury report to go unquestioned and unchallenged was to give approval to an injustice. Throughout its report the committee refuted many of the grand jury's findings while making several recommendations, many aimed at improving police-community relations.[76]

Black activists also blamed Locher for the disturbance. Many felt that the Hough riot could have been avoided if Locher had shown more compassion to his black constituents throughout his tenure. Two area residents, in particular, considered the riots to be the black community's breaking point with Locher. Nona Bailey, a housewife, and Charlie Day, a truck driver, spearheaded a recall effort to remove Locher from office. By law they had thirty days to collect forty-seven thousand signatures from people who had voted in the 1965 mayoral election. If they succeeded, Locher would have four days to resign. If he refused, the city council would set a date for a referendum on his removal. If a majority voted for his removal, he would be ousted and the safety director would serve as acting mayor until a special election was held. Asked why he was trying a maneuver that had never been tried before, Day gave an uncompromising answer: "I find the city has been lacking in leadership for four years. There have been broken promises. There have been riots for no reason."

Although Day was echoing the sentiments of black residents, local political figures, both black and white, repudiated the recall effort. Ester E. Spaulin, director of the Citizens League of Greater Cleveland, felt that the recall effort would exacerbate the tension: "I think it's most unfortunate, the community is already torn by dissension. There would be nothing to gain from this." Council member George Blaha, who represented Ward 33, a white area, also felt that the recall would divide the community. James Stanton, the city council president, called the recall effort unfair. He added: "We hold an election for mayor every two years, that's enough for the voters to approve or disapprove of the incumbent or to choose any mayor." Black politicians also lashed out at the recall attempt. One black city council member feared that the recall would make Locher a martyr by evoking both support and sympathy for him. Another predicted flatly, "They won't get the signatures."[77]

Many Locher supporters were not convinced that this effort was solely the idea of Bailey and Day. Some believed that Stokes was behind the move and that he was just getting an early start on the 1967 campaign. An editorial in the *Press* also suggested that Day and Bailey were "politically inspired." Suspicions about Stokes's involvement arose after Geraldine Williams, Stokes's 1965 campaign secretary, aligned herself with the effort. But Stokes flatly denied any association and even criticized the recall attempt. Critics of the move felt that the recall drive could actually backfire and help Locher. Anthony Garofoli, city council representative from Ward 19, a white ward, predicted that the move would not harm Locher, "and it may just have a beneficial effect for him." Harold Smith, councilman from Ward 22, believed that many of his constituents were "thoroughly disgusted" with the recall move. "I really believe people will get behind [Locher] solidly," he said. In response to these and other criticisms, Day accused many politicians of opposing the recall effort "because they know what it represents—a tool that the people could also use against them."[78]

Clarence Rogers, a lawyer for Day and Bailey, released an angry statement to the press answering his clients' critics. Rogers said the recall effort presented a threat to politicians "who had long forgotten that this is a government by the people and for the people." Rogers further asserted that Day and Bailey would gather the necessary signatures for the recall to show Locher, other politicians, the press, the chamber of commerce, and all of the "mythical power structure," that "the people" were still in charge.[79]

Without the backing of the black power structure, which was critical of the effort, Day and Bailey were forced to recruit fifty volunteers to gather signatures. Many circulators went door to door and found a black community receptive to their efforts. One volunteer, Richard Norris, took the day off from work to collect signatures. Among the many residents he found eager to sign was Barbara Byrd of 10814 Hull Avenue: "I'll sign, Mayor Locher has not been interested in our problems. He should sit down with us and have a round-table discussion, but he doesn't. I believe it is right to recall him."

Clyde Witherspoon, a nearby neighbor, thought along those same lines: "In a way Mayor Locher has taken care of the problems of Cleveland, but in another way he has failed." Bertrice Amison agreed with Witherspoon. In her opinion Locher was "not very good." For Amison, Locher's constant refusal to meet with black leaders was the problem: "When our leaders went down to talk with him, he was always busy or he refused to see them. That's bad." Others, such as James Powers, felt that Locher's handling of federal grants was the issue: "I don't think Locher should be in office because he hasn't done a good job with all that federal money given to Cleveland. He hasn't used it for the benefit of all the people." But some, like Ledoris Menafee, refused to sign the petition, stating flatly, "I don't know whether he has done a good job or not, but I won't sign the petition."[80]

In the end Day and Bailey fell fifteen thousand signatures short. Kenneth McGhee, spokesman for the group gathering signatures, maintained that the Locher administration sent a directive to all city employees stating that if they signed the petition, they would lose their job. He also charged that local welfare officials told recipients that if they signed the petition, their funds would be cut. Nonetheless, McGhee felt that the campaign had achieved some positive results. Most important, McGhee claimed, "Politicians now know they are going to have to serve the people . . . all the time." He further argued that the failed recall attempt illustrated to voters that "they don't have to wait until the next election to be judge and jury, but can use the recall move." In closing, he declared, "This is not our last effort to improve city government." Although the grassroots drive to oust Locher was not successful, the effort itself demonstrated that black Cleveland was approaching political maturity.[81]

The Hough riots affected the city's business community in two ways. First, it increased white awareness of black frustration and forced the white community to recognize that Locher lacked the political sophistication to deal with the problems of the city. Second, whites were concerned about the possibility of further riots, fearing serious economic and financial repercussions. Corporate elites made it clear that Locher would serve the remainder of his term without their support. They needed an effective replacement. In the fall of 1966 they concluded that electing Carl Stokes would both increase the effectiveness of municipal government and reduce the probability of future racial violence. Consequently, they would use the twelve months before the 1967 mayoral election to help Stokes get elected.[82]

The riots also strengthened Stokes's position within the African American community. In a political sense the riots increased Stokes's chances of capturing the mayor's office. While the rebellion served as a catalyst for racial unity, it also solidified the black community's opposition to politics as usual. As black voters realized the need for strong leadership, Stokes emerged as their spokesman. In fact, he soon became a national figure because civil rights activists were moving toward using political power as the next phase in the black freedom struggle.

To the dismay of Cuyahoga County Democrats, Stokes had an undeniable lock on a third term in the state house. They had not forgotten that he had broken ranks with the party on several occasions, and in 1965 he had done the unforgivable, running for mayor as an independent against a Democratic incumbent. Although Stokes received the Democratic endorsement in 1966, the local party still considered him a traitor. On the eve of the 1966 elections Porter and Stanton instructed ward and precinct committeemen to do whatever they had to to ensure that Stokes did not get elected to a third term. However, this was a virtually impossible mandate, considering that Stokes's popularity was steadily increasing, Cuyahoga County had seventeen at-large seats in the state house, and Stokes therefore needed only to be among the top seventeen vote-getters to gain re-election. Nonetheless, party leaders also warned black Democratic candidates, "Don't line up with Stokes."[83]

Stokes used the 1966–67 legislative session to sharpen his image. He was active on the house floor, articulating the needs of his largely black and poor constituents. He opened a discussion about increasing support for housing, education, health, and welfare, and he mobilized colleagues to block the passage of a controversial stop-and-seizure bill. No other black politician in the state could match his legislative enthusiasm. Meanwhile, he kept a close watch on the political situation in Cleveland.[84]

In the spring of 1967 Locher's popularity reached an all-time low when Robert Weaver, the HUD secretary, froze the city's urban renewal funds and withdrew an additional $10 million committed for downtown commercial development because the city had failed to complete a single urban renewal project. Locher was further embarrassed when Weaver rejected Cleveland's application for Model Cities money because the application was incomplete. As the 1967 mayoral elections approached, business leaders officially ended their affiliation with Locher.[85]

On June 16 Stokes declared his candidacy for mayor. Although he had entertained the idea of running again as an independent, he filed as a Democrat, largely because President Lyndon B. Johnson and the Democratic National Committee (DNC) had promised him support. In a press release announcing his candidacy, Stokes emphasized that the problems of Cleveland were serious and that the Locher administration had failed the people. He mentioned that although he was proud of his "Negro heritage," he was not running as the candidate of the black community or any other special group.

Rather, he sought to serve all the people of Cleveland: "For the record, Carl Stokes will serve all the people without favor or unfair special consideration. East Siders and West Siders, senior citizens and children, rich and poor, whites and Negroes, bankers and busboys are all equally entitled to the best possible police and fire protection, sensible traffic regulations, and all the services and leadership the city government can provide to make this a better community with greater opportunities and attractiveness for everyone."

Stokes also introduced what would become a central theme in his campaign: that he was the only person who could maintain racial peace in the city. "My administration would not tolerate violence in the streets. However, we would also work diligently and determinedly to correct the root causes of this violence." Throughout his campaign Stokes would exploit the idea that he was the only politician who could keep the lid on black unrest. The business community agreed and threw its support solidly behind Stokes.[86]

In contrast to his previous attempt, the 1967 Stokes campaign would be a highly professional operation with a budget of more than $250,000. Stokes used a two-track campaign—the mass mobilization of black voters and a citywide media-based appeal to whites. A steering committee that included Dr. Kenneth Clement, W. O. Walker, and Geraldine Williams made the key decisions, while Stokes retained the public relations expert Al Ostrow to sharpen Stokes's image with white voters.[87]

When Stokes announced his candidacy for mayor, local civil rights activity came to a virtual halt. "Keep it cool for Carl" was the slogan that summer. Stokes and most other community leaders believed that any massive civil rights demonstrations could jeopardize his chances of being elected. To ensure business support Stokes needed to convince the white power structure that he was an insurance policy against black unrest. To maintain racial peace Stokes and Walker convinced two local power brokers, Ralph Besse, chairman of the Cleveland Electric Illuminating Company and of the Inner-City Action Committee, and Lawrence Evert, executive director of the Businessmen's Interracial Committee, to give $40,000 to local black nationalists in an effort to pacify their frustration. "Peace in Cleveland," as it was later referred to, was an outgrowth of meetings held at the *Call and Post* building after the Hough riots. Local residents and black nationalists agreed to remain calm because they assumed that a Stokes administration would be an extension of the civil rights movement.[88]

Geraldine Williams and Kenneth McGhee were Stokes's campaign coordinators in the black community, and they consistently stressed four major themes: that if all blacks voted, Stokes could win the election; that they could make history by electing Stokes; that Stokes would make black issues a priority; and that October 3 was the day to vote. Because of the widespread notion that black voters ignored primary elections, his campaign literature did not reveal that October 3 was only the primary.[89]

The mobilization efforts in the black community received a tremendous boost when the major civil rights organizations announced that they were "coming to Cleveland that summer to register every black voter." In fact, Cleveland CORE received a $175,000 grant from the Ford Foundation specifically to register black Clevelanders. Stokes understood why they wanted to come. With passage of the Voting Rights Act of 1965 and the Civil Rights Act of 1964, the civil rights movement had lost momentum and was groping for a way to regain it. As a result "Cleveland was where the action was, at the focus of the eyes of the black world," as Stokes put it. However, Stokes did not want them to come to Cleveland. "Well, we already had the black community organized, mobilized, and energized," he explained. "If the Big Six [NAACP, CORE, Student Nonviolent Coordinating Committee, Southern Christian Leadership Conference, Urban League, and the National Council of Negro Women] came to Cleveland with their various rhetorics, they would create an energy that would in turn create an opposite and probably more than equal counter-energy."

The threat of countermobilization was real. Stokes was particularly skeptical about the involvement of Martin Luther King, whose popularity was at an all-time low after his failed campaign to end housing discrimination in Chicago. Stokes feared that King's "coming would only release the haters and the persons looking for an issue to excite racist reaction to what we were doing." During a meeting in Cleveland, Stokes desperately encouraged King to leave the city. "Martin, if you come in here with these marches and what not, you can just see what the reaction will be. You saw it in Cicero [Illinois] and other Northern towns. We have got to win a political victory here. This is our chance to take over a power that is just unprecedented among black people. But I'm very concerned that if you come here you're going to create problems that we do not have now and may not be able to handle. I would rather you not stay."

King refused to leave, but he promised Stokes that he would do nothing to inflame whites. "I will have to stay," King said, "but I promise you there will be nothing inflammatory. We'll try to do a job here and our people will get in touch with your people, and any time that you feel there is something harmful to your overall campaign, just let me know." That summer King "did limit his visits and he did conduct his activities in a very restrained manner." Although Stokes did not particularly welcome the voter registration efforts, he was pleased that the Big Six registered thousands of black voters. This effort cannot be overlooked because 30 percent of black registered voters had been dropped from the rolls since 1965 because of confusing election laws.[90]

To some degree Stokes's concerns about King's involvement were valid. As the election approached, white voters were in a frenzy over the possibility of a black mayor. One white group, the Save Our Homes Committee, distributed a memorandum in white areas when King announced that Cleveland would be the focus of a major voter registration drive in order to get Stokes elected. The memo asked the following questions regarding the implications of King's involvement:

1. City Hall will be "open" to "Civil Rights" leaders Mr. King, Stokely Carmichael & Rap Brown and revolutionaries in the event of Mr. Stokes's election?
2. School Children will be bussed from white neighborhoods into colored areas and colored children bussed into white schools?
3. Housing in the City will be forcibly integrated?
4. Mass demolition of thousands of Cleveland houses to make way for integrated housing projects?
5. White job-holders will be displaced by Stokes?

Other conservatives predicted that if Stokes was elected, "there will be a large migration from other states, as to Cleveland, and we will be witnesses to overcrowding, vandalism, and pushing around and other insults." Conservative whites were resorting to any and all tactics to defeat Stokes.[91]

Locher and Porter used the Democratic Party's newsletter to introduce to some and reinforce to others the idea that a Stokes victory would lead to a black nationalist takeover. One headline read: "DICTATORSHIP IN CLEVELAND: PREVIEW OF STOKES AND MLK AS MAYOR. DO YOU WANT MLK AND HIS DISCIPLES RUNNING YOUR CITY?" In a later issue Porter argued that a Stokes victory would give Martin Luther King, "the noted racist, control of his first city in the United States." Both issues closed with the warning: "Keep Stokes and MLK out of city hall." The Stokes campaign countered by publishing a brochure called the "Cleveland Democrat," in the hope of attracting more white Democrats.[92]

Because of white hostility, the Stokes campaign did little canvassing on the West Side. In the early days of the campaign Stokes workers were verbally assaulted, and the harassment got progressively worse. Volunteers were attacked, his West Side headquarters was vandalized, and someone fired gunshots at a security guard who was protecting that office.[93]

Stokes was eager to debate Locher, but the mayor, who was seeking re-election as a Democrat, refused: "I appreciate his willingness to debate, but I will conduct my campaign in my own way, period." Stokes then wrote a series of letters to the mayor, repeating his request for a debate. Locher still refused, realizing that he had nothing to gain by debating Stokes.[94]

Locher increased his visibility on the East Side as the primary date neared, but he had little luck attracting black voters who were firmly behind Stokes. Locher then took his appeal to the city's black employees. At an all-black rally for Locher, two black Stanton lieutenants, Jack Oliver, a well-known black conservative who was a city employee, and Clarence Gaines, a former city council member, labeled Stokes a pawn in an effort to place a Republican in city hall. Oliver repeatedly stressed that Stokes took the black vote for granted while paving the way for a Republican takeover. "Stokes is on the way up alone, and he's not taking anyone with him. . . . Where are you going to be when the GOP takes over?" Other speakers at the rally characterized Stokes as an Uncle Tom. For many city workers racial solidarity was secondary to job security.[95]

The Stokes team received a big boost when the *Plain Dealer* endorsed him in the primary. The editors argued that Stokes could provide the kind of leadership the city needed to repair its reputation. Plus, Stokes could pull the city out of its "doldrums" by revitalizing the city to attract new residents and new business.[96]

Stokes won the Democratic nomination by more than 18,700 votes, 110,769 to 92,033. As expected, he swept the black community, but he received a remarkable 15 percent of the white vote. That night a crowd of more than five thousand celebrated in front of Stokes's headquarters.[97]

His opponent for the general election was Republican Seth Taft, a wealthy suburbanite whose only previous political experience was as mayor of Pepper Pike, an exclusive East Side suburb. Nonetheless, Stokes knew that he was in for a tough campaign. He knew he had to maintain his black support, but a significant problem was the early decision to stress the date of the primary election, October 3. In fact, many black voters thought that Stokes had already been elected. The larger obstacle was convincing white Democrats not to vote Republican. The Stokes media blitz stressed three themes to white Democrats: that Stokes's primary victory entitled him to the support of all Democrats, that he would be mayor of all the people, and that his background in urban politics qualified him to be mayor.[98]

In an effort to foster party unity, Stokes invited Albert Porter to occupy the head table at a "Stokes for Mayor" banquet sponsored by the Democratic Party. Virtually every well-known local Democrat except Locher and several white council members attended. But while the Democrats put on a good show of unity for the public, much dissension remained in the ranks. Stokes realized that many of the white politicians were making only a pro forma appearance and had no intention of helping him gain election.[99]

Stokes and Taft agreed to three debates. On paper a debate seemed to favor Stokes, because Taft was relatively unknown and not a great public speaker. However, Taft held the most important asset. He was white. The first debate was held on the East Side at Alexander Hamilton Junior High. Throughout the debate Taft argued that Stokes lacked a specific program and that he was under the influence of the Democratic National Committee. Stokes, meanwhile, labeled the mayor's race as a contest between the "grandson of a slave and the grandson of a president," subtly implying that Taft was unfamiliar with the lifestyle of the poor. Stokes contended that Taft was "accustomed to the remote security of Pepper Pike" and had no idea what it meant to be "hungry, without shoes, without clothes, or for his children to go hungry." Although Stokes acknowledged Taft's intellect and integrity, he asked audience members whether they would be willing to "entrust the problem of finding jobs to a person who never knew the shock of the unemployment line in his own life or in his family." Throughout the remainder of the campaign, Stokes would stress how his poverty-stricken childhood made him the most qualified candidate.[100]

The second debate was held on the West Side at John Marshall High School. Once Stokes took the rostrum, he focused on Taft's inability to address urban problems. Stokes then suggested why Taft would win the election: "Seth Taft will win the November 7th election for only one reason. That reason is that his skin happens to be white." The crowd erupted and the moderator had to restore order. Taft then pulled out a Stokes campaign poster to illustrate to the crowd that Stokes was the racist in the campaign. It read: "Don't vote for a Negro, Vote for a Man." Although Kenneth Clement, co-chair of the Stokes campaign, was angry at Stokes for playing the race card, "it was probably worth 10,000 votes in the black community," said one campaign supporter.[101]

With two weeks remaining before the election, the *West Side News,* a weekly, also endorsed Stokes. The *Plain Dealer's* endorsement said that the paper believed that he had the courage to try new solutions to the problems that plagued Cleveland. It further praised his experiences as an assistant police prosecutor and state legislator and asserted that his "personable" and "articulate" personality prepared him for the job. The *West Side News* echoed these sentiments, writing that Stokes would provide a "fresh and sensible" approach to the needs of the city because he was a man of vision and purpose.[102]

Despite these two influential endorsements, Stokes realized that he could not count on traditional Democrats to support him. In particular, sixteen white Democratic council members refused to endorse him. Many of these council members represented white communities that were ferociously against having a black mayor, and the council members realized that pushing for Stokes could jeopardize their own careers. Several black political leaders likewise refused to support Stokes. In particular, Jean Murrell Capers, a former Stokes supporter who had since turned on him, and her League of Non-Partisan Voters believed that Taft's qualities were superior to those of his opponent and that he had the knowledge necessary to govern the city. The league's endorsement also claimed that Stokes's program was superficial and that he was ill equipped to solve the city's problems.[103]

Taft's popularity skyrocketed on the West Side as a Stokes victory became more likely. White conservatives held parades, rallies, and festivals in a broad effort to get out the white vote. But Taft still trailed in various pre-election polls. To attract voters Taft began questioning Stokes's integrity. He criticized Stokes for buying his mother a house in Shaker Heights (an incorporated suburb) and raised questions about Stokes's visibility in Cleveland during periods of racial turbulence. "Do I have to be ashamed my mother was a scrubwoman?" Stokes responded. "When I have an opportunity to give her a house all of us would want to have, should a snide remark be made about that?" In response to Taft's allegations that Stokes had been absent during the school crisis and the riots, Stokes quickly retorted that he was in the streets of Hough, while Taft was in his "mansion out in Pepper Pike."[104]

On election day Stokes won by 1,679 votes, 129,396 to 127,717. Stokes enjoyed high black turnout and moderate white support. When the election results were announced at 3 A.M., Stokes gave a brief victory speech in front of four hundred enthusiastic supporters. "I can say to you that never before have I known the full meaning of 'God Bless America.'" Now an even bigger struggle lay ahead: the application of power.[105]

Charles and Louise Stokes, parents of Carl, with Carl's older brother, Louis (ca. 1925).

Carl Stokes at thirteen months, shortly before his father's death in 1928.

Carl Stokes as a G.I., soon after going into the army in 1945.

Members of the United Freedom Movement demonstrating in front of the headquarters of the Cleveland school board in April 1964. Ralph McCallister was the school board president.

Carl Stokes on the campaign trail during the 1965 mayoral race.

Carl Stokes giving his inaugural address in November 1967.

Carl Stokes (right) stands next to Harllel Jones, leader of Afro-Set, as they participate in a black nationalists' rally just three days before Ahmed Evans declared war on the police, sparking the Glenville riots in 1968. Note the man in the background who is holding a rifle.

Fred "Ahmed" Evans in dark sunglasses and kufi, being interviewed by local reporters in front of his black nationalist headquarters on May 29, 1968.

Baxter Hill, center, and members of the Mayor's Committee patrol the streets in an effort to maintain the peace after the killings in Glenville, 1968.

Carl Stokes and his chief nemesis, Council President James Stanton, share a platform in October 1968.

Carl Stokes engages in a heated argument with a local homeowner during a Lee-Seville area town hall meeting designed to lessen community opposition to his public housing proposal. (Cleveland Press/Van Dillard)

David Hill of the House of Israel speaks at a Operation Black Unity rally during the McDonald's boycott, 1969. (Cleveland Press/Timothy Culek)

Retired general Benjamin O. Davis Jr., being sworn in as safety director by Mayor Stokes. (Cleveland Press/Herman Seid)

3. Cleveland: Now!

ON THE AFTERNOON following his election Stokes gave a victory address at the annual Future of Cleveland luncheon. His central theme was that the citizens of Cleveland had to work together to revitalize the city. Stokes asked the attendees to forget about the election and look forward to the future. He closed by stating prophetically: "I promise you a lot of interesting things will be happening in our town in the next few years."[1]

Stokes later acknowledged that, having campaigned so hard to get elected, he had no idea what to do when he took office. "We went into those sessions with wild-eyed dreams of the reforms we would wreak on this corrupt machine, only to discover that we didn't even know where the buttons were." He was also overwhelmed by the widespread publicity his election generated. "The first days of our administration were awkward, to say the least. My unprecedented victory had made me an international celebrity, and reporters from all over the country were descending on our office asking for interviews." Black residents also flooded city hall. "Everybody wanted to talk to me," Stokes recalled, "to see me, to touch me. So many people who had spent their lives feeling disenfranchised by the system now felt that I was their mayor."[2]

Stokes also confronted the burden of being "a credit to my race." As the first black mayor of a major city, Stokes realized that his administration would be the most scrutinized and analyzed of any in history. Everything would be in the limelight. "That meant I had to be more creative, more honest, more intelligent, more available, more witty, more thorough, than any other mayor in the country." Consequently, days after his election Stokes retained a local public relations firm to help him gauge how the public might react to his conduct. Stokes knew that "all of my actions would reach the public through the interpretative structure of the white media."[3]

With only six days between the election and his inauguration, Stokes named his cabinet with careful thought to the concerns of his supporters and to the racial divisions in Cleveland. He was deluged with applications from "ambitious white liberals" and from African Americans "who hadn't been given chances elsewhere." Stokes promised himself that he would not appoint political hacks, only real professionals. He recalled that the people he chose "for the most part didn't like politics anyway."[4]

To allay white concerns about black governance, Stokes chose Joseph McManamon and Michael Blackwell, both whites, to be safety director and police chief, respectively. Under Cleveland's city charter the safety director was in command of the city's safety forces—police and fire—and Stokes expected McManamon and Blackwell to reform the Cleveland Police Department, which had a long history of institutional racism. Next, the mayor appointed three African Americans to important posts. He named Municipal Judge Paul D. White to be city law director (city attorney), the second-highest official in Cleveland city government; Ralph Tyler to head the service department, and Rev. Arthur LeMon to serve as executive assistant for liaison with church and youth groups. In other appointments Stokes named Dormand Witzke the city finance director and Ben Stefanski Jr. to head the utilities department. The interracial nature of his cabinet dispelled fears in the white community that his election would mean a black takeover of city hall. Stokes was explicit in stating that he was seeking the most qualified people without regard to race or color. But like the mayor, many of these appointees were inexperienced, with little knowledge of municipal government. Stokes also named many African Americans to other, less visible cabinet positions and to the city's various boards and commissions. And Stokes established initiatives to place African Americans throughout the entire municipal workforce. By the end of his first year in office Stokes had added 616 new black employees, while 340 white city workers were removed from the payroll. The biggest increase in black employees came in general administration, finance, and human resources. In fact, before Stokes entered office the Human Resources Department did not have a single black employee. One year later the department had eighty-nine employees, and sixty-four of them were African Americans. Throughout his tenure city hall would begin to reflect the racial makeup of the city.[5]

Shortly after his election Stokes initiated a series of weekly meetings with members of the business community to demonstrate that they would play a prominent role in his administration. Ralph Besse, chairman of the Cleveland Electric Illuminating Company and director of the Inner-City Action

Committee, was chosen to coordinate the formation of the informal group, which labeled itself the Urban Renewal Task Force. In addition, Besse would become Stokes's chief liaison to the city's white business sector. After announcing the formation of the task force, Stokes said: "It's common sense for businesses to become involved in upgrading their cities, because this is the same as upgrading themselves." He believed that "business and industry built these cities. If they are going to be rebuilt it will take that same investment and ingenuity that was originally employed."[6]

Stokes next made an unprecedented move by hiring William Stein, a lawyer, as a city lobbyist to work primarily in Washington. The Stein appointment was critical to Stokes's overall plan. Having a cabinet-level representative in Washington solely for the purpose of lobbying for federal funds showed a degree of political sophistication. Stokes was determined to build a healthy relationship with Congress and the federal agencies, and Stein's appointment was a step in that direction.[7]

In late November 1967 Stokes and several cabinet members met with Ohio governor James Rhodes to secure a commitment for matching funds, which would assist the city's efforts in getting the HUD freeze lifted. Stokes contextualized his request by noting that what was good for Cleveland, the state's largest city, was also good for the state. But Rhodes flatly denied his request by arguing that the state had little power to help cities solve their problems. Stokes left the meeting annoyed because he knew that the governor's support was critical to Cleveland's urban renewal efforts. In essence, Stokes needed to show HUD authorities that Cleveland had the support of its own governor. Stokes could not exactly understand why Rhodes had denied his request because the problem of urban decay did not stop at Cleveland's city limits; it affected the surrounding communities as well. Nonetheless, Rhodes did offer several suggestions, albeit rather generic ones. For instance, although Rhodes saw the lack of low-income housing as Cleveland's biggest problem, he advised Stokes that the way to gain more was to petition Congress for pertinent legislation. While Stokes did not get the support he wanted from the governor, he left with the impression that Rhodes would take into consideration the city's needs in the upcoming legislative session. Witzke, the city finance director, summed up the feelings of many: "We came out with a batting average of .000, we asked for money and didn't get any. But we learned how they gradually say no." Still, Rhodes pledged to cooperate with Stokes. In fact, Rhodes asked Stokes to accompany him on his annual trip to New York City, the specific purpose of which was to attract new industry to Ohio. Stokes accepted the invitation, knowing that he could not afford to pass up the opportunity to meet approximately two hundred top executives.[8]

In speaking before the assembled business leaders in New York in late November, Stokes told them that they were welcome and wanted in Cleveland: "Cleveland needs industry, Cleveland wants industry. We deeply appreciate your investments in Cleveland but we're not satisfied." Stokes promised them that "in Cleveland you will find a new attitude, you will find that we really care about your problems. This is a personal commitment." He went on to explain why their support was critical to Cleveland's revitalization: "Jobs are so essential, so basic to Cleveland's success, I need your help. I humbly ask your help." In closing Stokes remarked that just as he was creating a city government responsive to the needs of the people, he was creating a city government that would be responsive to the needs of the business community. The speech was well received, and Stokes went home ready to begin his job of managing the city.[9]

The support of the business community was critical to Stokes's overall plans. First, he realized that he could not effectively implement his programs without strong business backing, and, second, he was well aware that as a black man, the influence of the city's business establishment would go further than his appeals, especially in gaining the cooperation of the Cleveland City Council. Although twenty-seven of thirty-three council members were Democrats, he had the unqualified support of only ten, some black, some white. City Council President Jim Stanton, a Democrat who had worked to keep Stokes from becoming mayor, had the support of the remaining seventeen. Even four of the city's black council members were in the Stanton bloc.[10]

Stanton, who was born in 1930 on Cleveland's West Side, learned politics at an early age from his uncle, Edward Stanton, a former Cleveland city prosecutor and prominent lawyer. After the younger man graduated from the University of Dayton in 1957, he returned to his hometown, and two years later at the age of twenty-seven he was elected to the Cleveland City Council from Ward 4. Early in his career he exercised considerable independence when he opposed the 1962 mayoral candidacy of Ralph Locher. When Locher won, he banned Stanton from official Democratic Party affairs. The breach was healed a year later when Stanton engineered a coup that ousted longtime City Council President Jack P. Russell from his powerful post. With the help of several black council members, Stanton used his power to control the city's legislative body. Although there was talk of his running for mayor in 1965, he declined, preferring instead to retain his city council presidency.[11]

Stokes recognized from the beginning that his administration would be under intense public scrutiny, held to a higher standard than other mayors had been. Just weeks after his inauguration local journalists began to look for any hint of mismanagement or scandal, and early on they found one. While

Stokes was vacationing in the Caribbean in early January 1968, the *Cleveland Press* revealed that Geraldine Williams, one of Stokes's executive assistants and long-time supporters, was active in the business affairs of an after-hours night-club. Stokes had first heard rumors about her involvement just days after his election, and he asked her about the allegations. She responded that she had divorced herself from the operation. The *Cleveland Press* broke the story with the headline "MAYOR'S AIDE LINKED TO CHEAT SPOT." A reporter for the *Press* had gathered information over a five-week period by purchasing beer and whiskey on Sundays, which was against state law. The reporter also revealed that although the club was allowed to sell alcohol only to its members, he had freely purchased the alcohol without anyone asking about his membership status. The reporter had confirmed Williams's involvement by finding her signature on the state liquor permit, club minutes, and canceled checks.[12]

Because Stokes was away, the *Press* reporter Dick Feagler sought comment from acting mayor Paul White, who immediately called Stokes in the Virgin Islands. Stokes told White and Executive Assistant Ken Clement to have Safety Director Joseph McManamon acquire the written evidence and take it to a handwriting expert for analysis. The handwriting expert reported that all the signatures were Williams's. Now faced with the first crisis in his administration, Stokes struggled about what to do. Some supporters wanted her fired immediately because of her dishonesty, while others wanted the mayor to defend her because she had been instrumental in both of his mayoral campaigns. Making the situation even more difficult was that Stokes was out of town, he was inexperienced, and the local media were all over the story. After conferring with White and Clement, Stokes decided to fire her, feeling that he needed to keep his administration above reproach. In a statement to the press Stokes explained his decision: "The imperatives of this administration require maximum integrity and the public must be able to maintain confidence at all times in those administering their efforts."[13] The black community's reaction to Williams's dismissal was mixed. People understood that Stokes needed to maintain the integrity of his administration, but some found it difficult to accept Stokes's decision because Williams had been so instrumental throughout his political career.[14]

Stokes's supporters saved much of their criticism for the *Cleveland Press.* The carefully timed publication of the story made the city's black residents skeptical—the editors were well aware that Stokes was out of the country and would be unable to do much damage control. Furthermore, many citizens could not fathom why the paper had called the club a "cheat spot," because it had been in business for twenty years and cited only twice for illegal sales. Some even questioned the credibility of the entire exposé. For example, Elliott Pogue, owner of the club, believed that the reporter's story about what he had been able to buy was a complete fabrication. Even if it were true, he argued, "This record compares favorably with that of the exclusive Union Club," an all-white club downtown. Pogue accurately assumed that the story was designed to weaken the Stokes administration, because no one ever asked specifically about Williams's involvement or the operating procedures of the club. W. O. Walker, editor of the *Call and Post*, labeled Williams a "sacrificial lamb" caught up in a calculated attempt to smear Stokes. In his autobiography Stokes recalled that when the crisis arose, he panicked and later regretted the way he handled the situation. "I wish I could undo what I did," he wrote. "I lost probably one of the four or five most trusted and loyal people I have ever been around in public office." The Williams incident would be the first of many attempts by the local press to embarrass the Stokes administration.[15]

In the aftermath of the Williams controversy, Stokes faced more serious problems with the Cleveland Police Department. Police reform was high on his agenda. "I took my election as a mandate to reform the police department. I saw as one of my most important tasks the reform of the police, the return to having our police as our protectors, men who would enforce the law, do their job, be responsive to the needs of the people." For decades black residents had complained of a dual standard of law enforcement. Police brutality was a reality, crime went unchecked in black neighborhoods, and the force had few black officers. Once on the force black officers were not allowed to patrol white areas and were often denied promotions. The police department also suffered from low morale, poor leadership, outdated equipment, and primitive procedures. Stokes was determined to use the power of city hall to rectify many of these problems.[16]

Shortly after his election black officers gave Stokes a list of recommendations:

Stop the promotional list now.

Integrate all the cars on the eastside as far as the Negro Patrolmen go, even by transferring some to the third district so they can work on the cars in the downtown area.

Integrate the Mounted Unit by putting Negroes in the downtown area at least eight men.

Transfer more Negro officers into downtown traffic unit so they can work in the downtown area. Also investigate the practice of the large companies such as Electric Illuminating Co. hiring policeman at $4.00 per hour to do traffic duty ask why the Illuminating Co. and other companies do not hire Negro Patrolmen for this part-time work.

Transfer out all the Negro Patrolmen who have obtained so-called good jobs in the police department through the former administration, only because they were and still are in the eyes of the police department so called "Good Negroes with the right attitude." These officers can be replaced with other Negro Patrolmen who in the past have been reprimanded for speaking out against the illegal conduct of the police department.

See to it that a Negro Patrolman works in the office in each district, around the clock to prevent any illegal treatment of prisoners or alleged acts of brutality.

Automobile transfers of all white police officers every six months to prevent any so-called "findings of homes" and any other condoning of other illegal activity.

The most important is that a unit be set up to work out of the director's office to make spot checks of the districts and other various units at unannounced times to prevent any illegal practices towards prisoners.

Eliminate district vice officers or district vice units.[17]

After taking the black officers' recommendations into consideration, Stokes asked McManamon and Blackwell to implement some of the suggestions. They then placed black officers in white areas, integrated several of the elite units such as the department's undercover task force and the SWAT team, and ordered all officers to stop wearing their traditional white helmets, largely because black citizens argued that it created a Gestapo-like atmosphere. A team of lieutenants, sergeants, and captains supervised the reorganization, to the dismay of the white rank-and-file but to the applause of black residents.[18]

The administrative moves ignited a wave of controversy. White officers believed that Stokes and McManamon had no legal right to make the transfers of personnel. In their opinion it was against the city charter. Other officers believed that Stokes was interfering with Chief of Police Blackwell's duties by not leaving him alone to run the department. When the reorganization was completed in late January, white officers were outraged. Mayor Stokes was sending a message that he planned to play an active role in the affairs of the police department.[19]

White officers responded by coming down with "blue flu." They stopped enforcing the law in high crime areas, and throughout January 1968 the city had a noticeable decline in arrests, particularly for running numbers, prostitution, and drinking after hours. Their intention was to block any administrative efforts to put more officers on the street. The police protest ultimately fizzled out, and Stokes stuck to his plans to reorganize the department. The reorganization fiasco was the first showdown between Stokes and the police department. In many ways Stokes's organizational ideas and the response of the police department set the tone for future relations.[20]

Stokes then turned his attention to urban renewal. "The Urban Renewal Department was a scandal," Stokes said. Adding to the department's failure to complete the projects it began was that throughout the 1950s, city officials told property owners to let their dwellings deteriorate because they were going to be torn down. As a result, they would lose value, and the city would be able purchase the land at a low price. Stokes labeled this policy "callous, contemptuous, and inhuman." In January 1967 the U.S. Department of Housing and Urban Development (HUD) agreed and took the unprecedented step of cutting all of Cleveland's federal funding until "the mess was cleaned up."[21]

By mid-February Stokes still had not named a community development director, partly because Cleveland was still ineligible to receive federal funds for urban development.[22] To help him bring the city's urban redevelopment efforts into compliance with federal guidelines, Stokes retained Edward J. Logue of Boston, "the best urban renewal man in the country," to draft both short- and long-term plans. Logue found that although the city had pioneered several approaches to urban renewal and city planning, it had foundered in their execution. In submitting his recommendations, he suggested that Stokes first recruit a top-flight urban renewal director at a salary of $30,000, which was $5,000 more than the mayor's salary. Logue knew that finding such a person would be difficult, and he told Stokes to use money as a drawing card and to solicit the support of political, civic, and community groups at all stages of the project. Next, Logue stressed that Cleveland needed a bold and workable program: "Cleveland does not have such a program today. In fact, few cities do. The city must have a program big enough to do the job, bold enough to capture the imagination of the people, sound enough to be workable, and feasible enough to restore federal confidence."[23]

For the first phase of the program Logue suggested that Stokes streamline several projects, such as public housing, code enforcement, a model neighborhood program, and the construction of public facilities and place them under the jurisdiction of the community development director. For the second phase he suggested that Stokes establish a department that would integrate housing, city planning, and community development. The department was not for Stokes to manage, however; rather, he was to assemble a task force of "urbanists" to handle the day-to-day issues.[24]

Stokes and the Urban Renewal Task Force implemented many of Logue's recommendations. In early February, Stokes and Paul Unger, chair of the task force, prepared a detailed summary of their actions since Stokes's inauguration to illustrate to HUD authorities that they were serious about urban renewal. They emphasized the creation of the task force, stricter code enforcement, and a reassessment of all existing urban renewal projects. They hoped the report would lead HUD to release the city's urban renewal dollars.[25]

Although Stokes had begun to move the city's urban renewal programs along, he still needed the support of the city council in order to hire a first-rate urban renewal director. When council member Leo Jackson introduced the legislation to authorize the $30,000 salary, Richard Harmody, Michael Zone, and other white conservatives questioned the feasibility of a cabinet member having a higher salary than the mayor. Other council opponents questioned the logic of bringing in an expert to handle the city's urban renewal problems. Zone asked whether a local person could do the job, because in his opinion any member of the council's community development committee knew as much about urban renewal as anyone in the city. Pressure from the business community nonetheless convinced the city council to authorize the salary. Days later Stokes appointed Richard Green, a graduate of Harvard and MIT, to lead the city's urban redevelopment efforts. He became Stokes's fourth African American cabinet appointee.[26]

Green's appointment sent optimism throughout the city because it represented an attempt to get the city back on track. In many circles across the nation Cleveland had become an embarrassment, mainly as a result of its inept urban renewal plan, which was the main underlying cause of the Hough riots. The selection of Green was seen as the all-important first step toward bringing the community development department "back to life." Still, many observers realized that Green had a tough job waiting for him in a department that had suffered from years of neglect, bad planning, and incompetence. One writer observed, "There is plenty of trouble for Green to shoot. Cleveland's urban renewal program is bogged down and have [*sic*] been stuck in the mud of inertia and federal disapproval."[27]

Once Stokes had made his most important cabinet selection, he still faced the task of restoring Cleveland's urban renewal funds. This was critical for two reasons. First, since the city was losing its tax base as a consequence of white flight and deindustrialization, Stokes needed as much federal funding as he could get. Second, getting Cleveland's federal dollars restored had been one of his campaign promises, and now he had to deliver. One week after he appointed Green, Stokes met with HUD Secretary Robert Weaver in an attempt to get the freeze lifted. Stokes was confident of success because his Urban Renewal Task Force had been hard at work and because he had hired Green. Joining Stokes at the meeting with Weaver was the entire congressional delegation for northeastern Ohio, which helped Stokes argue his case. Persuaded, Weaver released the funds, ending the fourteen-month freeze. Weaver said that he was not entirely satisfied with the city's progress, but because Stokes and the city had taken considerable steps to rectify the problems, he felt confident in lifting the freeze and approving additional funding. Stokes also persuaded Weaver to not to require Cleveland to make monthly reports to HUD.

The local media, city council, and area residents all applauded Stokes. The *Plain Dealer* characterized HUD's reversal as a triumph for Stokes that put Cleveland back in business while vindicating the faith of voters. The *Call and Post* echoed many of the same sentiments under the headline "STOKES MAKES GOOD ON CAMPAIGN PROMISE." While Stokes took credit for getting the ban lifted, those inside the Stokes camp knew that President Johnson had worked behind the scenes. In the midst of urban unrest nationally, Johnson had instructed Vice President Hubert Humphrey to stay in close touch with the mayors of key cities. Since Stokes's first run for mayor in 1965, he and the White House had maintained a healthy relationship.[28]

Black residents were especially pleased by Stokes's success in Washington. Days later, at a press conference in Hough on March 9, 1968, Stokes announced plans to build three hundred units of low-income housing, the first step in his efforts to revitalize the city. "Urban renewal, under any administration, is going to be what the people want, it's going to make this and other neighborhoods better places to live," he told residents. "Right here is where we are going to start making headway against the problems which piled up in the last twenty years and which almost wore down your patience."[29]

Stokes achieved another legislative goal weeks later when he secured a pay increase for the city's director of public health. When he took office, "the health department simply wasn't doing anything. It had been limping along with little funds and providing almost no real services." To revitalize the office he selected Dr. Frank E. Ellis, an African American, to head the department. Stokes was particularly impressed with Ellis's dedication to public health because he had given up his thriving practice.[30]

The mayor's early success also increased his popularity in the white community. Not only had he appointed an integrated cabinet but he had also secured the release of federal aid to rebuild Cleveland. After several months in office Stokes had quieted many of his critics. Likewise, Stokes's black supporters were delighted at many of his early administrative moves and ecstatic that for the first time in history their issues were a priority. But as his popularity escalated, Stokes faced his first potential crisis.

On the evening of April 4 Stokes occupied a platform with the noted journalist Carl T. Rowan at Baldwin-Wallace College. In the middle of Rowan's lecture the mayor was informed that Martin Luther King had been assassinated. Visibly shaken, Stokes told the stunned audience, "I am going to have to leave." Violence erupted throughout the country as soon as King's death became known. In all, 110 cities experienced rioting that left thirty-nine dead and millions in property damage. Stokes could not afford an outbreak of racial violence in Cleveland.[31]

The mayor headed for local TV stations to urge the public to remain calm, telling viewers, "I appeal to all Clevelanders to do honor to the memory of MLK by reacting to this tragic loss in the peaceful manner in which he lived." Stokes said he understood the bitterness expressed by black youth, but he reminded them that a violent reaction would be an injustice to King's legacy. As white law enforcement officers patrolled black urban communities throughout the country, Stokes used a different strategy. He ordered white police officers to stay out of the black community. Instead, Stokes formed an all-black peace patrol to maintain order. Consisting of cabinet members, black nationalists, ministers, professional athletes, and other community volunteers, the peace patrol traveled throughout the black East Side, urging frustrated black youths to "keep it cool." Most responded positively. To facilitate timely communication Stokes established a command post and gave volunteers the use of city vehicles. The peacekeeping effort by Stokes and other leaders paid off. While virtually every other major city experienced massive rioting, Cleveland was spared. Stokes's timely actions and the commitment of his peace patrol combined to keep Cleveland free of racial violence, much to the delight of business leaders.[32]

The mayor's ability to keep Cleveland calm after Martin Luther King's assassination was cheered throughout the metropolitan area. The *Plain Dealer* led off by labeling the effort "GOOD WORK BY CITY LEADERS." The paper attributed Stokes's success to his ability to communicate with the people, which enabled Cleveland to escape the immediate "madness" that had erupted throughout the country. Neil J. Carruthers, president of the influential University Circle Development Foundation, a wealthy fund-raising body for the University Circle area, offered Stokes his sincere congratulations and appreciation for saving lives and preventing "substantial property loss." Likewise, A. I. Davey, editor of the weekly *Cleveland Citizen*, gave Stokes credit for calling in the peace patrol to keep the lid on unrest. In Davey's opinion Stokes's actions following the assassination had done more to bring the races together "than has ever been accomplished previously in one full year."[33]

Although black Clevelanders did not resort to violence, they felt considerable frustration at King's death. Cleveland CORE called for an official day of mourning, asking all 300,000 black citizens not to report to work in observance of "black Tuesday." Don Bean, local chair of the Congress of Racial Equality, went to all three television stations and called for a citywide work stoppage. In Bean's eyes the community response was tremendous— many employers even agreed to give their black workers the day off. CORE also used a bit of coercion by threatening to boycott companies that refused to honor the request. Stokes responded to CORE's appeal by giving all nonessential employees a half-day off, insisting that all emergency workers, such as police, fire, and utility personnel, report to work. "If tragedy were to result because someone left his job to observe the memorial, it would be a great disservice to the memory of Dr. King," explained Stokes. IBM gave all its employees the day off, while local department stores remained closed until noon. Classes at both Case Western and Cleveland State were suspended for part of the day, and memorial programs were scheduled throughout the public school system. After King's death the mayor's popularity reached new heights, and he received tremendous kudos in the national media as an excellent politician and community leader. His versatility puzzled some, as they marveled at how he was able to speak the language of both the boardroom and the poolroom.[34]

The decision by Stokes to withdraw white police from the frustrated black East Side was unprecedented. It was also dangerous, but it worked. After King's assassination Stokes was quickly emerging as the most popular African American in the country. He would exploit his popularity and launch Cleveland: Now! a large-scale urban redevelopment program.

After King was slain, business leaders asked Stokes how they could help maintain racial peace. Stokes reiterated that because of the socioeconomic conditions in the inner city, the slightest incident could trigger an outbreak of violence. They told him to come up with a plan and they would support it. In the week after King's death the mayor instructed his cabinet members and other city leaders, such as Irving Kriegsfeld, the recently appointed director of the Cuyahoga Metropolitan Housing Authority, to outline a series of needs and priorities as soon as possible. They presented their list at an April 12 meeting with Stokes, cabinet officials, and business leaders. The latter included Thomas Patton, president of Republic Steel; Cleveland Indians owner Vernon Stouffer; and Francis Coy, president of the May Company, which owned department stores. At the meeting Stokes asked for a $10 million commitment and eleven thousand jobs for the hard-core unemployed. The business community agreed. Two weeks later Stokes released the details of the program to the news media and the marketing for Cleveland: Now! began.[35]

Cleveland: Now! subsequently became a $1.5 billion plan to improve housing, employment, and urban renewal during a ten-year period. The short-range goals called for spending $177 million in the next twelve months to attack major urban problems in six areas—employment, youth resources, health and welfare, neighborhood rehabilitation, economic revitalization, and city planning. The funds were to be a mixture of city, state, federal, and private contributions. To erase unemployment Cleveland: Now! would undertake to train and employ at least 11,000 full- and part-time workers. The new jobs were to be a mixture of public and private positions; some others would be part time and seasonal. The Aim-Jobs program of the Council for Economic Opportunities in Greater Cleveland was to create 4,000 jobs, and the National Alliance of Businessmen was signed up to supply another 4,000. Additionally, the job-training program of the city, in conjunction with the Cleveland Urban League, promised 1,800 jobs, and the U.S. Department of Labor's Office of Development and Training pledged 2,500 positions. For the city's youth Cleveland: Now! would oversee a $750,000 program that would provide a wide array of programs such as neighborhood cleanups, work training, cultural enrichment, education, and recreation. In health and welfare Stokes planned to establish ten multiservice health centers and ten day-care centers.[36]

The City Planning Commission under Cleveland: Now! would receive $1.75 million in city and federal funds to create a policy planning and program evaluation center to be used to avoid duplication or overlapping projects. The city earmarked $61 million for economic revitalization to accelerate the existing urban renewal projects, with particular emphasis on downtown development. The greatest expenditure, $86 million, was set aside for neighborhood rehabilitation, largely to make available forty-six hundred new and rehabilitated housing units throughout the city for low- and middle-income families. Of that amount, $20 million was to be used for housing inspection, while the remaining $10 million was to be set aside for homeownership programs. Funds were also earmarked to expand small business opportunities.[37]

Cleveland: Now! was the centerpiece of the Stokes administration. Although political pundits realized that many of these projects were under way before Stokes's arrival at city hall, urban redevelopment had never been marketed like this. It represented something new. Stokes recalled that much of Cleveland: Now! was pure public relations: "People had to have a feeling that the building they saw, the progress in evidence around them, was the result of their effort and determination to see their city move."[38]

Stokes announced Cleveland: Now! in a half-hour prime-time program that all area television and radio stations ran. He stressed that the redevelopment program was critical to the city's revival: "To stop that downhill slide, to start the city moving forward to create a climate in which our city can someday be a great one, we must take that first difficult, giant step." Although Stokes was the initiator of the program, he opined that he needed the support of the entire Cleveland community. "Cleveland Now! is a program which enlists the aid of the total community . . . business, civic groups, professional people, the news media, and the general public in a concerted effort to assist Cleveland in attacking some of the these most urgent problems, now, in 1968."

In Stokes's eyes this was not his program but the "city's program, which reflected the combined thinking of the entire community."[39]

The bulk of the $177 million that would underwrite the short-term goals of Cleveland: Now! was to come from the federal government, which had agreed to supply $143 million. These various grants were to trigger $22.75 million in state and city matching funds. Donations from private contributors were to make up the balance of $11.25 million. Stokes asked the business sector to contribute $10 million and individual citizens to donate a total of $1.25 million. Handling the financial end of the program was the Cleveland Development Foundation, along with John Sherwin, president of the manufacturer Pickands-Mather and Company, and George Dively, president of Harris-Intertype Company, a printing company. The foundation, Sherwin, and Dively were responsible for raising the $10 million from the business community. Heading up the committee to raise the $1.25 million from private citizens was Group 66, an organization of young businesspeople led by George Steinbrenner, president of American Shipbuilding. Other key players in the program were William Adams, director of the Cleveland Growth Association, and William Silverman, the local publicist whom Stokes put on the city payroll to help him get his message across. The close involvement of white business leaders gave the massive redevelopment package instant credibility.[40]

Local media reaction to Cleveland: Now! was excellent. The *Cleveland Plain Dealer* asked city residents to support Stokes's plan, which it described as bold, exciting, and imaginative. The editorial stressed that Cleveland: Now! represented an opportunity for civic cooperation, "never before proposed," and that the challenge should be answered and the opportunity grasped. The *Cleveland Press* echoed many of these themes in its editorial, which ran under the headline "LET'S BLAST OFF WITH CLEVELAND: NOW!" The *Press* characterized Stokes's proposal as a break from the past. "This time things are different," the *Press* declared.[41]

The optimism created by Cleveland: Now! easily trickled down to many of the black poor, who assumed that the mayor's urban redevelopment proposal would improve their standard of living. James Terrell, a part-time construction worker, told reporters that Cleveland: Now! was a "wonderful program . . . we should of had someone like Mayor Stokes here years ago." Hough resident Arthur Danley was equally excited: "He's the best damn mayor Cleveland ever had." Even suburban whites were ecstatic about Cleveland: Now! "He's the best thing that ever happened to Cleveland," a suburbanite told a *Press* reporter. "He has brought new blood and new ideas to Cleveland. He has shown who can influence important people with money. Now he seems to be revitalizing the downtown area and I'm for him all the way."[42]

The Stanton bloc did not share that optimism. The council's concerns centered on whether the city could provide its contribution without raising taxes. Council members thought that Stokes was exploiting Cleveland: Now! to attract support for a 0.05 percent tax increase that he had proposed. County Prosecutor John T. Corrigan wondered "where will that money come from. . . . It seems this program will require additional taxes." Council member George Blaha expressed similar feelings: "There was no mention of a city income tax increase, but I don't know how else Cleveland can come up with its share of the necessary money." Other council members, including Harold Smith, were much more direct: "This is leading up to an income tax increase and I don't know if I can support an increase.[43]

Stokes successfully mobilized a broad base of support for Cleveland: Now! by exploiting white fears of racial unrest. He constantly stressed to the business community that unless it supported a massive redevelopment program, he could not guarantee racial peace. Although Stokes had maintained order after King's death, he said he could not guarantee it in the future. These arguments instilled fear throughout the business community, which still felt the effects of the Hough riots and had recently witnessed massive property damage in other metropolitan areas in the aftermath of King's assassination. The business community was determined to keep Cleveland peaceful by any means necessary, and Stokes took advantage of these fears.

To attract widespread support for Cleveland: Now! Group 66 launched a massive advertising campaign. Within days the slogan "Cleveland: Now!" began to appear on billboards, posters, buttons, bumper stickers, and pennants throughout the city. Another marketing program was aimed at the middle-class worker under the phrasing "A Day's Pay Will Lead the Way, an Hour's Pay for a Better Day." Robert Fearry, chairman of the Group 66 subcommittee in charge of employee solicitations, asked area employers to encourage their workers to give. However, Ferry made it particularly clear that the employee solicitation was separate and distinct from the contribution sought from employers themselves. Group 66 also asked that area corporations contribute volunteers to Cleveland: Now! Lawyers, engineers, accountants, and other professionals were asked to give specific amounts of time. By May 15, less than two weeks after the program was announced, Group 66 had met its goal of $1.25 million, and the Greater Cleveland Growth Association had met its goal of $10 million, largely as a result of a donation from the Cleveland Development Foundation. Because Cleveland: Now! had collected more than $11 million, the federal government agreed to release $74.8 million, more than half of the $143 million commitment that Stokes wanted by the end of 1969. Cleveland: Now! was on its way, and Stokes was the darling of the national media.[44]

Stokes was especially pleased that his administration would be able to provide $750,000 for the Mayor's Summer Youth Program, which gave low-income youth job and recreation opportunities. The program was critical because because until Cleveland: Now! came along, the Summer Youth Program had had a hard time securing private-sector jobs, and the jobs provided by antipoverty dollars had strict income requirements. The Summer Youth Program's staff expressed relief, knowing that thousands of youth who lived just slightly above the poverty threshold would otherwise be unable to find jobs, a recipe for idleness and violence during the upcoming summer. But with Cleveland: Now! money, city hall undertook a massive summer youth project.[45]

Cleveland: Now! served two purposes. First, it was designed to redevelop the city; second but equally important, it allowed Stokes to distribute much of the money as he desired. Because it was not tax money, the city council had little say in how the money was disbursed. Although the Greater Cleveland Growth Association would collect and handle the donations, Stokes was literally in charge of all disbursements.

With Cleveland: Now! off to an unprecedented start, Stokes began a campaign to raise the city income tax, just as council members had predicted. The Little Hoover Commission Study, which examined the status of all phases of city government, suggested raising the tax increase from 0.05 to 0.08 percent by April 1. However, Stokes sought to raise taxes by a full 1 percent. In pushing for the increase Stokes emphasized that the additional $15 million would go toward pay increases for city employees, most notably police and fire personnel. As expected, the Stanton bloc actively opposed the increase. At a hearing on the issue Stanton asked how the Hoover Commission could predict a tax increase when new buildings were being built, which would generate more tax revenue. Stokes countered by buying a full page in local papers to run a letter asking voters to support the increase. In it he listed the home phone number of all the council members so that their constituents could reach them. The mayor's tactic infuriated Anthony Garofoli. "I will not be intimidated," the council member thundered. "If they're looking for open warfare I'm ready." Stanton concurred: "I'm not impressed by the newspaper campaign, to stampede this council without proper documentation." Criticized for listing the home phone numbers, Stokes did not express regret: "In our enthusiasm to get Cleveland on the move we have applied pressure everywhere . . . pressure on the administration and on City Council. We have urged City Council to move as quickly as possible on the income-tax measure because there is an urgent and immediate need."[46]

Stokes's efforts on behalf of an income tax increase were aided when city sanitation workers staged a four-day walkout that left 116,000 homes without garbage pickup. More than a thousand tons of garbage went uncollected each day. The workers were angling for higher wages, and they wanted to bring the issue to the attention of Stokes and Stanton. Many of Stokes's critics suggested that he was actually behind the strike, hoping to get his stalled tax proposal out of the blocks for a vote. Although it appears that Stokes did not engineer the walkout, the strike did motivate voters and city workers to pressure the council for a vote.[47]

At a May 27 council meeting scores of municipal employees picketed city hall, and other workers packed the council chambers to hear debates on the tax proposal. However, Stanton adjourned the meeting before the legislation ever was mentioned. It came out that the Stanton bloc had bottled the legislation up in the joint finance-legislative committee. Stanton also attempted to compromise the measure by calling for its adoption as of October 1, as opposed to Stokes's date of July 1. The later date would have made the additional money available only after January 1, 1969, effectively delaying raises and other improvements for a full year. As Stanton stalled, the public began to apply pressure. The tax issue came to a vote on June 11, 1968, and passed easily, with only 3 dissenting votes. Afterward Stokes stated simply, "I'm very gratified." Although Stokes had succeeded, Stanton would never forget that the mayor had published the home phone numbers of council members in the city's newspapers. Stanton conceded the battle, but he was prepared for a long war.[48]

In addition to generating millions in city revenue, the tax initiative allowed Stokes to build a base of support in the largely white city bureaucracy. The allegiance of city employees was critical because their jobs were protected by civil service. Although Stokes expected a certain degree of "bureaucratic resistance," he sought to lessen the tensions by granting pay raises and higher salaries.[49]

As Stokes looked back over his first eight months in office, he was elated. He had restored the city's urban renewal dollars, managed to keep the peace after King's assassination, launched Cleveland: Now! and secured a tax increase. More important, he had experienced no major scandals or controversies. In many ways he had convinced the city's white voters that he could govern the entire city and that his administration did not necessarily translate into a black takeover. This was critical, because as long as he satisfied his white critics, his efforts to improve the lives of the city's black residents would go unchallenged.

The national media was captivated by Stokes's success. With King's death the civil rights movement lacked an icon. Stokes filled that void. As the cries of "Black Power!" captured the attention of angry black youth across the United States, Stokes showed that political power was the next phase of the black freedom struggle. He was proving that the system could work. By the summer of 1968 he was clearly the nation's most popular African American and one of its most popular politicians, period. In fact, his name was mentioned on several occasions as a potential running mate for Hubert H. Humphrey. An editorial by the *Call and Post* political columnist Woody Taylor summarized a widespread perception: "The Mayor of Cleveland is on the move. The people of Cleveland are getting on the move with him." The honeymoon would come to an abrupt end on the night of July 23, 1968.[50]

4. Glenville

WHILE THE NATIONAL press was applauding Stokes as the golden boy of black America, the myriad black nationalist groups throughout Cleveland were not sold on the idea that power could be attained through the ballot box. They believed that the quickest avenue to power was through blood and iron. Throughout his early political career Stokes had managed to capture the attention of the burgeoning nationalist element, because he realized that it represented a sizable segment of the black community. Stokes felt that it would be hypocritical of him to enter office as the first black mayor of a major city, then keep the black power faction marginalized. Rather, he took a pro-active approach. He made it clear to the nationalists that they represented an essential part of his constituency and that their support was critical to his success.

Soon after he entered city hall, he told representatives from the Afro-Set, the Republic of New Libya, and the Federation of Black Nationalists that he considered their support to be of paramount importance: "I want you to work with me, cooperate with me. The extent [to] which you will, I am going to help you all I can." The relationship between city hall and the nationalists got off to a tremendous start, especially when they helped him maintain the peace after the King assassination. But the actions of Fred "Ahmed" Evans and the Republic of New Libya would cause many to question this approach.[1]

Fred "Ahmed" Evans was born in Greenville, South Carolina, in 1931 and moved with his family to the East Side of Cleveland in the mid-1930s. Like most black children of the period Evans grew up surrounded by filth, poverty, and squalor. As a youngster he wanted to know "why things never changed" for black residents. All he ever heard from his parents and neighbors were "promises and more promises." He left school in the ninth grade and enlisted in the army in 1948. He briefly served in Guam with the Seventy-third Combat Engineers Battalion before being sent to Korea. As a soldier, Evans saw "the useless waste of lives. I saw people stacked like cordwood. I viewed all these things and saw how cheap life can be." After a year abroad he returned to Cleveland briefly, then re-enlisted. Shortly after he returned to the military, he struck his commanding officer and was sentenced to two years of hard labor at Fort Crowder, Missouri. After serving his sentence, he returned home in 1956 and found work with the Pennsylvania Railroad. While Evans was readjusting to civilian life, two events left a lasting impression. The first was the 1959 lynching of Mack Charles Parker in Poplarville, Mississippi. "It was the Mack Charles Parker thing that first got me interested in the cause," he recalled. "After that, I became what you would probably call an agitator. At this point in my life I had given up to the system. That is to say I had come to realize that my pursuit of happiness was irrevocably blocked because I was a Negro. But when the Parker thing happened, something was born in me."[2]

Then, in 1962, Evans saw a UFO hovering over the heart of the black community at Seventy-ninth and Kinsman. "It hovered for a while and disappeared. That started me thinking about the stars and the God and I thought that here I was thirty-three and Jesus had died at thirty-three and I hadn't even got started yet. So I moved off by myself to study the science of astrology and philosophy. In astrology I found a never-failing relationship of cause and effect which teaches one lesson: that which ye sow ye also reap." He then "heard of a group of people who were in the process of forming a sort of unity among members of the community" and he found them to be honest. They were not "a bunch of people stuffing their pockets with other people's money, having no interest in the people at heart but living high lives, driving beautiful automobiles, wearing fancy clothes, eating elaborate meals, and giving elaborate speeches to a bunch of people who couldn't understand what they were talking about. So I joined these people." In 1964 he visited several groups in Harlem before joining the Republic of New Libya. "I was a slave until 1964 when I became a Black Nationalist. By this time I had become Ahmed. I wasn't Fred Evans anymore."[3]

Sometime between 1964 and 1966 Evans emerged as the leader of New Libya, and he became a popular figure in the black community. Evans believed that a black nationalist was a man who "had grown out of the bonds of being a Negro. He is a black man, the same as a Negro, but he doesn't think the same as a Negro. He thinks for himself. He does for himself. He doesn't need anyone to guide him by the hand. This man has aspirations and he has ambition and he has love and desires. He has pride." Evans's philosophy also had a strong religious component. Although he took on a Muslim name, he believed in Jesus, and he was quick to use the Scriptures to support his beliefs. "The principles of Black Nationalism are to believe in God, to know and understand God. We have the words of Jesus and Jesus is saying that we cannot serve God and Mammon." For Evans this meant that a black nationalist was obligated to serve God "in all circumstances. If it means your life it means your life." On the subject of violence, Evans was explicit in believing that a "black nationalist will fight back in self-defense." Which, he acknowledged, "I have done myself." He believed that African Americans had been oppressed long enough. "This is where you stand up like a man and dish out what is necessary to dish out." Evans's philosophy was "to fight fire with fire. If I am attacked by anybody or anything, I will defend myself at all costs. But I would not attack someone who is not attacking me."[4]

Evans gained a significant amount of attention in 1966 as he traveled throughout the black East Side lecturing on African culture and history, black economics, and black self-determination. In the early part of that year Evans accurately predicted that the East Side ghetto of Hough would explode. "I predicted that there would be trouble in Cleveland. I said it would happen in the months of June or July, and the Hough riots happened in July. I could do this through the studies I had undertaken in astrology."

In the aftermath of the Hough disturbance the part-time astrologer and pseudomystic emerged as a community leader. He "began to speak out even more." He told members of the black poor that he was a soldier and that he had a role to play, just like members of the traditional leadership class. "I said I was willing to follow if they were willing to lead. But they disappointed me, and it seemed that we were all heading for the streets." In March 1967 Evans and his New Libya followers opened the African Culture Shop in Glenville. "We had sets of carving tools, art materials, paints, hammers. We decorated it and had hangings on the wall, with the signs of the zodiac and information relating to astrology, numerology, and philosophy. And we had a Black Nationalist flag there, black, red, and green. It had the crescent and the star on it." They stayed in the shop for a year "until the police drove us out. They used an order from the sanitation department and condemned the building."[5]

Evans and company then relocated to 6605 Hough Avenue "and started to clean it up. It was in terrible shape, rubbish two feet high on the floor. We cleaned it out, scrubbed the premises and disinfected it. We painted inside and out." Evans intended to make the new location a community center. He recalled, "We had seamstresses. We had artists, brothers who dealt in oil paints and all the arts. We had carvers and sculptors. We had musicians and danc-

ers. We had just about anything you can think of. You name it, we had it."
By showing these skills to the young people of the community, Evans hoped
to "stop them from killing each other."[6]

Evans and his followers also caught the attention of local police, who were
eager to either infiltrate or dismantle the group. The police made the first of
many moves, arriving at the cultural center, which was also Evans's primary
place of residence. "They came to ask questions first," he recalled, "then they
came with a sledgehammer and wrecked the joint. They came in numbers,
sometimes forty or fifty. They had various weapons, submachine guns and
sometimes grenades. I heard once they brought a bazooka, but I didn't see
it. We were always under surveillance." They frequently stopped Evans during routine patrol. "I was clubbed in the head any number of times," Evans
said. "Once I was taken to the fifth precinct while walking my girl home. I
was never charged with anything but they clubbed me on the way to the station." This was mild: "I have been clubbed, stomped, spat on, kicked." On
one occasion his girlfriend was forced to strip in front of policemen. Another time, while Evans was in police custody, he "was beaten unmercifully at
the station house by officers," and then he was visited by a lieutenant who
"spat on my chest and said, 'That's you, Ahmed.'" But Evans believed in self-
defense. "Officer [William] Payne came to the shop with a sledge hammer
and broke the window and then attacked me. I disarmed him and we had a
little altercation," Evans said. "He made an effort to draw a gun and I pinned
his arms to the side." Evans was later charged with assault and sentenced to
jail in connection with his run-in with Payne.[7]

Two events in the spring of 1968 convinced Evans that the only way for the
black man to get justice was in the streets. The first was the assassination of
King. He and King had met several times in Cleveland. Although the local
civil rights establishment tried to neutralize Evans by dismissing him at times
as a madman, King understood Evans's importance to the black community. Whenever King came to Cleveland, he would meet with Evans. At one
meeting arranged by local ministers, King took them to task for not inviting
Evans. King told them that violent nationalists like Evans made it possible
for whites to accept King's philosophy of nonviolence. In fact, in the summer of 1967 King publicly embraced Evans in front of reporters. At least one
observer still believes that King's acknowledgment of Evans prevented riots
that summer.

"Martin Luther King was a great friend of mine, but a nonviolent man in
a violent world is a fool," Evans said. "I felt he was leading the people astray."
Nonetheless, Evans grieved King's death deeply. Then Evans was evicted from
his astrology shop for failing to pay the rent. With no advance notice, court

officers changed the locks and moved all his belongings to the sidewalk. When community leaders failed to assist Evans in his desire to fight the eviction, he grew discouraged.[8]

In July, Evans and his followers rented an apartment in Glenville, at the intersection of Auburndale and Lakeview. They soon began stockpiling arms. The building owner notified police; Evans refused to allow Sgt. Bosie Mack and Det. Michael Taylor, both white, to enter. Evans later told building inspectors that if they returned to the apartment, they would not make it out of the area alive. "These inspectors were really shook-up," said one observer. For the next two weeks Ahmed Evans and his group prepared for a showdown with police by purchasing high-powered weapons and ammunition. When Evans was notified that he and his young followers would have to vacate the building immediately, he grew angrier still.[9]

On the morning of July 22, Evans went to Detroit and Pittsburgh to purchase additional weapons. Word soon spread throughout Glenville that the Republic of New Libya was getting ready for the "enemy." When police got a tip that Evans would strike on July 23, they grew nervous. Complicating the situation was that Stokes was out of the city; he had left Clarence James, the new law director, an African American, in charge. The following morning James and police officials, including McManamon and Blackwell, as well as several black council members, decided that the police would set up a roving surveillance in front of the apartment building. A moving reconnaissance was significant because Evans often stationed guards outside his home, and on occasion he sent followers to hunt for police on adjacent streets. City leaders also agreed that council member George Forbes and Walter Beach, director of the mayor's youth programs, both African Americans, would go to Evans's place to monitor the situation. The meeting ended between 6:00 and 6:30 P.M.[10]

After the meeting Mack grew concerned when he overheard Insp. Lewis Coffey, head of the police undercover task force, tell his subordinate to establish a stationary detail at the Auburndale building. Mack repeatedly reminded Coffey that it was to be a moving detail. Coffey replied that his lieutenant was a good man: "He will know what to do." Mack then went to Capt. George Sperber, chief of the intelligence division, and asked him to make sure the task force members knew that they were supposed to keep moving. "Coffey is an Inspector. He knows what he is doing. Who am I to tell him what to do?" Sperber declared. Mack continually tried to do something about the task force's instructions, even volunteering to conduct the surveillance himself. All his suggestions were brushed aside.[11]

As Forbes and Beach approached the apartment building, they saw two cars "full of white people." These were members of the police task force who were sitting in parked city vehicles in front of the apartment building. Evans noticed the police, and when he saw Forbes and Beach, he quickly summoned them to his backyard to express his displeasure with the surveillance and the eviction. Forbes was shocked to see Evans and other New Libya members wearing bandoleers and carrying rifles. The council member tried to assure Evans that the surveillance would be discontinued. Evans seemed convinced and sent them back with a message for Stokes: "Tell the big brother downtown [Stokes] everything will be alright." Forbes and Beach left Evans's at 8:05 P.M. with the impression that there would be no trouble.[12]

When Forbes returned home, he spoke with the mayor, who had just returned to the city. Minutes later McManamon broke in on their conversation to inform Stokes that trouble had begun at Auburndale and Lakeview. At 8:30 P.M. Evans and his followers came out of the apartment complex firing weapons at two tow-truck operators whom they misidentified as police officers. As police rushed to the scene, they were fired upon as well. Members of the task force were terrified. "They are coming out, they have automatic rifles, thirty of them," shouted a task force member over the police radio. The first man out of the apartment fired a shot toward a surveillance car but missed. As the police retreated, two New Libya members followed closely, firing their weapons. The gun battle was under way.[13]

The first officers at the intersection were ambushed. "Get somebody, get a tank down here . . . get tear gas, get more rifles," they yelled frantically. By 8:40 three white police officers and two New Libya members were dead. A sniper's bullet hit the motor of the patrol car driven by Officer Willard Wolfe. The resulting explosion killed Wolfe and blew his body into the intersection of Auburndale and Lakeview. Seconds after Wolfe died, Patrolman Louis Golonka was killed as he searched for New Libya members, and Lt. Leroy Jones was shot and killed by a New Libya member as well. Harllel Jones recalled that "them young brothers hit anything that moved." The standard-issue police weapons were no match for the armor-piercing bullets and tracer ammunition that Evans and his followers used.

The two New Libya members who also died in the early minutes of the siege were Malik Ali Bey, twenty-three, and Nondu Bey, twenty-five. Sgt. Sam Levy, one of the first officers to arrive, recalled the tense moments: "As I started up the driveway . . . I was hit. . . . They kept shooting and I was hit again. They shot at anybody who moved." Bertice Fleming, who lived next door at 1395 Lakeview, had a front row seat as police and New Libya members exchanged gunfire in her apartment complex. "They started shooting and I was afraid to look out. I looked out and there was an army of police there. I begged the police to stop shooting but they wouldn't listen. I barred the door because I didn't want anybody to get in and then I just got back down on the ground." The shooting ended around 9:30 but not before another New Libya member and a black passer-by were killed.[14]

After the gunfire stopped, the police began to look for Evans and other New Libya members. Police were determined to avenge the deaths of officers Wolfe, Golonka, and Jones. The police first searched the popular Lakeview Tavern, which was next to the apartment building. They found the bar's patrons hiding in the basement. Louise Brown, twenty-one, was one of several women who were sexually assaulted by police. "The policeman ripped my clothes off me, he felt me in between my privacy, in between my legs." Her friend Jean Grisby was next, as white officers "searched" her by putting their hands up her skirt. The humiliation continued once the women were outside the bar. Angry officers forced Peggy Finley to remove her clothes. The black men trapped inside the tavern were next. They knew the police were coming back when they fired shots and tear gas into the tavern. John Pegues caught a bullet in the thigh, then was brutally kicked and beaten. He was forced to sit in jail for several hours although he needed medical attention. Officers repeatedly hit Arthur Radan with the butt of a shotgun. When he told the officers that he was unarmed, they showed little concern. "We're going to kill this black motherfucker," they yelled. They brutally beat Trenton Irwin, who suffered several cracked ribs before he was knocked unconscious.[15]

After the tavern's bruised and battered patrons were taken to jail, white police looted the Lakeview Tavern's liquor supply. Alfred Reed, who was standing on his porch after the shoot-out, saw the police take the liquor and drink it on the sidewalk. "I could see the police come out with some boxes . . . and putting them in the police car," he explained, "and then I could see them coming out individually, with bottles in their hands, drinking from them." When Lakeview Tavern owner Leola Williams returned to the bar later that night, she could not find $200 in cash, ten cases of beer, and thirty-six bottles of whiskey.[16]

Although most of the battle occurred at the intersection of Auburndale and Lakeview, police confronted black residents throughout the Glenville area. As Andrew Wright and his wife headed home around 9:00 P.M., they got stuck in a traffic jam at the intersection of East 123d and Superior. There, a police officer told Wright to take Lakeview Avenue instead of Superior, a major thoroughfare. Police opened fire on Wright as soon as he turned onto Lakeview. Miraculously, he avoided injury. Blocks away, Albert Forrest narrowly escaped with his life after he was told to stop helping a wounded black passer-by. "Get away from him," the police warned. When Forrest failed to obey, police fired at him. Nonetheless, Forrest and several friends tried to remove the body of one of the three dead New Libya members from an alley later that night. This time the police showed no mercy. "One of them jammed a shotgun in my ribs and told me he was going to blow my guts out and the police behind him came across his shoulder with his rifle butt and jammed me in my face and knocked me down; then a number of them stomped and beat me and kicked me," Forrest declared. As Sandra Parks tried to check the pulse of a gunshot victim, police drew their weapons on her; as she retreated, they kicked and mutilated the corpse.[17]

Then there was James Chapman, who was last seen that night walking home with his wife and children. As they approached the bullet-ridden intersection, Chapman was told that it was not safe to walk through the area. When a police officer offered to escort him through the area, he instructed his wife and children to go to the home of a friend. The young husband and father of two never made it. He was later found dead in the middle of the intersection, with a gunshot wound to the head. Police and the local media reported that he was killed by a sniper while assisting a wounded officer. A week later an independent pathologist found gunpowder residue on Chapman's face, which means that he was shot at point-blank range, not by a sniper. No one was ever charged in his death, and the police department never acknowledged how he really was killed.[18]

As word spread throughout Glenville that white police officers had killed three New Libya members, black youth wanted revenge. After the disturbance began, black youths gathered blocks away on Superior Avenue. As white motorists drove through the area, they were bombarded with rocks, bottles, and Molotov cocktails that failed to explode. By 9:30 P.M. black youth were on the offensive against white police officers. Twenty-one-year-old Officer Herbert Reed was pulled from his patrol car and severely beaten. Later a Molotov cocktail obliterated a police cruiser on Superior. Two other brand-new police cars containing valuable equipment were set ablaze and destroyed.[19]

Evans was captured at 12:24 A.M. When the officers arrived at 1384 Lakeview, where Evans had gone during the shootings, he emerged from the house shirtless. As police placed him in the patrol car, he asked: "How are my people?" When he was told that at least three had been killed, he replied, "They died for a worthy cause." Officers also asked Evans about his weapon, and he pointed to the bushes in front of the house. Lying there was a toga, a loaded carbine, five boxes of ammunition, and a first-aid kit. At police headquarters an officer asked him the reason for the shootings. "You police have bothered us too long," Evans replied.[20]

As the night continued, black youth decided to take their frustration out on white-owned property. Looting in the area began early in the evening, and by 11 P.M., as the shooting ended, looting and rioting increased. Crowds of looters and arsonists moved east along Superior and west toward Rockefeller Park. Stores all along East 105th Street were looted and burned, and the violence even spread to St. Clair, more than a mile north of Superior. There were also incidents in the Hough area and as far west as East 55th Street. The looting and other incidents continued into the next morning.[21]

By the morning of July 24, seven people were dead: three police officers, three suspects, and one area resident, Chapman; fifteen were wounded or injured, including eleven officers; at least forty people were arrested, largely for looting. Property damage was in the tens of thousands of dollars. As the first night came to an end, all eyes were on Stokes, the mayor whom voters and big business considered to be an insurance policy against this type of violence.[22]

After the shootings erupted, Stokes had met with his top aides to decide on a course of action. Stokes plainly admitted that he did not know what to do. He asked Blackwell. Blackwell responded, "To tell you the truth, I don't know." Stokes then shot back, "Chief, we've got to stop this thing, police and citizens are being shot out there." Stokes then issued an appeal for peace over local radio and television stations. After conferring with Chief Blackwell and McManamon, the safety director, Stokes asked Governor Rhodes to mobilize the national guard. At 3 A.M. two hundred guardsmen arrived in the riot-torn area, and the police were told to report any sniper activity to the national guard. Early that morning Stokes asked black community leaders to meet him at 8:30 A.M. at city hall.[23]

More than one hundred people arrived at city hall to discuss the situation. Attendance at this meeting was limited to black leaders; not even white cabinet members were allowed to take part. Stokes was well aware of the police actions the night before, and he was cognizant that looting, burning, and rioting had taken place as well. He put the matter before the community: "What do we do?" The group discussed several options, including imposing a curfew, strengthening police and national guard units, or withdrawing white police from the area. "We tried to get a true cross section of the black community. They were almost equally divided on the issue of pulling the police out or leaving them in, and we reached no decision then," Stokes recalled. "Most of the older, middle-class Negroes were against pulling them out. The

younger, more militant blacks wanted to pull them out." The meeting ended ninety minutes later with no consensus. About twenty "militants" continued to meet. Later that afternoon they again recommended that Stokes pull
the police out of the area and let community leaders patrol. Stokes was hes-
itant. However, he "had the feeling that black people were not going to kill
black people. And I knew that in that room that morning there were at least
two people who knew whether there would be further shooting, because of
their personal knowledge and involvement." Stokes called a press conference
later that afternoon and announced that he "was going to pull the white
policemen out and allow black leadership to patrol the area." The national
guard cordoned off the riot-torn area, and no white police officers were allowed in, only black law enforcement personnel and community leaders.
When reporters questioned the strategy, Stokes said, "The program is in the
black community and the black community will handle it." The group that
would patrol the area was labeled the "Mayor's Committee," and its members wore bright red armbands so they could be easily identified by white
police.[24]

The Mayor's Committee was headquartered at the office of PRIDE, a self-
help organization operated by Baxter Hill. Stokes gave the committee access
to city cars equipped with police radios. Throughout the night five hundred
patrol members toured the area, usually stopping to talk to groups of youths
gathered on the streets. Sometimes members of the patrol would stand in front
of looted stores to prevent further damage. Although they could not contain
the many sporadic acts of looting, by and large the peace patrol was effective,
largely because of the efforts of militant leaders such as Harllel Jones, Baxter
Hill, and DeForrest Brown, a community organizer. More important, no one
else died. Three fires were reported, thirty-six stores were looted, and thirteen
arrests were made, but no more deaths occurred. Nonetheless, Stokes's enemies did not consider the black patrol a success, largely because of wholesale
property damage. For many whites, property damage represented Stokes's
endorsement of lawlessness.[25]

When they first learned that the mayor planned to exclude them from the
riot-torn area, white police officers were outraged. Police radio dispatches that
night burned with their hatred of the mayor. A call requesting police assistance for a heart-attack victim was met with the reply, "White or nigger? Send
the Mayor's Committee." The response to a fire call was "Tell Stokes to go
piss on it," and answers to other calls for assistance included "Fuck that nigger mayor." White officers were also annoyed when McManamon told them
that they could not carry their rifles while patrolling the perimeter of the
cordoned area. Despite specific instructions to stay out of the area, white

police were visible throughout the cordoned-off neighborhoods. However, whenever they appeared in the riot-torn area, members of the Mayor's Committee asked them to leave.[26]

Nonetheless, the all-black peacekeeping effort was a success, and Stokes was pleased: "There was some looting, but no more shots were fired, no more lives were lost." However, many of the mayor's critics thought otherwise. "If you want to say what happened last night—no shootings, no snipers—was a success, then it was, but if you consider the looting, the destruction, the breaking of windows, the wholesale gutting of buildings, last night's activities, it was a total failure," declared Leo Jackson, the council member representing Glenville. "People of the area were scarred stiff . . . and I am upset." Stokes strongly disagreed: "Police records show no instances of looting, black leadership did a splendid job, the people stayed home. There have been no shootings of any kind, no deaths. Our greatest concern was for the safety of individuals."

Jackson was not alone in criticizing the unchecked looting of the second night. Area merchants were also upset—several area stores were totally wiped out, including a furniture store and two dry-cleaning establishments. In fact, members of the Mayor's Committee admitted that "they just couldn't handle the problem of looting. Some reported the presence of professional looters and cars from Michigan," Stokes wrote in his memoir.[27] Stokes realized that although his intent was to protect life, he could not allow looting to continue for another night. Later that day he dismissed the Mayor's Committee, announced a curfew, and sent the national guard back into the riot-torn area. He was confident that the tensions had cooled and that the guard would enforce the law.

However, Stokes and his advisers still hesitated to send in white police officers. After a meeting with police officials, Stokes decided to allow white officers back into the area to preserve morale and lessen the force's increasing hostility. But Stokes and McManamon suggested that only integrated two-man patrols be allowed to re-enter. White officers responded to the mayor's proposal by going on strike for two to three hours. White police demanded four white officers to a car and departmental permission to carry high-powered rifles. They compromised: three officers to a car, two white, one black. Once they re-entered the area, some police apparently still wanted to provoke another confrontation. "There would be people in the streets and the police would pull up and jump out of their cars with their guns out and tell them to get the hell off the street. The people cooperated and moved away despite the provocative behavior of the police," Stokes recalled.[28]

Thursday and Friday were relatively calm as the national guard presence cut down on looting and rioting, but Stokes could not digest the sight of armored personnel carriers patrolling his streets: "We got to Superior Avenue and were greeted by a tank. Not a half-track. A tank. In the center of my city, an army of occupation had taken over. My reaction to the sight, as a mayor, as a citizen, as a man, was a bottomless revulsion, an uncontrollable visceral churning. I was cast down."[29]

By Saturday morning things were quiet in Glenville. After conferring with national guard officials, Stokes lifted the curfew and pulled them out. When the police resumed regular patrol on Saturday night, they were still fuming about Stokes's management of the crisis and were eager to get revenge for their three slain brothers. But this time reporters felt the iron fist of the Cleveland Police Department. Late Saturday night a disturbance occurred at the Haddam Hotel on Euclid Avenue, just one block from Fifth District Police Headquarters, a precinct notorious for its brutality. When the reporter Julius Boros and the cameraman Charles Ray of NBC's national staff arrived to cover what was going on, they noticed that a large throng of partygoers had left various nearby bars and taverns to watch the altercation at the hotel. At the same time, white police officers were flooding out of the Fifth District station. The officers immediately began assaulting people in the crowd, which then began to disperse. Ray proceeded to film the brutality. Two white officers grabbed his camera, his wallet, his press credentials, and his glasses, then slammed him against a wall. Within seconds six or seven officers were punching him in the face and chest. Then they took him to jail and forced him to sign a disorderly conduct waiver, which immunized police against any charges of brutality. Boros was nearly knocked unconscious by police, who continued to assault him even after he was taken inside the Fifth District headquarters. At the hospital later that night medical personnel found that Boros had one broken rib, three fractured ribs, and severe kidney damage. Boros was later charged with assault and battery on a police officer.[30]

As the city returned to normal, Stokes became embroiled in a public relations nightmare after reporters learned that Ahmed Evans had received a $10,000 grant from Cleveland: Now! to open up an "African Cultural Shop." The purpose of the center was to "broaden the youth's knowledge of his heritage" by studying black history, Swahili, philosophy, numerology, astrology, and art. Membership in the shop was to consist of only black nationalists "or individuals that embrace that philosophy." What made this project unique in Evans's words was that "the poor are to guide and control the operation and policies" of the shop. In submitting his original proposal, Evans requested a grant of $25,000, with the bulk earmarked for salaries. For instance, Evans was to receive a director's salary of $5,000, while other New Libya members such as Lathan Donald and Jessie Harmon, both high school dropouts, were to receive $1,250 a piece as "instructors." Evans hoped that through his shop "the wide gap between the Black Nationalists and the rest of society can be narrowed to the point of acceptance." Stokes approved $10,000 for Evans's program as part of a $30,000 Project Afro grant, $10,000 of which went to Harllel Jones and the Afro-Set, and the balance went to yet another nationalist organization. The money was funneled through the Hough Area Development Corporation (HADC) and then distributed to Evans.[31]

After the riots Stokes learned from sources within the black nationalist community that Evans had used the majority of the grant to purchase weapons that were used in the gun battle. A storm of protest followed. Many critics interpreted the grant to Evans as a way of trying to buy peace in the ghetto. Although political observers acknowledged that buying peace was not a new phenomenon, many were enraged that the money had bought the weapons that killed white police officers.[32]

Stokes defended the grant. "What is the alternative to such a grant? Do you leave a man like Evans free to float in the community, to justify his resentments and nourish hatreds? Do you leave him in isolation, or do you try by any means at your disposal to reach him? It seems to me that you have no alternative but to embrace the socially dispossessed person, especially when he is a leader." Stokes would later add that as long as the black nationalists were excluded from the governing process, "you are guaranteeing the fact that they will be enemies rather than participants." Dean Ostrum, a member of the board of Cleveland: Now! and a vice president of Ohio Bell, stood by Stokes. Ostrum later recalled, "His program [was] to reach 600 young people in ghetto areas (Project Afro), we endorsed the original proposal and we still have confidence in [DeForrest] Brown and the HADC." Many of Stokes's black supporters agreed, but white business executives did not. For example, J. E. Wilhelm, president of Avery Engineering and a one-time supporter of Cleveland: Now! did not object to the involvement of militants in city government, but he did oppose "giving them money." Wilhelm wanted to know how and why Evans received a grant for educational programs, when he had little or no experience in teaching. Wilhelm also attacked Cleveland: Now!'s disbursement procedures. He wanted Cleveland: Now! to implement controls to ensure an accurate accounting of funds. Likewise, Tom Patton, president of Republic Steel, made a public demand for an audit of Cleveland: Now! disbursements. The business community slowly withdrew its support for the program. "The businessmen, against my constant reminder that I was not an insurance against violence, had continued to believe it anyway," Stokes recalled. "Glenville was their rude awakening, and when they found out that they had risked an independent mayor as an insurance policy to no avail, they turned away."[33]

Stokes said he regretted the misuse of funds, but he stood firm about his decision to allocate the money. He now was in a fight for his political life. Three policemen had been killed, he had pulled white law enforcement out of the black neighborhoods, and he had given Evans a Cleveland: Now! grant, which was used to purchase weapons.

As things slowly returned to normal over the following week, much of Stokes's white support vanished. Although the mayor did not condone the actions of Evans, many whites held Stokes responsible for the deaths of the three officers. In addition to the dubious grant, white residents were unhappy about Stokes's participation in a parade just days before the riot. On July 20 readers of the *Plain Dealer* awoke to learn that their mayor had led a parade through Hough; he was flanked by two rifle-carrying black nationalists. Although the guns were not loaded, readers still got the impression that Stokes was a black nationalist in a good suit.[34]

In the weeks after the Glenville riots, white residents sent hundreds of letters to city hall expressing their displeasure with the mayor's decision to remove white police officers from Glenville. One West Side resident asked Stokes to "admit" that the group responsible for the shooting was his "own black, Afro-American race." The writer then informed Stokes that he held him personally responsible for the tragedy because Stokes "used this same group to help him gain sympathy as well as tremendous financial terms for the entire Negro race." A Cleveland Heights resident felt the city could have avoided trouble if Stokes had not discontinued the helicopter surveillance (that the police department loved to use for patrolling the black community) or reorganized the police department. She labeled these decisions irresponsible. An observer calling himself a Goldwater Republican pronounced himself shocked by the mayor's refusal to protect white-owned property. He wanted to know how a "criminal" could order white national guardsmen out of a city that had been overrun by "insane black rampaging mobs." In closing, he promised "bloody retribution." Equally angry was another anonymous writer who wanted to know why Stokes could not keep things cool: "You should've been able to deal with these people." A majority of whites in Cleveland agreed.[35]

Despite the controversy about his decision to bar police from the riot neighborhood, Stokes received considerable support from all areas of the city. Among those who backed Stokes's decision to preserve life over property were Robert Morse, president of Case Western Reserve University; Rev. Donald Jacobs of the Greater Cleveland Council of Churches; Robert Ginn, president of the Cleveland Welfare Federation; the Catholic Interracial Council; and the Jewish Community Federation. Local civil rights organizations expressed their support in a full-page thank-you letter in the *Plain Dealer*. The support of Cleveland's civil rights organizations mirrored that of the broader black community. In a survey taken one week after the riots, 82 percent of black respondents believed that Stokes had made the right decision in pulling white police out of the area, whereas only 47 percent of whites did. Asked if Cleveland: Now! was a "good thing," 85 percent of blacks said yes, compared to 51 percent of whites.[36]

The decision to ban white police from the riot-torn area was a bold and risky strategy. For Stokes, the decision to protect life over property was not a difficult one. When Stokes learned that the police were preparing to storm the rioters and search for New Libya members, he had a good idea of what was likely to happen: The Cleveland Police Department had historically conducted itself as an antiblack organization. As the first black mayor of a major city, Stokes understood his obligation to the black community, and he offered no excuses for his decision.

Members of the black community offered little criticism of the Evans grant largely because thousands of black youth had spent a fruitful summer in hundred of other programs funded by Cleveland: Now! For instance, the Afro-American Youth Cooperative received $25,000 to provide employment and on-the-job training for youth aged fifteen to eighteen, and Baxter Hill and PRIDE received $20,000 for employment and training of poor youth. Cleveland: Now! awarded $16,500 to Case Western Reserve University's Junior Scholar program, which was designed to prepare graduates of inner-city high schools for college. The program also provided low-income youths with financial aid for college. The Pace interdistrict summer school received $25,000 to enroll youngsters in suburban districts so they could take classes not offered in Cleveland public schools. And the Black Economic Union Project received $7,000 to help inner-city youth prepare for leadership positions. Another grant of $25,000 went to a broad-based educational and cultural program designed to address a variety of problems that inner-city youngsters face. Cleveland: Now! also financed the start of six day-care centers across the city, as part of a broader commitment to establish a series of multiservice health and welfare centers. The day-care facilities were especially appreciated by low-income teen mothers like Charlotte Thomas, who sent her children to the Mt. Pleasant Community Day Care Center: "I probably would have to stop working if the center wasn't here . . . since I would have a hard time finding a good baby-sitter. . . . Plus it would be hard for Terrell [her son] to get the training he does here." In all, Cleveland: Now! spent $780,000 for summer programs for 1968, making Cleveland: Now! a success in the eyes of the city's black community.[37]

Meanwhile, the Fraternal Order of Police (FOP) considered the mayor's decision to bar police from the riot area an affront to law enforcement. In early August at the largest meeting in the local chapter's history, the FOP called for the resignations of both Stokes and McManamon. The biggest gripe against the mayor and the safety director was that officers were not warned that Evans and his followers were armed, and that helicopters were not used even though one was made available by the national guard. In airing these grievances the FOP believed that community sentiment was on the side of the police: "At least 95% of the people in Glenville wanted police in the area. . . . Only the militant black nationalists and the hoodlums didn't want them," one officer claimed. FOP officials also demanded that the mayor arrange for the police department to immediately gain the use of tanks and high-powered weapons for sniper control. FOP members also voiced much dissatisfaction with Blackwell, whom many officers believed was "letting the mayor and safety director push him around." The call for his resignation was tabled only because of his age (mid-sixties) and because of his lifelong membership in the FOP.

Stokes rejected calls for his resignation even as he took full responsibility for the decisions he had made during the crisis. Days after Stokes's refusal to resign or dismiss McManamon, posters appeared on precinct bulletin boards with pictures of Stokes and McManamon and the words "Police Killers: Wanted for the Murder of Three Policeman."[38]

When the FOP was unable to dislodge Stokes and McManamon, it asked Governor Rhodes to remove them for neglect of duty. Leading this campaign was Sgt. Louis Bors, who sent the governor a ten-page affidavit requesting the ouster of Stokes, McManamon, and James. Rhodes ignored it. Then the newly formed Citizens for Law Enforcement Committee (CLEC), led by Robert Anable, a well-known local white supremacist, began a recall effort. The basis of the recall drive was the mayor's failure "to act properly in the Glenville area." CLEC also demanded that all Cleveland: Now! funds be given to the widows of the three slain officers.[39]

But local black nationalists were impressed with the mayor's actions during the crisis. During a rally at Cory Methodist Church in early August they affirmed their support for Stokes. Jay Arki, prime minister of the Federation of Black Nationalists, quashed the rumor of a plot to assassinate Stokes, and Arki warned that if angry whites "do anything to Brother Stokes or Ahmed—they talk about Red China—they'll have something worse than Red China right here." Wilbur Gratton of the Afro Unity Circle echoed Arki's remarks and then expressed his opinion on the shootings: "It was a plot on the part of the police, the establishment, and the white power structure. The black men who died are comrades. We salute them. The white press has called for peace and supports the cops. If they escalate an arms race, you better get in on it." Harllel Jones probably summed up the mood of the meeting when he remarked: "In the next five years, we're going to rewrite history. The white man is going to have to give us our freedom or he is going to have to kill us all."[40]

The Glenville shoot-out effectively ended Stokes's political honeymoon. Since taking office the previous November, he had made a number of moves toward getting the city back on track: He reorganized the police department, got the city's HUD funding restored, passed a tax increase to raise salaries, kept the peace after King's death, and launched Cleveland: Now! He also had solidified the support of the business community, the press, and black nationalists. The crazed actions of Ahmed Evans caused many to forget about Stokes's accomplishments. Yet Stokes's nightmare was partly of his own making. Since the summer of 1967 he had constantly emphasized that if elected, he would keep Cleveland cool. Although he was successful after King's murder in April, his attempts to placate the frustrated masses did not succeed with Evans. Although other militants were content to let Stokes reform the city's discriminatory institutions, Evans was not one of them. In essence Stokes was being attacked for not fulfilling his promise to keep the peace in Cleveland.

In 1969 Evans was convicted of murdering the three white police officers and sentenced to death. At his sentencing he told the judge: "I fully understand the ways of life as they are now, and the truth of the matter is I have no regret. The electric chair or fear of anything won't stop the black man of today. Like, I fully understood what I might encounter when I became a Black Nationalist; but I didn't become a Black Nationalist to sell out my people or to use them for malpractice. I became a Black Nationalist because I wanted to help. I felt that I had something to give them, to aid them, and I did." Evans died in prison before Ohio could execute him.[41]

The Glenville rebellion gave the Stanton bloc on the city council new ammunition to fire at Stokes and his programs. And at the first city council meeting in September, they let loose. "I believe the East Side of Cleveland is in a state of anarchy," said council member Edward Katalinas. "My ward is literally being taken apart by hoodlums, thugs, and murderers." Although Stanton did not specifically refer to Stokes's attempts to establish a relationship with the dispossessed, he implied that the mayor was preventing the police from doing their job: "We have young hoodlums walking the streets in broad daylight carrying flags, carrying spears, carrying knives, carrying swords, some even carrying guns." Other council members, such as Lawrence Duggan, Anthony Garofoli, and Ralph Perk Jr., implied that Cleveland was becoming a haven for criminals because of the mayor's distrust of local law enforcement. Members of the Stanton bloc continued their attacks at the next council meeting, only to be confronted by several groups of nationalists that packed the city council chambers. When Katalinas went into a long monologue about the need for law and order, they heckled, booed, and laughed as they waved the black nationalist flag. Stanton tried unsuccessfully to quiet the crowd. The protests continued until James asked the audience to tone down. The presence of black nationalists at council meetings cost Stokes support among the white moderates on the council, who were increasingly being won over to the conservative Stanton bloc. Sensing that the council wars were under way, Stokes decided to take his message directly to the people in the form of town hall meetings and televised speeches.[42]

Stokes held his first post-Glenville town hall meeting in the white working-class community of Collinwood in September. The crowd was initially hostile, but Stokes cooled the anger by answering and addressing the concerns of audience members truthfully and honestly. When one concerned resident asked why the police department did not have the equipment it needed to handle the disturbance, Stokes accepted full responsibility, although the budget for police equipment had suffered from "twenty years of neglect," he said. When another citizen suggested that Stokes purchase tanks and bazookas so that the police would be prepared for future disturbances, he answered: "I am not going to permit the City of Cleveland to be turned into an armed camp. Anytime we descend to the point when tanks and policemen with bazookas are required to keep the peace, then we have lost any semblance of democracy." Another concerned citizen asked why he had marched with armed nationalists on the anniversary of the Hough riots. He responded simply, "I do lots of things that I don't want to do. I do them because I am the mayor." By the end of the evening Stokes had carefully managed to quiet many of his critics; he stayed for thirty minutes to sign autographs and shake hands.[43]

Also in September Stokes started a monthly television program designed to win community-wide support for his programs. His first televised speech dealt with law and order or, more specifically, his relationship with the police department. Stokes opened by stating that the Glenville tragedy had been fomented by a group of "sick, misguided men" who had given up on democracy. He stressed that he hoped that the citizens of Cleveland would not let Evans's vendetta poison the city while acknowledging that Clevelanders no longer were united behind his Cleveland: Now! program. He described what happened in Glenville as an unfortunate event that turned "police against citizen, citizen against citizen, government official against government official, and black against white." In discussing his own responsibility to maintain public safety, Stokes emphasized that although he inherited a police department that lacked discipline, was understaffed, and poorly trained, he had recently initiated a police training program for all patrol officers and that he was in the process of replacing much of the department's outdated equipment. In closing, Stokes asked all Clevelanders "to erase the misunderstanding, to support the police, and to uphold the laws." With the town hall meeting and the televised address, Stokes hoped to recapture the civic enthusiasm of his first months in office, but he was not successful. Meanwhile, the local press added to the anti-Stokes atmosphere.[44]

In late September the *Plain Dealer* began a series headlined "THE CLEVELAND POLICE: WHAT'S ON THEIR MIND." Stokes eagerly anticipated the series because he and the paper's editor, Thomas Vail, agreed that it should discuss the obstacles the mayor faced in reforming the police department. In one of Stokes's weekly meetings with local media figures, Vail asked Stokes if his paper could help the mayor's efforts. "I told him yes—if he could get someone to really write about the malingering [in the police department], the continued protection of numbers and policy operators, the nearly complete work stoppage the police were engaged in after the Glenville shoot-out," Stokes said. He was under the distinct impression that staff writers were going to conduct an in-depth study of black attitudes toward the police department.[45]

The first article set the tone for the series. It measured the attitudes of white police officers toward Stokes, McManamon, and Blackwell. For instance, when asked about their leadership qualities, one officer responded: "Mayor Stokes can't lead. Maybe he doesn't know how. . . . McManamon won't lead. He can't. He wasn't even a good policeman. Chief Blackwell won't lead. He can, but City Hall won't let him. He's nothing but a puppet." Officers also claimed that the mayor protected black nationalists and that he wanted to put them in uniform. One officer remarked, "He wants to get them into the police department . . . then these blacks will have an 'in' in the department."[46]

"We're like a British outpost in Africa," read the introduction for the second installment. One officer wanted to know "what good are .38s against automatic rifles?" Another questioned the lack of riot-control gear: "We're not prepared for another one of these (Glenville) . . . when you have to go up against automatic fire with shotguns and handguns not only is the public going to be in danger, but you're going to have a lot of dead policemen."[47]

The third installment discussed racial attitudes within the department. "This business about putting a white and Negro policeman in the same car won't work. You got to have a close relationship between partners. If you're not buddies, forget it," read a drop quote on the front page. The article went on to relate how the majority of blacks favored "good" law enforcement but that militants strongly influenced the Stokes administration's policy of public safety. One veteran of the force characterized police-community relations on the black East Side: "The responsible citizens of the ghetto proved they are for law and order and that they are not responsible at all to the radical groups in their midst." Another patrol officer was much more direct: "In my book Negroes are not the biggest problem in any way. The problem is the dissidents."[48]

The major theme of the series was that Stokes was the enemy of good law enforcement. Although the editors at the *Plain Dealer* had promised that the series would separate fact from fiction, it was based entirely on the attitudes of white officers. More important, however, was that the paper gave no space to the views of Stokes's supporters within the department. Stokes later recalled that the articles had one purpose: "to show the hatred and animosity the police department had for Carl Stokes and for what he was trying to do."[49]

In response to the series local civil rights organizations announced a boycott of the paper. The articles had shown Stokes and his supporters that the local media were also caught up in the hysteria. Throughout the remainder of his tenure the relationship between Stokes and local journalists grew increasingly antagonistic: "In the next three and a half years there was almost no time that one or both newspapers did not have some kind of investigation going that concerned me or my administration." As the relationship between Stokes and the all-white media worsened, he came to realize that local reporters did not understand his predicament. "They had no understanding of how I, as a black man, had gotten elected," Stokes said. "They had no understanding of the things I must do as a black man in power."[50]

Stokes dismissed Blackwell in October, largely because he had lost control of the police department. The mayor then decided to promote from within, in an attempt to heal the stormy relationship between city hall and the police. Days later he named twenty-eight-year veteran Patrick Gerity to replace Blackwell. What impressed Stokes about Gerity was that he was not a member of the "ruling clique" but was a loner, a straightforward cop. Stokes gave Gerity a mandate, telling him to carry out his duties "anyway you want— but do it." Shortly after Gerity's appointment the new chief gave an exclusive interview to the *Call and Post* in which he outlined his plans to improve the volatile relationship between the black community and the police.[51]

Asked what specific steps he would take to curb police brutality, Gerity explained, "If a policeman violates departmental regulations, he can certainly expect to be punished." The paper also asked Gerity how his officers would deal with black nationalist organizations, which were growing in popularity throughout the city. "As long as any organization operates according to law they will be treated like everyone else," Gerity replied. "We're trying to open lines of communication with them, to reduce tension." Black residents enthusiastically welcomed Gerity as chief, but the FOP questioned his appointment. Perhaps FOP members realized that as long as Stokes was mayor, they would not have a chief sympathetic to their approach to law enforcement.[52]

After naming Gerity, Stokes answered some of his critics by announcing a series of changes in police policy. He and the city council agreed to take steps to end racism in the department, to support police in enforcing all laws, to discipline rogue officers, and to work toward a more realistic goal of integrating the department. Moreover, they also agreed to stop "coddling" lawless elements throughout the city. These symbolic gestures by Stokes were overt attempts to recapture some of the support he had lost within the police department. Stokes also rejected black nationalist demands for a civilian review board and for an all-black police force in black communities.[53]

Despite all that had happened, the mayor was still quite popular throughout the country. The Democrats asked Stokes to give one of the nominating speeches for Hubert H. Humphrey at the 1968 Democratic National Convention in Chicago. As he approached his second year in office, the mayor understood that much of his momentum had died on the night of July 23. But he nonetheless remained committed to reform and began a battle to place public housing units in the black middle-class community of Lee-Seville.[54]

5. Lee-Seville

WITH NEW HOME construction in the inner city virtually nonexistent since the 1920s, much of the housing stock in the black community was either substandard or dilapidated when Stokes became mayor. Because the second great migration exacerbated the housing squeeze, some black families had to live in garages, alleys, sheds, attics, and cellars. Although home construction in the suburbs peaked in the 1950s, these developments were off limits to blacks, either because of discrimination by banks, restrictive covenants, exclusionary zoning laws, or outright intimidation and violence. By the mid-1960s Cleveland's poorly planned urban renewal programs had forced thousands of black families to relocate into already overcrowded areas. To alleviate some of the housing tensions Stokes embarked upon an ambitious plan to build 274 single-family homes in the black middle-class neighborhood of Lee-Seville.

With approximately twenty-five hundred homes, the Lee-Seville community was in many ways a testament to black progress. With its spacious homes, manicured lawns, wide streets, and broad sidewalks, the community was unlike any other area of black Cleveland, and Lee-Seville homeowners took pride in that fact. Like their white counterparts out in the suburbs, black residents of Lee-Seville relished their quiet streets, large yards, better schools, and most especially their mortgages. Equally important, however, was what homeownership in Lee-Seville represented: upward mobility. Buying a home in Lee-Seville meant that one had arrived in Cleveland's black middle class.[1]

However, as black homeowners made their way to Lee-Seville, a subdivision within the larger southeastern community of Lee-Miles, they faced harassment and intimidation from conservative whites. In fact, residents chose to arm themselves on several occasions after police failed to provide them with protection. They also confronted a host of structural problems, including few recreation facilities, overcrowded schools, and a neighborhood drainage system that did not work. Thus, although the community was a delight to onlookers, local residents often considered its physical beauty to be superficial and felt considerable dissatisfaction.

Much of the community outrage centered on the 120 acres of vacant land on both sides of Lee-Seville Road. It served as a community junkyard, sprouting discarded furniture, refrigerators, garbage, rubbish, hot water tanks, and old automobiles, and residents wanted the land to be cleared and developed. The land was originally zoned for semi-industrial use, but homeowners convinced the city to purchase sixty-seven acres in March 1967 for residential use. The city then designated the land for families displaced by the urban renewal program. The Cuyahoga Metropolitan Housing Authority (CMHA) owned the remaining acreage, which had been the site for a never-built 900-unit high-rise public housing complex in the early 1950s.[2]

In May 1968 Mayor Stokes announced plans to build 274 new single-family homes in Lee-Seville that residents could either rent or purchase with mortgages carrying an interest rate of 1 percent, to ensure community stability and to give low-income residents an incentive to take care of their property. When complete, the development would include 48 one-bedroom homes for the elderly, 122 with three bedrooms, 80 with four bedrooms, and 24 with five bedrooms. The houses were to sit on huge lots, recessed from the street, in lots of colors and designs comparable to those of the existing homes in the Lee-Seville area. Eligible families would pay rents of $40 to $80 a month. Stokes was particularly excited about the development because it would shorten the housing authority's waiting list of seventeen hundred families and encourage private developers to build housing for low-income residents. Although Stokes could have chosen any community within the county, he chose Lee-Seville largely because the land was available, and he was confident that area homeowners would be more receptive to the idea of lower-income blacks moving into their community. Later that month Stokes named local fair housing advocate Irving Kriegsfeld as executive director of the Cuyahoga Metropolitan Housing Authority to help the mayor better articulate his plans for Lee-Seville and to better coordinate the mayor's overall housing program.[3]

Although the Lee-Seville development was to be built on fifty-one acres of vacant CMHA land, the housing authority still needed Cleveland City Council's approval to make the necessary street and neighborhood improvements. Stokes considered the council's approval to be a mere formality. Although the council had begun to more openly oppose many of his measures in the aftermath of Glenville, he was firmly convinced that he could acquire the support he needed. But when Stokes announced his plans in the late spring of 1968, two Lee-Seville area council members, Clarence Thompson and George White, both African Americans, immediately objected that the existing level of city services could not handle the population increase. Upon hearing their concerns, Stokes realized that getting the legislation passed by the council would not be easy.[4]

At an emotional city council meeting in early July, White and Thompson attacked the mayor's proposal. "We don't have adequate schools now; we don't have adequate recreation now; we don't have adequate police protection now," said White. To the surprise of those in attendance, White suddenly shifted his criticism from the lack of city services to an implicit attack on working-class blacks: "We learned that it takes a lot of struggle for the fine things in life. You don't get it by thinking that the Federal government is going to make everything right." White also attacked the mayor for making the black middle class the subject of an experiment. "I want you to go to Shaker Heights [a Jewish suburb] and plead for housing there," he said. When council member Charlie Carr and Richard Green, the community development director, rose to support the proposal, Stanton held them to a strict time limit for their statements. Stokes then took the rostrum and argued that the development would provide quality housing for the people who needed it most. He also said that any delay in passing the legislation was virtually signaling the "death-knell" for decent public housing. Stokes was passionate about the Lee-Seville project because he recognized that there was "no more serious crisis today than the poverty-stricken, the ill-fed, the ill-clothed, the ill-educated, and the ill-housed."[5]

Although White and Thompson claimed to be speaking for their constituents in opposing the project, the mayor felt otherwise. At an emotionally charged town hall meeting on July 9, Stokes supporters presented the two conservative council members with a petition signed by more than five hundred area citizens who favored the proposal. But White and Thompson were not convinced that these were legitimate signatures from actual Lee-Seville homeowners. White believed that the signatures came from people outside the community. When White asked about the source of the signatures, Rev. Claude Cummings asked him to sit down. A visibly upset White then stormed out of the building. Next, Kriegsfeld addressed the concerns about overcrowding by promising that city services would increase and that property values would not decline, an unmentioned yet obvious concern of White and Thompson. Kriegsfeld also remarked that the petitions were proof that the local citizenry favored the project.[6]

At the following Monday night council session on July 15, tensions flared again as White tore into the housing authority and more than 150 of his constituents cheered and applauded. "My opposition is not an attempt to embarrass this administration," he proclaimed. "But if you don't have enough police protection now, how are you going to have it with more houses? Anyone who can tell me 1,000 more children won't cause a problem can call me a bigot and a man who is against his own people." As White took his seat, his supporters showed their approval by waving orange and black signs calling for no project, while those in favor of the project showered him with insults. In response, Stokes reminded White that the conditions of the city could not be changed overnight: "Whatever we try to do in two years cannot possibly replace what hasn't been done for the past quarter century." In closing, Stokes reiterated the obligation of the city to provide decent housing for low-income people: "We have to give the poor people a chance to have their own garage, their own piece of property. We have to give these people a chance to be a part of the affluent society."[7]

Days later Stokes issued a press release outlining the city's commitment to increasing municipal services in Lee-Seville. The mayor promised new access roads, with lighting and sewerage, as well as additional police patrols, a small fire station, new playgrounds, including a swimming pool and basketball courts, stricter code enforcement, and housing rehabilitation. Council member Thompson was not convinced. He argued that Lee-Seville residents deserved something for their tax dollars now, not later, and that such improvements for the area should not be contingent on approval of the new housing development.[8]

The opposition by White and Thompson was significant for several reasons. First, it confirmed Stokes's belief that the city's black council members were only interested in their respective wards, not in working collectively to solve the problems of the black community. Stokes was now beginning to understand why black residents saw little change in the conditions of their community, although at least eight African Americans had served on the city council since the late 1950s. The resistance of White and Thompson also represented the first time that any of the city's black council members had openly opposed any of his proposals. While they may not have agreed with his recommendations and policies, pressure from the black community generally convinced them that they would be wise to support Stokes, lest they be labeled sellouts. Last, their resistance gave the Stanton bloc an opportunity to defeat a Stokes proposal. Although this was purely a black issue, Stanton and his followers seized the chance to enforce an informal council rule: that council members defer to the wishes of the member whose district is affected.

Although White and Thompson were able to gain the support of the Stanton bloc, they received little support from the other eight black council members, all of whom supported the mayor. But with White and Thompson vociferous in their objections, and the Stanton bloc eager to work against him, Stokes faced an uphill battle in his efforts to provide the black poor with quality housing.

At a special council meeting in September, Stokes nominated Kriegsfeld to the city planning commission in the hope of broadening his base of support for the Lee-Seville development. Chaos soon erupted in the council chambers as Thompson convinced the Stanton faction to reject the nomination on the ground that Kriegsfeld's appointment to the commission represented a conflict of interest. "There must be a tremendous study regarding the conflict of interest issue which the Kriegsfeld appointment to the Planning Commission poses here," said Thompson. Stokes supporters knew this was just an excuse because Ernest Bohn, Kriegsfeld's predecessor, had chaired the planning commission for an entire decade. However, Thompson stood firm: "My stand is for the taxpayer in my ward. The taxpayer must be represented. There are many others who could be put on the planning board." There was no discussion before the vote, which was unusual. Stokes was irate: "The community is concerned and wherever there is an issue where the community is concerned there should be some discussion from the Council floor." This convinced Stokes that the issue was bigger than Kriegsfeld. "This was not a vote against a man, but what he stands for, low income housing for all of the people who need it in the city of Cleveland," said Stokes. After the council rejected the Kriegsfeld nomination, Stokes called it a blow to city planning and to low-income residents across the city.[9]

The rejection of Kriegsfeld inflamed William O. Walker, editor of the *Call and Post*. He blasted the actions of the city council in an editorial entitled "CITY COUNCIL TAKING A DANGEROUS ROAD." Walker opened his harangue by stating that "prejudices of all kinds" were involved in the rejection. Council President Stanton and other white council members "who don't want Mayor Stokes to succeed because he is a Negro" had shown racial prejudice. Sectional bias was evident because a number of council members "are against any housing program involving Negroes if it isn't confined to the already established ghetto areas." He concluded by arguing that class prejudice was involved because it was mainly middle-income blacks leading the opposition. According to Walker, Kriegsfeld's only shortcoming was that he was nominated by Mayor Stokes. In Walker's opinion "this was sufficient for Council's bigots." In closing, Walker told his readers that Cleveland should not suffer in its efforts to develop quality housing because of the "petty prejudices" of council members. He warned the opponents of the project that it was time for the council to end these tactics before "this town really erupts."[10]

As the controversy continued, Stokes resorted to confrontational and heavy-handed politics to win support for his project. In October he stated publicly that two African Americans on the city council were unconcerned about the welfare of the black poor. The dispute became ugly when Stokes labeled opponents of the project "black bigots." He explained: "If you permit bigoted black middle-class persons with a bigoted black public official representing them to stop the utilization of unused land in Lee-Seville for housing . . . you will have failed to support everything we want to do with housing in this city and you will have struck a blow against expanding opportunities for all persons to live anywhere in the city and in the greater community." Stokes also accused the foes of Lee-Seville of adopting tactics similar to those that white suburbanites used to exclude blacks from their communities.[11]

Thompson responded by deploring Stokes's comments. "To be called a black bigot I don't like, I am not a bigot, this is sickening." Thompson went on to stress that although he was concerned about the black poor, he and his family had worked hard for everything they had attained. "We are concerned about the poor in our city. How many of us have been poor? Many have come from farms. I never lived in metro housing. My dad was a farmer. We have struggled hard for what we have attained." Thompson then shifted his argument to the more practical theme of overcrowding. "A street at the end of my street is a dead end. There are 47 acres of land owned by the Metropolitan Housing that have no storm sewers, water backs up in my basement. This is why people in Lee-Seville oppose the development." Despite their legitimate concerns about overcrowding, the real issue, according to White, was that "it takes a lot of struggle to get the good things in life, you don't get them by having someone else give them to you."[12]

Many black homeowners shared the view expressed by White. "I had to work 14 hours a day and seven days a week to earn the down payment on my house, why should I say 'Come on Charlie you can have it all for free?'" remarked the Lee-Seville resident Fred Butler. While some residents saw public housing as a handout, others feared the decline of property values. "I don't want them up there because of my home. You put life savings in a home and I think it would depreciate my property. I rented to some of their type . . . and I know how destructive they were," said one anonymous homeowner. Another equated lack of homeownership with lower-class values: "If they can't afford to build homes of their own like ordinary people, how are they going to keep up those they propose to build for them?" Area homeowner Sherie

Guilford feared that the newcomers would not paint their homes, mow their lawns, or place trash in garbage cans, while her neighbor was not convinced that the proposed homes were any different from other CMHA properties: "First thing you know it will be another ghetto, even though they plan to make it lease-own developments. Those pictures look like plain old projects. Only difference they have added is, what looks to me as far as I'm concerned, a board in front." One concerned resident stated that the controversy was simply an issue of "homeowners vs. renters."[13]

Council member Thompson came under intense scrutiny and pressure to support the project after he opposed the mayor and publicly objected to the initiative to help the black poor. Thompson and his supporters could accept criticism from other African Americans who favored the project, but they could not digest the insults from "blue-eyed liberals" and white "suburban guardians of the poor." He was referring to white liberals who did not live in Lee-Seville but who nonetheless questioned the racial loyalty of Lee-Seville homeowners. On several occasions Thompson and his supporters called upon white suburbanites to make arrangements with the housing authority to place the proposed homes in their communities and put them, the "black bigots," to shame.[14]

Stokes did receive support from a small contingent of Lee-Seville residents who looked beyond the rhetoric of overcrowding and declining property values. Asked why he favored the development, one Lee-Seville homeowner responded, "Because everyone needs a decent place to live," while another answered that there was a "need for more housing for low-income families." Harry Powell, a local grocer, said that he could not object to the project because "we've been kicked around so much we can't afford to kick anyone else." Local black nationalists like Baxter Hill were adamant about constructing the much-needed housing: "We are going to build these houses, even if we have to tear down Lee-Seville to do it."[15]

Stokes received considerable support from the wider black community. The most active of the groups supporting Stokes was the Community Fighters for Large Families, which distributed literature attacking White and Thompson for feeling "that people in low-income homes should not be provided decent housing in neighborhoods where middle-income people live." Throughout December and January its members were visible at council meetings, where they demanded that Thompson bring the legislation out of committee for a hearing.[16]

The controversy reached a showdown in late January and early February 1969, when the city planning commission held hearings on the proposed development in the Cleveland City Council chambers. Throughout the evening the partisan crowd heard members of the Stokes administration answer critics of the project. Those in attendance listened as Stokes's cabinet members spoke of a "dream community" with radial streets, underground wires, improved police and fire protection, and a well-equipped park. Paul Briggs, superintendent of Cleveland public schools, promised to build new schools, and a representative from the City Transit Service told residents that new bus routes would be added to handle the enlarged population. Stokes supporters, who wore large lapel badges reading "BUILD IT," applauded and cheered after the administration made its presentations. After listening to these promises, Thompson shouted, "Do something now!" He argued that the improvements should be made before the new housing was built, not after. Albert Pottinger, council member from neighboring Ward 13, drew applause when he informed the crowd that the new homes would be different from those in the community because they would not have garages or basements. He provoked further cheers and jeers when he remarked that the low-income residents would be unable to afford to make routine repairs. But Stokes supporters did not let these attacks go unanswered. Franklin Anderson of the Hough Area Development Corporation received wide applause when he told Thompson and Pottinger that "you don't have pretty houses out there, anyway." Likewise, John Barnes, who chaired the Lee-Seville Development Corporation, a Lee-Seville civic group that backed the mayor, informed opponents of the project that they had been lied to in order to get them to oppose the development.[17]

At the end of the volatile hearings, the city planning commission approved the plans for the 274 single-family homes. The planning commission's stamp of approval was critical because it guaranteed Lee-Seville homeowners that the city would make the public improvements to accommodate the subdivision. Now the issue was clearly in the hands of the city council. Although the housing authority now had permission to build the development, it could not begin construction until the council passed legislation to make the infrastructure improvements. In February, Stokes sent the council measures for new sewers, roads, a fire station, and other improvements.[18]

Despite the city planning commission's approval, the fourteen bills were stalled in council committees—and Stanton allies chaired all of them. Michael Zone and George Blaha presided over the Real Property Committee and the City Planning Committee, respectively, while Richard Harmody chaired the Public Development and Service Committee, and John Cimperman chaired the Air and Water Pollution Committee. Although they claimed to be abiding by the informal courtesy rule, Stokes knew otherwise. He understood that the Stanton bloc had little concern for the affairs of the black community;

rather, these council members actively sought to discredit the Stokes administration by opposing any and all of the mayor's proposals.[19]

While Stokes and Thompson sparred in council sessions, factions developed in Lee-Seville. The Lee-Seville Development Corporation (LSDC), directed by Kenneth Johnson and John Barnes, strongly favored the project and kept Stokes apprised of neighborhood politics. The LSDC also mounted a massive public relations campaign championing the housing proposal. However, these efforts were met with little success because Thompson and Stanton countered with an aggressive marketing campaign of their own that exploited the fears of Lee-Seville residents. Carrying out their plans within the neighborhood were Jack Oliver and Jean Murrell Capers, who emerged as the principal spokespersons. Oliver manipulated Lee-Seville residents by telling them that their beloved community would turn into a slum if they allowed the development. Likewise, Capers became an active foe of the development when she became lead counsel for the infant Lee-Seville Homeowners Improvement Association (LSHIA).[20]

The LSHIA had organized in 1967 in response to plans to use vacant land in Lee-Seville for public housing. Re-energized in 1968, the association fought to "maintain and to perpetuate a high standard of community stability" in what it considered to be a "model residential community." Members were particularly concerned that residents have the right to exercise what they called "neighborhood determinis," the ability of homeowners to determine the fate and future of their community. The LSHIA emerged as the chief organizational vehicle for blocking the housing proposal.[21]

At one point LSHIA members issued a three-page manifesto to better articulate their objections to the mayor's proposal. It began by arguing that public housing units never met the moral, spiritual, and inspirational needs of its tenants, regardless of the design. Rather, the development would merely perpetuate an awful system. After presenting concerns relative to overcrowding, the manifesto declared that the LSHIA did not want the black poor "colonized" and "stereotyped" in a public housing ghetto, because the organization believed that the housing authority created all-black high-density areas. In closing, it said that members were looking to the future and did not wish to relive the past: "Most of us are well aware of our origin but we do not want to go back to public housing days and those beautiful days on the farm, we could not do better in those days, now we can."[22]

Because the housing authority could have put the development anywhere in Cuyahoga County, LSHIA members wondered why Stokes insisted on building it in their community. They did not consider their position to be one of "black bigotism" but one they had to take to maintain a "first-class community." Last, they argued that the development would lead to increased residential segregation, when they wanted their community developed along lines of racial, social, and economic "inclusion." Instead of concentrating families in a particular area, the housing authority should use the "scattered-site approach," the LSHIA suggested. This was a valid argument. Although blacks represented 47 percent of all public housing tenants, more than 80 percent of black public housing tenants were concentrated in three East Side projects. Conversely, 99 percent of all white tenants lived in all-white projects on the predominantly white West Side.[23]

Members of LSHIA felt that it would be a mistake to view their stance as being against the black poor; they sincerely believed that their position would enhance the upward mobility of the black poor by forcing them to be self-reliant and not dependent upon government handouts. The position taken by the LSHIA clearly reflected the class divisions in Cleveland's black community. What made the group's stance even more interesting was that although many members were raised in public housing, they were not willing to give the black poor a chance to improve their living conditions. Though never explicitly stated, the LSHIA had two major concerns, the loss of property values and the loss of status. The thought of living near the black poor was depressing, because many had sought to escape the masses by moving to Lee-Seville.[24]

As the controversy continued, Stokes resorted to his riot-insurance rhetoric. Speaking at Yale University in early April, Stokes described his inability to get council approval for his housing proposal and warned: "If trouble comes in Cleveland this Summer it could well be over City Council's failure to approve housing for the Lee-Seville area." He further declared that if riots did occur, the entire city would be responsible because it had failed to respond to the needs of the black poor. Stokes was adamant in getting the units built because he knew the long-term consequences if the homeowners in Lee-Seville succeeded: "If we can't get council's approval for the Lee-Seville project, is there any reason why Bratenahl or Shaker Hts. should be more progressive? This is why the fight is so important, we can't go to the suburbs with such a plan if we can't demonstrate we can do the same thing in Cleveland." Stokes also pushed for Lee-Seville while speaking at a Martin Luther King commemoration at Cleveland's Olivet Institutional Baptist Church. Halfway through his address Stokes remarked: "Some of you are from Lee-Seville, I want to make it clear. Don't you people sit here and remember Martin Luther King, Lee-Seville is what Martin Luther King was all about—giving people a chance to live in dignity." Stokes's threats and appeals had little effect on Thompson and Pottinger.[25]

Weeks later Stokes took the matter of Lee-Seville directly to the people with an impromptu on-site, hourlong television special in April 1969. The mayor criticized Thompson and the Stanton bloc for keeping the legislation in committee, and he made a public appeal for them to set aside their individual concerns and work together for the "common good of this city." Stokes also remarked that it would be politically expedient for him to drop the issue because it was really the housing authority's fight, "but I have made Lee-Seville my fight and I bring this controversy to you tonight because this city cannot afford to lose this battle."[26]

In the hope of calming neighborhood fears about property values, Stokes and Kriegsfeld decided to build seven model homes on the site to give residents an opportunity to see exactly what type of homes the city intended to build. They didn't need city council approval to do it because the addition of only seven homes did not require new streets, sidewalks, and utilities. But shortly after Stokes announced the plans, Jean Capers sought an injunction against the model homes on behalf of the LSHIA in U.S. District Court. She argued that the housing authority had selected the Lee-Seville location because the community was 99 percent black and the new development would thus maintain a long-standing policy of segregation. The LSHIA focused on segregation because throughout its history the housing authority had intentionally segregated its tenants. However, U.S. District Judge Ben C. Green denied the injunction, saying it was outside his jurisdiction because the Common Pleas Court was already handling a similar request.[27]

As the power struggle between Stokes and Thompson approached an impasse, Thompson's supporters showed their appreciation by sponsoring a testimonial dinner in his honor in May 1969. More than four hundred residents fêted and praised Thompson as a "symbol of honesty and dedication," for not succumbing to the "powerful pressures" to vote for the development in Lee-Seville. The keynote speaker was newly installed Municipal Court Judge George White, the former Lee-Seville area council member. The appreciation dinner was designed to encourage Thompson to continue his fight against Stokes.[28]

With the city council scheduled to recess on June 30, Stokes and his supporters intensified the pressure on Thompson and Stanton. In late May Stokes sent letters to Stanton and to council committee chairs requesting that they hold public hearings on the legislation. They ignored him. In fact, Stanton suggested that the housing proposal be put to a vote of the residents in that area. "I believe that through the ballot box this difficult issue can be resolved. This is an attempt on my part to seek a solution," said Stanton. Stokes labeled Stanton's suggestions as a "clear evasion of his responsibility." The city law department later ruled that the city charter had no provision for such a referendum.[29]

At a city council meeting on May 19 seven black council members took the floor and demanded that the requisite committees hold hearings on the fourteen pieces of legislation. Charlie Carr from Ward 17 stated that in his twenty-four years on city council he had never known it to refuse to hold a public hearing on a piece of legislation introduced by the mayor. John Armstrong, James Bell, Warren Gilliam, Carrie Cain, Virgil Brown, and George Forbes supported Carr. Bell mentioned that he favored Lee-Seville because it would alleviate some of the suffering and give the community hope. Cain, Brown, Armstrong, and Gilliam called for hearings. "We have an obligation to hear both sides," said Cain. "My people are fed up with the 'councilmanic courtesy' routine. I'm fed up too."[30]

As the council recess date quickly approached, Stokes again took his appeal to the public, this time with a guest editorial in the *Plain Dealer*. He used the opportunity to make the distinction between the Lee-Seville development and the generally accepted notion of public housing: "People remember the old days when public housing often meant stark high-rise developments that hurt property values by literally forcing large numbers of people into a neighborhood whose residents had little in common with newcomers." Lee-Seville bore no resemblance to that, he wrote. "The proposed development is totally in keeping with what the people there need and want." He then told readers that according to local realtors and insurance executives, property values would actually increase rather than decline. Stokes was firmly convinced that if the development was called "XYZ" housing instead of "public" housing, "the public would be clamoring for it." The mayor ended the editorial by stressing that the opportunity for homeownership was why the project was so critical. More than twenty-five thousand Clevelanders lived in substandard conditions, "never . . . able to scrape together enough money for a down payment." The Lee-Seville development would give them that opportunity. This, Stokes wrote, was the best way to end the cycle of poverty.[31]

On Monday, June 1, council members were greeted by protesters from the League of Women Voters who supported the proposal. "This legislation must not continue to be used as a political football," said their president, Mrs. Henry Snead. Once inside the council chambers, members were shocked to see the gallery jam-packed with supporters of the mayor's Lee-Seville initiative. Black council members once again gave impassioned pleas for public hearings, but Thompson and the Stanton bloc stood firm. "On election day the people can and will express themselves. I believe it can be decided in the ballot box," Pottinger shouted. The community would have its say the next time he and Thompson ran for re-election.[32]

As the council's summer recess approached, the mayor sponsored the Citizens Rally for Lee-Seville Housing. A crowd of several hundred heard Stokes and other community leaders argue the importance of the development. The event was designed to be a pep rally for that evening's council session, one of the last before the summer break. At the council meeting Bell blamed Stanton for the stalling tactics. "I saw thirteen pieces of legislation to make various improvements, lighting, sewers, sidewalks, streets, playground facilities, and a promise to build new schools and better recreational facilities. The legislation is not unreasonable. If the people of Lee-Seville don't want it, we do in our neighborhood," he said. "I am concerned and sorry that such an important service to the people of Cleveland has been dropped into a struggle for power." Bell closed his dramatic statement by telling council members that they should represent the hopes and desires of the people they serve and alleviate the suffering of the black poor. Edward Katalinas agreed that the council should hold hearings, arguing that that was the only way to resolve the matter.[33]

Stokes made one last appeal for his housing proposal when he held a town hall meeting in the Lee-Seville area on June 12. In attendance were approximately four hundred Stokes supporters and a handful of black homeowners who objected to the project. Stokes immediately came under attack as opponents of the project expressed their by-now familiar criticisms. Stokes became visibly upset at their failure to understand that the development would not cause community deterioration. The tension increased when area homeowner Henry Simon questioned Stokes's commitment to providing the necessary city services. Stokes immediately made the exchange personal by mentioning that Simon had a police record. The meeting was marred with similar attacks, which left little time for meaningful discussion.[34]

On June 21, at the last session before its summer recess, the city council voted 20-13 not to bring the fourteen pieces of legislation out of committee. Stokes denounced the vote and claimed that the democratic process had been hindered. In closing, Stokes made another plea to the council: "Ladies and Gentleman of Council, from this point forward, the issue of public housing in Lee-Seville is entirely up to you. My responsibility as mayor has been fulfilled, and while I am open to suggestions on what more can be done, I must state candidly that I am at a loss to know what it could be." Stanton responded: "When two councilmen object as strongly as they did . . . risking their political lives,

I must stand by them. I make no excuses, no apologies." The session recessed without a hearing on Stokes's Lee-Seville housing proposal.[35]

It was a major setback for Stokes and his urban renewal plans. Although Thompson was out front, voicing the opposition, the Stanton bloc was actually responsible for the project's failure. The Stanton power play on the Lee-Seville development was simply another step in the council president's effort to fulfill his promise to block the mayor's initiatives. Stokes had hoped to use the project to demonstrate that public housing outside the ghetto could be one solution to the city's housing problems. However, the status-conscious black middle class surprised Stokes by effectively mobilizing against the development and by forging a coalition with the foes of black progress. Stokes would encounter similar disappointment when he undertook a battle to place more blacks on the police force, but he would achieve a degree of success in his efforts to replace white owners of businesses in the black community.

6. Police Reform and Black Capitalism

AFTER REORGANIZING the police department shortly after his election, Stokes launched a broad-based effort to place more blacks on the force. Although black Clevelanders represented approximately 37 percent of the city's population, they held only 5 percent of the positions on the police force. Basing its ratio on a 1965 article in the *Call and Post,* the Cleveland Police Department appointed one African American patrolman for every fifty-five white police. When former safety director John T. McCormick was asked why more African Americans had not qualified, he responded: "We would like to get more Negroes appointed but they just can't pass the examination." Similarly, the force's black officers had trouble gaining promotions; they accounted for less than 1 percent of the administrators.[1]

To increase black representation within the police department, Stokes changed the makeup of the five-member Civil Service Commission by securing the resignations of three board members and replacing them with Marvin Chernoff, a businessman and campaign worker; Jay White, an attorney; and Charles Butts, also a campaign worker, in January 1968. These appointments were critical because the Civil Service Commission was responsible for all testing of city personnel. The mayor told the members to make recruiting black police a priority. Such efforts under previous mayors had failed for several reasons, including the negative state of police-community relations, biased testing procedures, the lack of black administrators, the five-month wait from appointment to employment, and the obvious negrophobia in the department.[2]

To circumvent these obstacles Stokes approved a Cleveland: Now! grant of $15,600 in September 1968 to help the local NAACP and other civil rights organizations conduct a thorough recruiting program. The program would prepare potential applicants for the Patrolmen Civil Service Exam to be held on October 19. In coordinating the program, Bill Packard, executive secretary of the local NAACP, hired seven neighborhood recruiters to spread the word in the black community.[3]

Weeks before the exam the NAACP held four training sessions that covered such topics as test-taking techniques, mental preparation, and the role of the police in the community. Community response was excellent: 150 potential candidates took the classes, and 347 blacks submitted applications to join the department. The community was well aware that Stokes was launching an all-out effort to place more blacks on the force. Once the NAACP training was complete, White, Butts, and Chernoff—the new members of the Civil Service Commission—invited the instructors to a meeting to draft the upcoming police exams. Veteran Civil Service Commission members Clayborne George and Thomas Ryan were not invited to attend.[4]

On October 19 approximately twelve hundred applicants took the test. But this time the Civil Service Commission added an interview phase for those who passed the written portion. Only 43 percent passed the written portion, the lowest pass rate in decades. While the Civil Service Commission made only minor changes in its testing for patrol officers, it completely overhauled the promotional exam for the police department. Past exams had simply measured precise knowledge of rules and regulations. The new exam tested the police on their role in the community. The commission also required all officers seeking promotion to read twenty-five books on police-community relations. Among the titles were *Dark Ghetto* by Kenneth Clark; Ralph Ellison's *Invisible Man;* Charles Silberman's *Crisis in Black and White; The Police Role in Racial Conflict* by Juby Towler; and the Kerner Commission report. When officers learned of the new procedures, they were outraged. In particular they felt that Stokes was lowering the standards for both tests in an effort to place more blacks on the force. One officer remarked, "Our men are virtually in a state of shock due to City Hall intervention with the civil service examinations." This officer was especially upset by the interview portion of the test: "We understand there will be oral interviews given too, we are going to stop this by law." In sum, this officer felt that the exams would not be on the "up and up."[5]

After complaints from the Fraternal Order of Police, the Civil Service Commission postponed the promotion test twice. When it was finally administered on December 21, 1968, Police Chief Pat Gerity nullified the results, charging that proper security measures were not maintained. "His original charge was that there was cheating, but that reflected poorly on the policemen taking the test, so he changed it to a security failure, to make it reflect poorly on the commission," Stokes said. Common Pleas Court Judge Thomas Mitchell invalidated a second test given on January 23, 1969, after the FOP filed suit alleging that the exam asked questions unrelated to police work.[6]

In March, after a white officer testified that copies of the promotion test were available before the test date, Mitchell ordered the grand jury to look into whether any cheating had occurred. He also instructed the grand jury to look into whether there had been testing irregularities in the patrolmen's exam. As a result of the grand jury investigation, and upon receiving legal advice that it had acted incorrectly, the Civil Service Commission decided to nullify the police appointment list, which was based on the results of the patrolmen's exam; this decision meant that the police department was under a hiring freeze.[7]

While the tests were still under investigation, the Stanton bloc demanded the ouster of Civil Service Commission members White, Butts, and Chernoff. Council member Anthony Garofoli declared that "something is drastically wrong" with the commission and that unless Stokes was satisfied with its members' performance, "he ought to ask for their resignations," since he was "essentially in control of the CSC." George Blaha expressed similar feelings, and council member Richard Harmody said he believed that Stokes's appointees did not "know how to handle the job." Even one of Stokes's black supporters on the council suggested that the Civil Service Commission controversy had created problems not only for the administration but had become a "tremendous concern" in the black community as well.[8]

In May, when council member John J. Prince called for an investigation into the conduct of the Civil Service Commission, Stokes cautioned the council to wait for the grand jury's report. As the investigation continued, Stokes warned his appointees that if the investigation revealed wrongdoing, they would be prosecuted to the full extent of the law. To appease the city council and to satisfy his critics, Stokes issued a public statement in June that was aimed directly at the conduct of his appointees. "The Commission works independent of any governmental body. However, as mayor I have the power of appointment and removal of its membership, and therefore, while their operations are outside of my jurisdiction, the Commission's membership is not." While everyone awaited the grand jury's report, Stokes's allies privately advised him to dismiss his appointees so that he could move on with his legislative agenda. They were also concerned that the grand jury was stalling in order to release its report closer to the start of the 1969 mayoral campaign.

After two months Stokes attacked the grand jury's delay: "I cannot imagine what is holding up the investigation." The length of the investigation had

convinced Stokes that the grand jury was engaged in a witch-hunt, search-
ing for any hint of misconduct by the mayor and his appointees, and that it
was preventing new officers from joining the force. Stokes charged that County Prosecutor John Corrigan and his assistant, George Moscarino, had "carefully orchestrated the proceedings, stretching them out over months, leak-
ing information that would indicate wrongdoing on the part of certain blacks,
Stokes appointees, and by implication, me." The mayor's criticism brought
a sharp reply from Moscarino: "The prosecutor's office is interested in getting all the facts, not just some of them." Moscarino went on to say that any
time an investigation centered on alleged misconduct and irregularities of
public officials, "it is necessary to make certain that no stone is unturned to
discover whether or not such charges are true or untrue. The public will only
benefit if there is a full and complete disclosure." Stokes's efforts to place the
blame for the lack of new police officers fooled no one. Many of his critics
wanted to know why only eight officers had been hired in eighteen months,
and they wanted to know how the city was spending the money from the 1968
income tax increase, which was supposed to guarantee a bigger police force.
These were questions that Stokes could not place at anyone else's doorstep.
He was responsible for the Civil Service Commission crisis.[9]

By June the intense demand for stronger law enforcement compelled Stokes
to place one hundred police candidates in training on an emergency basis,
despite the grand jury probe. "It is essential that we provide more police in
the streets to combat the admitted increase in crime," Stokes said. "We cannot wait until the Grand Jury Probe is completed." The one hundred cadets
had all passed the patrolmen's exam, and both Chief Gerity and McManamon cleared them to attend the academy.[10]

In July the Cuyahoga County Grand Jury issued interim indictments against
Jay White and Charles Butts on charges of perjury and destroying Civil Service Commission records. Many legal experts were shocked because the entire matter was still under investigation. The grand jury also handed up the
indictment of a white police lieutenant, John Apanites, charged with lying
under oath about where he had obtained a copy of the promotion exam. "He
had maintained he got the exam from the wife of a policeman but vowed to
go to jail rather than reveal who the woman was. Despite the indictment, the
newspapers pictured his criminal act more as an act of chivalry than anything
else," Stokes recalled. When the indictments were handed up, "it was Jay White
and Charles Butts they [the media] kept in criminal posture," Stokes recalled.
They resigned immediately, and Stokes appointed David Sindell, a local attorney, to oversee the Civil Service Commission. However, the grand jury still
had not released the full results of its investigation.[11]

The grand jury finally released its report in early September. As expected, it blamed Stokes, the Civil Service Commission, and the NAACP for "security leaks" that occurred in regard to all the examinations. The report stated specifically that police candidates recruited by the NAACP were given unfair advantages over other candidates by being allowed to file applications after the deadline, given fee waivers, and being allowed to register at NAACP headquarters, instead of the offices of the Civil Service Commission. It also found that the NAACP practice test given during the training sessions was identical to the patrolmen's test. Moreover, the psychologists who drafted the test were also instructors at the NAACP sessions. The report further noted that since Stokes became mayor, veteran Civil Service Commission members Clayborne George and Thomas Ryan were often excluded from meetings. The grand jury then questioned the January promotion test by noting that a copy of the exam had been found "folded and coffee stained." It labeled that test "the greatest tragedy and misuse of manpower and public funds and misapplication of both that any Grand Jury could ever expect to find." The report concluded by issuing a strong rebuke to Stokes: "The responsibility to correct the damage that has been wrongfully done, was and is upon those in command of the situation, the administration of the City of Cleveland."[12]

The black community was angry about what the report failed to mention. First, many wanted to know why the police officer who testified that he had acquired a copy of the test was not severely punished for refusing to disclose where he got it. Second, the community was eager to know why the grand jury had failed to mention that the NAACP program was open to all applicants, black and white. However, what really convinced Stokes and his supporters that the report was biased was that it praised the cooperation of the Cleveland Police Department during the investigation. Many concluded that the grand jury report was just a one-sided political ploy aimed at further embarrassing the mayor.

In response to the blistering report, Stokes defended the role of the NAACP by pointing out that there was no "direct evidence presented of any wrongdoing by NAACP recruiters." He then called for a more thorough investigation into the role of the police department. Stokes was concerned that the grand jury had failed to investigate the role of white police officers in acquiring copies of the promotion test. Before the grand jury released its report, Stokes learned that more than twenty white officers "had purchased the exam and the answers. The prices quoted ranged up to $1,500." In fact, those in possession were not rookies or younger officers but white veterans, "some of the worst white policemen and best-known racists in the department,"

Stokes said. While Stokes acknowledged in his memoir that some irregularities had occurred, "it involved more than the failures of Stokes's Civil Service Commission. White policemen had been cheating."[13]

But Stokes was particularly upset with Jay White, the lone African American appointee. "When he and other blacks I had brought into city hall let themselves get mixed up in things like this I would sit and think, 'the sons of bitches,' here I am trying as hard as I can to put something together for all of us and they go and get involved in something like this. I would feel so helpless." Stokes found White's involvement especially hard to understand because the mayor had specifically warned him about the need to maintain his integrity. "I had talked specifically with him, as I talked with others I appointed to significant positions, saying, 'You are going to have great latitude, and persons are going to try to influence you and literally want to purchase favors from you. You will have a chance to make money, but I want you to understand, I can't stop you from taking a dollar but if I find out about it I will be harder on you than anyone else.'"[14]

While Stokes did not condone White's participation in the scandal, he realized that White was being scapegoated, mainly because he was an African American. The investigation was officially closed weeks later when a deal was struck. The felony charges against White and Butts were dropped in exchange for their guilty pleas on misdemeanor charges of destroying records. The plea bargain convinced Stokes that the county prosecutor was engaged in a cover-up. Stokes was determined to learn who else might have been involved in the fiasco, largely because "I did not want my people singled out for persecution for something of which they were merely a part." He then made a public request that Corrigan reopen the investigation and "go after everybody."[15]

Stokes persisted because, although the grand jury report did not implicate him in any wrongdoing, the public was blaming him. "I was fighting desperately the tradition of blaming black people while white people benefit," he recalled. Many of Stokes's supporters urged him to stop pressing for a reinvestigation, partly because they felt that more blacks were involved, and it created the impression that "I was covering up for black people and attempting to shift blame to white policemen."[16]

The clumsiness of the Civil Service Commission hurt Stokes on two levels. First, white moderates came to believe that Stokes had taken illegal steps to place blacks on the force. Second, it exacerbated his already tenuous relationship with the Fraternal Order of Police and the proponents of strong law enforcement who expected to see additional officers on the streets of Cleveland. But Stokes saw the controversy as a direct and deliberate conspiracy to discredit him, just because he wanted to place more African Americans on the force. Lost in the entire drama was the basic cause of the commission's problems: negrophobia.[17]

While recovering from the testing controversy, the mayor found himself in the middle of a dispute concerning the ownership of local McDonald's franchises in the summer of 1969. By taking bold steps to improve the living conditions of black residents and to bring them within the mainstream of city government, Stokes had created a climate that convinced community activists that city hall would support them if an issue had merit. Moreover, since he was a firm supporter and proponent of black capitalism, community leaders believed they would get the influential support of city hall as they began to try to improve the economy in the black community. When "Rabbi" David Hill and the House of Israel launched a six-month fight to force the sale of four white-owned, inner-city McDonald's franchises to black owners, Stokes found he had to juggle yet another political hot potato.

Hill was born on November 28, 1928, in Nashville, Arkansas. After serving in the army from 1943 to 1946, he studied theology at Nashville Christian Institute. While pastoring a church in Little Rock, Arkansas, he became involved in the school desegregation crisis. During the 1950s, however, Hill was also involved in a string of illegal activities, leading to a conviction for forgery in 1951 and for grand larceny in 1959. In 1962 the state of Illinois convicted him on charges of running of a con game, and in 1964 the thirty-seven-year-old Hill was wanted in Cleveland on charges of writing more than $9,000 in bad checks. His multiple convictions eventually earned him a sentence in the Ohio State Hospital for the Criminally Insane.

The convicted con man re-emerged in 1966 and established the House of Israel on Cleveland's East Side. Next, he adopted the title of "Rabbi," because "calling myself a Reverend and a Christian minister was really supporting, condoning, and strengthening slavery." Hill was desperately trying to find a way "to a more meaningful religion, one that would help free my folks rather than promise them heaven, milk and honey and a mansion as soon as they were dead and in the grave." He became a black Christian nationalist. "It is what we preach in the House of Israel," he said. "It is a new church and a new theology. It means that Jesus is a black man, in fact a Black Nationalist, a man very concerned about the nation, Israel." Hill strongly believed that it was "humanly impossible for a black man to really be a man and be identified with what is commonly called Christianity." Consequently, he began to stress that African Americans, or the "so-called Negroes in America were the Children of Israel, the chosen race of God." The House of Israel catered to the black churchgoer. "We want to destroy what he [the black man] believes in the most, and that is the slavemaster's religion, with the white Jesus and white Mary and white Joseph." Hill stressed to his congregation that "there is no freedom for the black man as long as he's a part of the white man's religion."[18]

Like most Christian black nationalists, Hill did not center his teachings on the conventional Protestant belief in the Resurrection: "We believe that we have already passed from death to life through that resurrection whereby one is changed from being a colored boy or Negro to a black man." His theology stressed that "when one has been born again, he is resurrected. So long as he's scratching his head and saying 'Yes, sir,' and the things white folks want to hear him say he's a dead man." But, once "he accepts black theology . . . and once he begins to relate to a movement that is working for control of the black community and a new identity for the black man, he has been resurrected and he will have eternal life." Hill told his followers that there was no such thing as heaven: "There is no time to prepare man to die and go to heaven. We are trying to teach him how to live now, here on this earth: to control the black community, to control the dollars spent here, the school where his children must receive an education, the police department that sets out here on the plantation, the hospitals where he goes when he is sick." He firmly believed in the politics of black self-determination. While Stokes did not particularly subscribe to this theology, the mayor agreed that black capitalism had merit.[19]

Although the House of Israel started with just four members, Hill claimed a membership of 450 to 500, with "eight or ten times that many sympathizers and well-wishers throughout the black community." Although many of Hill's contemporaries would dispute these figures, his message was undeniably appealing on the poverty-stricken black East Side. But many members of the black clergy considered Hill a liar and a fraud, and Hill knew it: "Needless to say, my fellow ministers hate my very soul, in fact many of them claim I don't have a soul." Hill's theology was somewhat hard for black Clevelanders to accept, but many agreed with his views on black self-determination. Although the traditional leadership class expressed scorn for Hill, Stokes realized that the controversial minister had a role to play in the black community.[20]

The McDonald's protest began in early 1969 after Hill asked to meet with corporate officials about their hiring practices. At the meeting Hill told McDonald's officials "to hand over the keys" to all white-owned franchises in Cleveland's inner city. In fact, four of the franchises were among the nation's busiest in terms of gross revenues, with the East 83d Street location generating a remarkable $750,000 a year in sales, making it the most lucrative in the entire country. Although the outlets had a predominantly black workforce,

Hill wanted blacks to own these franchises because the majority of their customers were African American.[21]

When Hill told Stokes and other community leaders about his discussions with McDonald's, they told him to set up a meeting. Weeks later Rev. Arthur LeMon, Stokes's executive assistant; the local chair of the Southern Christian Leadership Conference, James Raplin; and Hill met with McDonald's officials and agreed that Rev. Ernest Hilliard of Cleveland, a Hill ally, would be awarded a franchise once he completed the company's mandatory training program. But when Hilliard completed the training and showed up to sign the paperwork, McDonald's "had run out of the right forms and told him the deal was off anyway," the *Washington Post* reported. Weeks later McDonald's executives agreed to honor their commitment and award Hilliard a franchise. But on the evening before he was to sign the documents, Hilliard was murdered in his driveway in what police labeled a "professional hit." Although no connection between the murder and his attempt to purchase a franchise was ever proved, Hill and others certainly believed there was one. It later came out that when Hilliard's wife asked him who shot him, he responded, "White folks," before dying. This convinced Hill and other community leaders of a direct connection between Hilliard's murder and their efforts to acquire a McDonald's franchise.[22]

Days after Hilliard was shot, McDonald's executives informed Hill that they had awarded a new franchise to Charles Johnson, an African American who had no involvement with Hill. Johnson was particularly attractive to McDonald's because he had completed the training program, had obtained bank financing, and was not working with the controversial Hill. Hill claimed that the emergence of Johnson as a potential buyer represented an attempt by McDonald's to work independently of the black masses, because Johnson had no known connection to the black community. Moreover, Hill may have been irked that this development cut him out of the negotiations and therefore left him in no position to receive remuneration, legal or otherwise, for his efforts. It was rumored that Hill was telling prospective buyers that he could deliver a franchise for the right price.

When McDonald's announced that Johnson would receive a franchise, Hill submitted his own application to buy one. It was rejected. When Hill told Stokes and other community leaders of the McDonald's attempts to work around him, they agreed to launch a protest. After a lengthy meeting at the *Call and Post* building, community leaders formed Operation Black Unity (OBU), a civil rights coalition. Hill was named chairman. The group decided to launch an all-out effort to place the lucrative East Side franchises in the hands of black owners. Stokes gave the effort his full support and used the power of his office to support the protest throughout the controversy.[23]

Operation Black Unity had a strong case against McDonald's and its policy of excluding black ownership. Of the approximately twelve hundred McDonald's franchise owners in the United States, only one, Theodore Jones of Chicago, was an African American. McDonald's apparently saw nothing wrong with its policies, even though a significant portion of the restaurants— "the biggest money makers," according to OBU—were located in the black inner city.[24]

With strong support from the mayor's office, OBU scheduled a July 5 meeting with McDonald's representatives, hoping that they would either negotiate through OBU to find qualified black buyers or set up special financing for potential buyers who would not otherwise qualify. In addition, OBU hoped that white owners would sell their franchises for less than their market value. Their optimism quickly disappeared, however, when McDonald's executives refused to even consider Hill because of his questionable background and unorthodox businesses practices. In a letter to OBU, Edward Bood, a McDonald's vice president, stressed that the company had made a sincere effort in previous meetings to establish a meaningful dialogue with the House of Israel. However, "the presence of body guards . . . at such meetings hardly contributed to a climate of reasonable and rationale discussions." Consequently, McDonald's representatives found those early meetings totally unproductive because of the "strident, emotionally charged, racial position" taken by Hill and his aides. The letter closed with a statement that McDonald's was ready, willing, and able to meet with the more "respectable" members of the community, such as Mayor Stokes, but not Hill.[25]

When McDonald's executives failed to attend a meeting that OBU had called for July 5, OBU decided to boycott the restaurants. Stokes assured the organization that as long as the picketers remained peaceful, he would make sure that the police department made no effort to disperse them. The mayor's support was critical because the police department had historically broken up mass protest demonstrations by the city's black residents. The first day of the boycott, July 10, was a success—two locations were forced to close by 1 P.M. Manager James Shafer closed his store at 12:35 P.M. after seeing "ten carloads of black nationalists in black jackets and berets" telling patrons not to enter. Picketing on the following day was equally successful; all five inner-city McDonald's restaurants conducted little or no business. At about this time McDonald's sent a directive to all white owners of inner-city franchises asking them to sell to blacks.[26]

A meeting between OBU and McDonald's representatives on July 12 ended after less than five minutes when McDonald's executives refused to accept members of the House of Israel as OBU's chief negotiating team. They would recognize the House of Israel only as a member of OBU, but they refused to deal with Hill and his people exclusively, partly because they felt that Hill was representing his "own interests and objectives and not those of the black community." In addition, the hamburger chain officials still felt uneasy about Hill's confrontational and coercive negotiating style, which they claimed bordered on extortion. "The threats and intimidation directed towards independent McDonald's licenses in Cleveland with the objective of having them sell their businesses to persons selected by the House of Israel is hardly compatible with our company's objectives," Bood said. The steadfast refusal by McDonald's to negotiate with Hill on these grounds was a pure power play. Hill did have a shaky reputation, but he had the support of the mayor and the entire civil rights community. Indeed, OBU members were familiar with Hill's background, but they agreed with his position on black capitalism. In their eyes McDonald's was just attempting to divide the coalition, with the hope that OBU would remove Hill as leader and in his place appoint a more conservative negotiator or one more willing to compromise.[27]

Negotiations soon reached an impasse, although the boycott kept the locations closed. McDonald's was now in an awkward position because of its refusal to negotiate with Hill. "We were most disappointed," Bood said. "We thought we would have an opportunity to talk with the moderate and responsible organizations. But Hill asked if we were prepared to recognize OBU. Then he asked if we were prepared to negotiate with the House of Israel alone. We were not."[28]

McDonald's executives may well have based their position on long-standing business practices, but they clearly were out of touch with the politics of Cleveland's black community, especially after the middle class–oriented NAACP and Urban League passed resolutions urging their members not to patronize McDonald's. On the heels of the NAACP resolution came another strong show of support, this time from the Reverend Donald Jacobs, executive director of the Council of Churches: "Businesses have to recognize that to succeed in the black community they must give equal opportunity at all levels to black persons including ownership." Charles Cook, Midwest director of CORE, summed up the community's reaction to McDonald's: "Whites can no longer choose the blacks they prefer to negotiate with nor dictate terms based on racist attitudes. . . . They are looking for good niggers." Cook later added that the black community would not recognize any sale to a black franchisee in which OBU did not participate. While the corporation's efforts to split the coalition might have worked at other times, Stokes had succeeded in unifying the black community to the point that divide-and-conquer tactics achieved few results.[29]

Days later the effectiveness of the boycott forced McDonald's to soften its stance against Operation Black Unity and Hill. Moreover, McDonald's came to realize that the OBU coalition would hold firm in its demand that the chain negotiate with Hill because the members of OBU still held the "utmost confidence" in Hill's leadership. However, despite McDonald's announcement that it would negotiate with Hill, picketing continued for another week before OBU agreed to return to the negotiating table. Two days before the July 26 meeting OBU, with Stokes's assistance, published a ten-page manifesto outlining its demands:

1. Ownership of the Five McDonald's Restaurants in the Black Communities of Cleveland.
2. Ownership of the unchanged boundary and/or territory rights of future McDonald restaurants in black communities.
3. Franchise royalties from these five restaurants normally received by McDonald's.
4. Irrevocable franchise rights.
5. The right to select and approve franchise buyers.[30]

The manifesto stated that McDonald's was representative of the institutional discrimination that pervaded U.S. businesses. It further charged that economic discrimination imposed on black people was a barrier to human rights and freedom. However, by turning over the inner-city outlets to black owners, McDonald's would be taking a significant step toward increasing the economic base in the black community.[31]

In the community's opinion, the OBU manifesto declared, McDonald's had "knowingly, willfully, and systematically approved and executed a policy of franchise placements that excluded black ownership." In response to OBU's claims that McDonald's failure to award franchises to blacks was deliberate company policy, the company contended that the financial resources and business acumen needed to own and operate a store were virtually nonexistent in the black community. This attack on black intelligence further motivated OBU to continue boycotting until white owners relinquished the franchises.[32]

As the boycott continued, Hill announced that "all of the proposals we took to the meeting are negotiable" but cautioned that OBU would accept no deal unless the black community would benefit economically. Echoing Hill's statement was Cook, who emphasized that OBU was interested in working out a solution whereby the entire community would benefit, not just a handful of black business owners: "We're not talking about making a half-dozen black millionaires. CORE is interested in a structure in which profits from the restaurants will benefit the total black community." In Cook's eyes this was simply the politics of black self-determination, "that means define your turf and control it." Rev. Jonathan Ealy, director of the United Pastors Association, agreed: "We must have black control of our businesses . . . ," he contended, "the black community has no other place to reap benefits but in the black community." Although the demands by OBU paralleled, to some extent, the tactics of earlier "Don't Buy Where You Can't Work Campaigns," all participants agreed that the economic demands made this protest different. "The objective is different from that of former picketing. . . . It is to make them hurt to the point that they stop playing games and consummate the negotiation that has been going on for some time," said Rev. Emmanuel S. Branch of the Urban League. "I think this form of picketing is just as ethical and just as moral."[33]

McDonald's agreed to three of the demands. However, it would not agree on the issue of irrevocable franchise rights, nor would it agree that franchisees should pay the franchise royalty fee of 2.2 percent of gross sales to OBU instead of the corporation. McDonald's officials said that the company charged its franchisees the royalty fee in exchange for "valuable assistance and consultation services" provided by headquarters; if a franchisee did not pay the fees, those services would not be forthcoming. The executives also said that they would never grant an irrevocable franchise license. So the picketing continued and the stores remained closed. Still, Hill remained confident that they were close to an agreement, announcing, "We expect to be able to reach agreement within a week."[34]

Rev. Arthur LeMon, executive assistant to Stokes, represented the mayor during the negotiations. After Glenville and the police testing scandal, Stokes's advisers told him that he did not have to be out front on every issue he supported. Rather, he should work behind the scenes. His visible involvement would solidify the white community's suspicion that he was indeed a black nationalist. However, Hill and OBU knew that Stokes was instrumental in resolving the dispute.

Soon members of the black middle class began to criticize the tactics of Hill and OBU. The NAACP and the Urban League came in for the harshest criticism. Dr. Kenneth Clement, who had been a Stokes assistant until he broke with the mayor shortly after his inauguration, called the tactics being used against McDonald's blatant extortion, "a just plain shakedown operation." Clement further remarked that he did not understand what "the NAACP and the Urban League and other responsible organizations are doing following Hill. Are they so bereft of leadership that they must follow the self-styled Rabbi Hill, an uncontrite man who brags of a life of crime?" Clement felt that it was inconceivable and unconscionable that the NAACP and the Urban League pursued their mission through such an "unholy alliance." Councilman Leo Jackson, a Stanton ally, chided the groups for "legitimizing" Hill and the nationalists and asked OBU to end the boycott. The conservative Negro Business and Industrial Association also expressed displeasure with OBU's position. "We are opposed to any group trying to force others to sell their business. . . . Negro people must build something of their own instead of taking from others," said President Charles Morris. Despite these pleas, the picketing continued. The opinions of black conservatives carried little weight because they were not Stokes supporters. Consequently, their status in the black community was virtually nonexistent.[35]

On August 8 McDonald's announced that it would reopen the stores the next day. In the eyes of management, the decision to reopen was not a difficult one:

1. The black employees need their jobs.
2. No black purchaser will buy a closed business.
3. No bank will finance the purchase of a closed business.
4. Government assistance is not available to a closed business.
5. Customers [are] developing other eating habits.
6. The longer the units are closed the greater disadvantage to any black purchaser.

In explaining the decision to reopen, Bood stressed that unless the businesses were open, black ownership would remain merely a dream, because no black owner would be able to get a loan until the outlets were operating and producing a profit. As McDonald's made plans to reopen, Wendell Erwin, president of the local NAACP chapter, and Emmanuel Branch, president of the Cleveland Urban League, sent a letter to the hamburger chain asking it to reconsider: "We feel that the atmosphere within the community is not conducive to reopening at this time. We are proposing a Monday meeting with all parties and we are hopeful that a reasonable settlement can be reached at the meeting." Although Bood was pleased at their offer to meet, he remained committed to reopening the stores: "We don't see how we can call off the opening at this point, we have been asking to meet with OBU daily without getting any response."[36]

The franchise royalty fee was the main source of disagreement. If this money was going to go back to the community, how would it be collected, handled, and distributed? Bood wanted to know. "Operation Black Unity has no trust fund set up, no funds to be administered through any trust fund, no foundation or anything. Who are to be the officers? Who'll get the benefits of any monies collected from royalties?" he asked. Meanwhile, the reopened stores did little business: "We hardly needed pickets at three of them, the black people showed they just don't want to patronize them," Hill declared.

In mid-August negotiations between OBU and McDonald's took a different turn; instead of dealing with corporate officials, Stokes and OBU decided to deal directly with the four local franchise holders; they were represented by lawyers Edward Greenwald and Seymour Terrell. As the stores' revenues dropped, three of the four owners expressed their willingness to sell if the price was right. Two owners set a purchase price of about $300,000 for each of their stores, and the owner of the 82d Street outlet wanted $600,000. The franchise holders were eager to settle because the boycott had been effective. "You could say there ain't no business, none," Greenwald said. To the astonishment of the parent corporation and local whites, the two attorneys agreed that the demands made by Hill and OBU were within reason: "We have taken a great deal of business out of the black community. Why should we not put something back?" said Greenwald. "Our franchise holders have agreed that these businesses should be sold to blacks because these are very different times."[37]

On August 19 they reached a tentative agreement on all five demands. Instead of the 2.2 percent royalty fee, the franchise holders agreed to give 2 percent of the sale price and $2,500 to OBU to set up programs in the black community. However, when the contracts were sent to McDonald's headquarters for approval, the company rejected them. "McDonald's will not give us the letter listing the three points they had agreed to in earlier talks," Greenwald said. "Without this letter the deal is off. If we want to sell our franchises, we gotta look to Big Daddy [McDonald's Corp.] for the blessing. Big Daddy has final control and Big Daddy said no. We can't move without their consent." Greenwald was especially upset at the corporate actions because the agreement "would not cost McDonald's one cent!" Seymour Terrell expressed serious disappointment as well: "I feel that all my efforts to settle this matter have been repudiated. I thought we had hammered out an agreement that was fair to all people." Stanley Tolliver, lead counsel for OBU, felt betrayed by the parent company's actions. He observed that "the action by McDonald's seems to make it clear that their franchise holders are not as independent as the company has tried to make them appear in the past." Instead of agreeing to the individual $2,500 donations and the 2 percent fee designed by the franchise owners, McDonald's agreed to contribute to a fund supervised by a nonprofit organization, with the guidance of OBU. Also, McDonald's promised to lead a fund-raising effort for a community swimming pool, play-ground, and recreation center. But OBU officials would not accept this ar-rangement. They wanted McDonald's to contribute to a project that would enhance the economic base of the black community; they were not interest-ed in recreational facilities.[38]

The moderate element within the NAACP and the Urban League tried to organize a break with Hill and OBU after negotiations failed to produce a consensus. Neither organization succeeded; their rank-and-file wanted to remain in the coalition. Still, at a September 8 meeting the moderates con-vinced Hill to voluntarily resign as the chair of Operation Black Unity's ne-gotiating group. The principle reason for Hill's resignation was to clear up confusion in the local media, which constantly referred to Hill as the leader of OBU, instead of his correct title, which was chair of the negotiating com-mittee. Some OBU members, moreover, believed that the negotiations would achieve greater results if Hill stepped down. "I don't share these beliefs," Hill responded, "but they will soon learn that I am not the problem, but the ene-my is." With the charismatic Hill removed from the negotiations, McDonald's became more rigid in its opposition to the trust fund. The corporation's lo-cal lead counsel, James Davis, even threatened to call off negotiations alto-gether.[39]

On September 26 Stokes announced to the press that he would mediate the dispute. He had hesitated to do so because campaign season was looming. If he sided with Hill, he jeopardized his white support, and if he sided with McDonald's, the black community would deem him a sellout. Privately, how-ever, OBU knew that Stokes had been involved from the beginning; he just hadn't talked about it. The mayor's silence on the issue had not gone unno-ticed by his critics, but he was consistent in telling them that he could do lit-tle more than provide police protection for both the pickets and store employ-ees. "So far as picketing and the boycott, they are no different than any other," said Stokes. "It is as American as apple pie, unions do it everyday. So long as there is no violence, they can picket and boycott as people have been picket-ed and boycotted before." Arnold Pinkney, one of Stokes's executive assistants, agreed: "They are exercising a constitutional right to picket. And they are sit-ting down at the negotiation table trying to settle their grievances with a com-pany regarding what they consider to be an injustice in the community." Many of the mayor's critics, including Robert Kelly, who planned to run against him, blamed Stokes for creating the atmosphere that allowed the controversy to exist. "This shows how little he knows about America or apple pie when he tries to compare legitimate picketing with the extortion at McDonald's," Kelly asserted. "If these extortionists are successful who will be next? . . . Our city is living in fear. Everybody knows that the situation at McDonald's is typical of what's going on. It must stop at once and the leadership must come from City Hall."[40]

In announcing his intervention, Stokes said the controversy "was causing serious division within this city." He also did not want to feel the white backlash at the polls in the upcoming election. In a two-hour meeting with attorneys from both sides, Stokes persuaded OBU to call off the boycotting and picketing and to go back to the negotiating table and resolve the main issue of the dispute, the trust fund.[41]

The controversy ended in January 1970, after Stokes and Davis negotiated a settlement under which the Hough Area Development Corporation would buy two of the franchises; the other two remained under white ownership. Because Stokes was a strong supporter of black capitalism, his participation was critical to the success of the boycott. He created the climate that allowed Hill and OBU to facilitate the protest.[42]

In early October, Hill and Raplin were indicted and subsequently convicted on charges of extortion by an all-white jury. Hill was sentenced to one to five years in prison, while Raplin was given probation. Nonetheless, Hill deserves credit for having the vision to launch the boycott. Within months McDonald's and other fast-food chains were taking a more proactive approach toward black ownership. African Americans soon acquired twenty-one franchises nationally.[43]

Stokes's involvement in the McDonald's boycott convinced millions of African Americans that political power was truly the next phase of the civil rights movement. By late 1969 Stokes had emerged as the most admired man in black America, according to a *Time* Magazine/Louis Harris poll. However, he now had to gear up for a tough re-election campaign.

7. Re-election

AFTER A ROCKY first term, Stokes found himself struggling to get re-elected in the fall of 1969. As he approached the campaign, he faced three challenges: the scandals and controversies of his first two years in office, attracting white voters, and how to re-energize black voters. This was not the emotional crusade of 1967—now he had to campaign.

The only serious challenger to emerge was Robert Kelly, who had been city service director under Mayor Ralph Locher. Rumor had it that Stanton and other county Democrats asked Kelley to run "simply to provide opposition to a black mayor." According to the local journalist Roldo Bartimole, "White politicians, including Stanton, don't want to face white constituents and be open to the criticism that they didn't field a candidate against Stokes." But they realized that Kelly had little chance of winning the Democratic nomination.

Kelly opened his campaign before a sparse crowd of two hundred at the Italian Cooperative Association Hall. In his kickoff address Kelly claimed that the city had become a "jungle" under Stokes's leadership. Using the Glenville shoot-out as a representative of the entire Stokes record, Kelly hit hard at the mayor. "The first obligation of a government is the protection of life and property, and the Stokes administration has disregarded this principle," Kelly told the cheering, all-white audience. He drew further applause when he remarked that he would not let the city be run by hoodlums and ruffians: "I'll ask the national guard to come in when the police department is incapable of maintaining law and order."[1]

It was a straight George Wallace imitation. In front of white working-class audiences, Kelly drove home two themes: that Stokes had created an atmosphere of lawlessness and that the Stokes administration had created too many controversies. Although Kelly realized that no city "can be entirely free from crime," he lashed out at the 100 percent increase in crime that had occurred since Stokes took office. "All this violence is the direct result of the city administration's bungling and cheating," Kelly contended. He consistently blamed Stokes for the city's escalating murder and overall crime rates by making a connection between the Glenville riot and crime: "Every homicide since then bears this stigma of permissiveness." He then told business owners that the rise in crime created a hazardous business environment. "Who wants to do business in a city where fear has resulted in the closing of four major movie houses?" asked Kelly. "Who wants to do business in a city where conventioneers are publicly warned against using the downtown streets at night?" As evidence that Stokes was responsible for the climate of violence, Kelly pointed to the mayor's attitude toward law enforcement during the McDonald's boycott. Kelly contended that "the mayor could not be a negotiator in the McDonald case because he has been an active participant in the extortion. . . . The entire affair has been under his direction." In Kelly's eyes "serious violations of the law went unsupervised in this community. . . . For weeks the McDonald's restaurant company was picketed and threatened with injury to its business and property purely in the interest of personal gain."[2]

At the annual City Club debates one week before the primary, Kelly continued his attacks: "You have divided the city's population. You have made irresponsible decisions. You have been a bad housekeeper and the people believe you have failed badly and that you should not be allowed to continue this thing for two more years." By making a link between Glenville, the escalating crime rate, and a spirit of lawlessness, Kelly struck a chord among white conservatives.[3]

Kelly repeatedly pointed to the scandals of the Civil Service Commission as representative of a larger problem within the Stokes administration. "Which one of his aides went to jail today? Who was indicted today?" Kelly would ask. In Kelly's eyes, Stokes's tenure was the worst in the city's history. "Almost any week you pick over the last two years is as bad in the history of the city. Things have been so bad that people have become anesthetized to the failures and corruption of this administration." In Kelly's words, Cleveland under Stokes's leadership "has been scandalized," "maligned," and "cheated." As Kelly was wrapping up his campaign he asked voters, "How much more of this can we afford? I believe I am the man who can get the job done."[4]

Although Kelly made headlines with his attacks on Stokes, his own platform rarely received attention, largely because he did not set forth a program of governance. The major part of Kelly's platform was a fifteen-point program to improve the Cleveland Police Department. These included plans for a new safety director, a curfew for Clevelanders younger than eighteen, improved weapons and rescue apparatus, and regular meetings with the governor and the Ohio National Guard to "prepare for disorders." With so much of his campaign focused on law and order, Kelly devoted little attention to housing, employment, or education. Then again, he was not running on those issues.[5]

As Kelly campaigned in white areas, Stokes reassembled his power base on the East Side. Gone was the emotionalism that had powered his first two mayoral campaigns. Stokes was forced to spend much of the summer registering black voters. Beginning in July 1969 Stokes launched Operation Voter Registration, a massive voter drive led by Rev. Arthur LeMon, who established a chain of field offices to provide advice, assistance, and transportation to those wanting to register. Although the voter registration effort was supposed to open with much fanfare, only two hundred of the five thousand invitees attended the political rally on July 17. The voter registration effort was important because thousands of black Clevelanders had been dropped from the voting rolls since the 1967 mayoral election, either because they had moved or they had not voted in the interim. Moreover, to vote in the upcoming elections residents had to be registered by the middle of August.[6]

Stokes kicked off his bid for re-election with an address to enthusiastic supporters at his election headquarters. In his speech Stokes gave an appraisal of his two-year term, and he attacked those who sought to further divide the city along racial lines. Stokes acknowledged that his administration had made some grave errors, but "we have faced up to them, admitted them, corrected them, learned from them." Despite these mistakes, a new spirit was alive in Cleveland, "the spirit of a city moving ahead." Stokes proudly listed his accomplishments as the nation's first big-city black mayor: the establishment of a city health department, the revitalization of a community development department that was in "shambles, with federal funds frozen"; new city equipment; a new department of human resources and economic development, as well as a clean water task force, a reorganized service department, new housing for the poor; job creation, additional law enforcement equipment, and downtown development. By virtue of these accomplishments Stokes felt certain that the city had gained momentum. Stokes's opening remarks revealed his campaign strategy: Admit the mistakes by emphasizing that they were learning experiences but stress the accomplishments, which even the most diehard anti-Stokes voter could not deny.[7]

Stokes made his first campaign trip to the West Side to give an "accounting" of his administration. At this gathering he stressed what he considered to be the major achievements of his tenure: more police, low-income housing, jobs, and recreation centers. But at this neighborhood event Stokes also acknowledged that the Glenville riot was a bitter experience. He then labeled the testing scandal a fiasco, even acknowledging, "I made a mistake of poor judgment in some of the members I appointed to the Civil Service Commission." Stokes realized that he faced tremendous obstacles in getting re-elected.[8]

The Stokes team accurately predicted that the mayor was vulnerable in four areas: public safety, the perception that he had not supported the police, his East Side bias, and fiscal mismanagement, particularly the revelation that Ahmed Evans had received Cleveland: Now! money. Thus the entire campaign was geared toward overcoming these problems. Illustrative of the Stokes strategy were the speeches he gave to two predominantly white working-class audiences. In both, Stokes opened by admitting his mistakes, then repledged his support for law enforcement, and finally argued that he deserved another term. "There is no question that we have made mistakes," he declared, "because you can't make mistakes if you are not doing anything." He then went on to state that he placed more patrols on the streets and improved the city's fleet of police cars. In closing, he pleaded with the all-white audience to re-elect him: "I've come to ask your consideration and help to be re-elected and have another two years in office, not only to carry out programs, but to use the experience we have gained and add to it."[9]

His strategy was designed both to win the Democratic primary, where he was the overwhelming favorite, and to help him retain white support in the general election. Stokes realized that Kelly was not a formidable opponent, but the general election would be different, and the Stokes team knew that the majority of white Democrats would vote along racial lines in November, giving their vote to the Republican candidate. Thus the Stokes campaign had to keep white Democrats from bolting, as they had in the previous two mayoral elections. Primary voters responded to the Stokes message and handed Kelly a sound defeat, 92,219 to 60,899.

As the general election approached, the GOP endorsed County Auditor Ralph Perk for mayor. His campaign strategy developed around the themes of law and order and fiscal mismanagement. Before making a formal declaration of his candidacy, Perk remarked early in the summer that if he became mayor he would have to "throw the rascals out of city hall." Perk promised that he would be an "on-the-job mayor" and that he would hire more police to patrol the streets to prevent "frightening and persistent increases in lawlessness and disorders." Continuing on the law-and-order theme, Perk declared: "Here in the city of Cleveland our streets are so unsafe that residents on the east side, the south side, and the west side, are afraid to come out at night. . . . The streets are so unsafe that people are even afraid when they come out in the daytime." If elected, he argued, "I am going to spend endless time here on the job at city hall to make the streets safe once again." Perk also used his June kickoff as an opportunity to attack what he termed Stokes's greatest accomplishment: "the spending of taxpayer's money and showing no results. The present mayor is spending twice as much or more to run the mayor's office than his immediate predecessor. The people of Cleveland cannot afford to support countless unnecessary jobs . . . when these jobs are not adding to the effectiveness of city government."[10]

As in several of his previous races, Perk sought to portray himself as the workingman's candidate. "One of his [Stokes's] youngsters attends University School and is regularly chauffeured to the school in a car driven by uniformed officers," Perk asserted. "The mayor's personal taste in clothing involving $250.00 suits has been commented on in the *New York Times*." Perk further exploited this image by sponsoring six 98-cent dinners, which were satirical references to Stokes's $100-a-plate fund-raisers. At a gathering at the Polish Women's Hall, the site of one of the 98-cent dinners, Perk played the average Joe to perfection. "I'm just an average neighbor and average citizen, like yourself. Your presence indicates you appreciate a bargain .98 dinner, and you understand that the people of Cleveland are getting no bargain at City Hall these days." He also raised questions about Stokes's fiscal management ability and promised not to raise taxes to support social programs: "I can assure you that whatever office in which I serve as a public official, I'm going to do everything I can to keep taxes down, to eliminate waste of taxpayer's money and to operate my administration within the bounds of good government."[11]

Perk's candidacy generated considerable excitement in white ethnic wards. At a GOP-sponsored Labor Day event, approximately forty thousand people braved the rain for a People for Perk picnic. At the park he delivered a brief but emotional talk on Stokes's ineffectiveness as the chief cause for the breakdown in law and order. Perk shouted that "words and charisma" could not revitalize the city, "only effort and zeal. Oratory and showmanship will not cut down the constant rise of crime on our streets. When darkness falls, Cleveland's downtown streets are deserted. . . . I promise to spend endless hours on the job as mayor of Cleveland to make our streets safe once more." He then went on to link Stokes's fiscal mismanagement and the rise in crime. "Cleveland's mounting crime rate is all the more shocking when we realize that we are spending more money than ever before in the history of our city. . . . With a budget of over 100 million dollars, why can't we have more policemen?" Perk clearly knew which themes to stress. By playing upon the fears of white citizens, Perk attracted thousands of supporters as the election drew closer.[12]

Perk's calls for law and order naturally attracted the rank-and-file of the Cleveland Police Department, who by this time could not imagine serving another two years under Stokes. Although Perk had the support of police, albeit by default, he nevertheless cultivated them by openly criticizing the leadership of the safety forces. In a televised interview Perk shocked no one when he said that if elected he would shake up the safety department: "Under no circumstances could I keep Joe McManamon. I'm sure Chief Gerity knows that if I'm elected his days are numbered." The moderator then asked what he would do to improve law enforcement. Perk responded that he would give the police the kind of equipment they needed to carry out their jobs, equipment "equal or superior to that used by criminals."[13]

In a speech before the Cleveland Police Patrolmen's Association, Perk hit at the police testing scandal: "I will work with you to re-establish faith in the Civil Service Commission . . . one free of scandal. Two of the three appointees of Mayor Stokes have been indicted. How can we, the people, have confidence in appointments made by the mayor?" Perk also disputed Stokes's claim that he placed more than three hundred additional police on the force. "No one knows better than you," Perk told the officers, "that there aren't three hundred more men on the streets. . . . The police chief knows it. The safety director knows it. But who do you think doesn't know it?" he asked. "The mayor!" they shouted back in unison. Perk was still on this theme a week later. Meanwhile, the *Cleveland Press* had revealed that Chief Gerity had refused to attend a swearing-in ceremony for new police recruits, largely because he felt that they were unqualified. "We are in the midst of a city scandal," said Perk. "There's something wrong at city hall when the police chief refuses to attend a swearing-in ceremony for new police officers because he regards one-third of them as unfit." Continuing, he said, "there is something wrong at city hall when the FOP demands an investigation of those appointments. That something goes right to the top, right to the mayor's office." Perk suggested that the police were not the only ones dissatisfied with the mayor, that "Stokes's own police Chief Gerity is disenchanted with the mayor, and he has lots of company. . . . It's time for new leadership in the city."[14]

On the campaign trail Perk questioned Stokes's relationship with local black nationalist organizations. "When I am elected," he remarked, "we will get rid of all these unofficial armies that now are parading the city." He specifically wanted to know about the mayor's relationship with Baxter Hill, the self-proclaimed black nationalist and ghetto troubleshooter for the mayor. "Who is Baxter Hill? Why does he have his own army? Who is paying for that army?

Is it being paid from out of Cleveland Now! funds?" he asked. "Why is he called the unofficial chief of police? Why does Cleveland Now! money support his unofficial army?"[15]

Perk was focusing solely on attracting the white voter. He gave no significant attention to the black East Side, making only token appearances. In one of his last campaign appearances, Perk implied that the whites who voted for Stokes in 1967 were foolish. "In 1967 Carl Stokes with his glib talk, his nice pretty smile and his debating skill persuaded 27% of the decent people of this community to vote for him. Are you going to be fooled again?" he asked.[16]

Perk spent so much of the campaign criticizing the deficiencies of the Stokes administration that he never laid out his own plans for leadership. Not until one week before the election did he reveal a platform; even then, it focused almost exclusively on stopping crime. Along with vague plans for fiscal management, he offered several solutions to the crime problem, including the appointment of a new safety director and police chief, reorganizing the Civil Service Commission, and appointing five hundred new police. Like Kelly, Perk said nothing about housing, employment, health, or welfare. In fact, on several occasions he implied that city hall was doubling as a welfare office and that when he became mayor, "all able-bodied people capable of leaving those welfare rolls will be pressed to gain meaningful employment." Perks's strategy worked. He picked up momentum in the weeks before the election. It was clear to all that Perk had much of the white ethnic vote. Stokes's only chance was to mobilize his black support and retain his base of white moderates. This would not be easy.[17]

Immediately after the primary Stokes began to mobilize the black community. Although everyone realized that the mayor still had considerable support on the black East Side, he could not afford to take the black vote for granted. Campaign workers emphasized that unless black voters turned out in great numbers, Stokes would lose the election. His campaign staffers used three avenues to spread their message: word of mouth, handbills, and the pages of the *Call and Post*. But according to preelection polls, black Clevelanders did not have to be convinced to vote for Stokes. In a random survey of seven East Side wards, black Clevelanders were asked, "What does Carl Stokes being mayor mean to you?" The two most popular answers were that "he is an inspiration" for the community and "he has shown the white people what an intelligent Negro is capable of doing." Along with these symbolic benefits, black Clevelanders pointed to tangible advantages. A twenty-eight-year-old black domestic remarked, "I never saw a snow plow on our street before." A recent home buyer gave Stokes credit for helping him buy a house: "Mayor Stokes got the loan for me, he called the finance company and said I was OK so I could get this house near the school for my kids." When asked if Stokes had been a mayor for the entire community, black respondents overwhelmingly answered yes: "He kept things quiet when MLK was assassinated," and they cited "his courage in ending the shooting in Glenville." Other residents fully subscribed to Stokes's riot-insurance rhetoric, that if Perk won, racial unrest would be inevitable. One supporter believed that "Negroes listen better since Stokes has been in," while another felt that Stokes's true value lay in his message of patience: "He can tell people not to tear things apart but wait for improvements." While this mood guided the Stokes team on the black East Side, his backers devised a rather elaborate strategy to attract white voters.[18]

The integrated team of Arnold Pinkney and Hugh Corrigan directed the Stokes campaign. As expected, they led a split campaign, one directed at the "soft" white community and another at the black East Side. The approach to moderate whites was that "Stokes has made a good start and that he deserves two more years to continue the job that he started in 1967." Since moderate whites were the focus, Stokes concentrated his stumping in the eleven wards west of the Cuyahoga River. Stokes conceded the white East Side wards to Perk, so he had no need to spend time there. But in focusing his campaign on the West Side, Stokes organizers had to overcome the perception, and to some extent the reality, that Stokes had been an East Side mayor who had neglected the concerns of his West Side constituents. To dispel this feeling the Stokes team drafted the "West Side Story," a journalistic piece citing Stokes's accomplishments on the West Side: increased public safety, recreation improvements, a renewed commitment to public health, and an air and water pollution campaign. Of these the most notable was the creation of additional police patrol zones, an ambitious street resurfacing program, and Cleveland: Now! expenditures for West Side programs. Although this brochure listed facts, it was clearly campaign propaganda. When Stokes's critics claimed that he focused exclusively on the East Side, they were right. The eleven wards on the West Side concerned the mayor only at election time.[19]

Gaining votes on the West Side would not be easy because Perk's candidacy was attracting two groups of white voters: "those who think that race relations have relaxed sufficiently so that taxes and other good government issues are more important, and those who seem to be itching for a showdown, police confrontation with the black East side," as a *Cleveland Press* reporter put it. Thus Stokes appealed to white voters who still believed that he could keep the lid on black unrest. A thirty-one-year-old white television repairman and former George Wallace supporter told a reporter that he wanted Stokes re-elected because "his being a darkie helps keep trouble down." The parents of a sixteen-year-old white girl who was taking cosmetology classes on the East Side explained why they were sticking with Stokes: "It will be bad for any white man to take over as mayor, Stokes has the colored with him. It's better to stay with a black mayor." A white housewife expressed similar thoughts: "Stokes will keep the trouble down. The colored feel happy when he's elected."[20]

Stokes also wanted to mobilize another group of whites: those who were both happy with his accomplishments and disappointed at his mistakes but who nonetheless felt that he deserved two more years in office. Selling this perspective were the white business elite, the local press, and white liberals. The support of the business community was critical to his chances for re-election. Since he entered office, Stokes had created an excellent business environment. In addition, Stokes had solicited the advice and support of the business sector throughout his first two years. The business elite was certainly impressed with many of his construction programs, including a building boom downtown, large federal expenditures toward public housing, a $100 million antipollution bond issue, increased city revenues, and a $65 million airport expansion. Corporate elites believed that although Stokes had made several mistakes, "he should be allowed to pursue his programs . . . now that he has more knowledge of the job, of the city, and of his mistakes."[21]

While several wealthy Republicans funded the Stokes effort, he had a hard time gaining the full support of his own Democratic Party. Although the countywide Democratic organization publicly endorsed Stokes, Stanton openly withheld his support, causing several of his council underlings to do likewise. Despite Stanton's silence, the entire county party put on a display of unity at the annual Democratic Party Rally where officials from all levels and branches of government attended in a symbolic display of support.[22]

At the rally Stokes emphasized the accomplishments of his administration, but he also attacked Perk. Besides the construction boom and increased federal funding, Stokes stressed his reorganization of the Cleveland Police Department, which put more officers on the streets and saw construction of a new $6.5 million police communications center. In the area of community development, Stokes spoke of the more than five thousand public housing units that were either built or rehabilitated on his watch and the stricter enforcement of the housing code. The mayor also spoke of his efforts to create new jobs through the human resources and economic development departments. He was particularly proud that thirty-one hundred hard-core unemployed had been placed in jobs through the various job-training programs. Stokes was also quick to mention the $1 million water pollution bond issue, which the city used to clean up Lake Erie, and his appointment of a clean water task force. In the area of city services Stokes made sure voters were aware of his efforts to replace the city's obsolete equipment and to meet the city's health needs by establishing the city's Health and Welfare Department. He also reminded voters that he had established seven new health centers across the city.[23]

Despite his accomplishments, some white voters were still not convinced that he deserved another two years in office. All they could remember was Glenville, the testing scandal, and the McDonald's boycott.

As election day approached, Stokes intensified his criticisms of Perk. He began questioning Perk's relationship with Robert Hughes and Saul Stillman, co-chairmen of the county Republicans. Throughout the campaign Stokes constantly stressed to voters that if Perk were elected, Cleveland would have a "three-headed" mayor, with two of the heads living in the suburbs. In essence, Stokes suggested that Perk was a bossed candidate, a puppet who would serve as a phantom mayor. "The Perk campaign is a well calculated, well financed movement to get control of City Hall and to carry out the personal desires of two very ambitious men for their own self-aggrandizement," declared Stokes. He contended that Hughes wanted to be a GOP power broker, while Stillman had his eyes on a federal judgeship. Stokes also linked Perk to the Nixon administration, telling voters that Perk wanted to be a "little Nixon." At a press conference Stokes remarked that a Perk administration would create drastic unemployment, as Nixon had when he slashed Model Cities funding. To further emphasize Perk's relationship with the fat cats of the GOP, Stokes also noted that Republicans had opposed a minimum-wage law while forcing reductions in Medicare, Medicaid, and education. As the campaign entered its final week, Stokes challenged Perk to a debate. Perk declined.[24]

As the election neared, the Stokes team went into high gear to mobilize voters on both sides of the Cuyahoga River. Stokes held three major rallies on the West Side and a host of campaign events on the black East Side. Among the East Side activities was a spectacular parade, the Women's Walk for Stokes, a rally with Jesse Jackson, and a rally at Shiloh Baptist Church. Last, on the eve of the election the campaign used a citywide gimmick: a "Turn on the Lights for Stokes" campaign.[25]

On November 4, 1969, Stokes defeated Perk by 3,752 votes, out of 238,843 cast. Still, the margin of victory was twice what it had been in 1967 when Stokes beat Seth Taft. The key to Stokes's victory lay in his surprisingly good showing on the West Side. In eight of the eleven West Side wards Stokes increased his support from 1967, but on the black East Side tallies for Stokes went down, primarily because the emotional campaign of 1967 could not be duplicated. In giving his victory speech Stokes thanked all his supporters: "It was a united effort by a unified party and those folks who supported me in my 1967 victory came out again to back up their judgment. (Perk) gave me a hard, tough fight and winning was not easy. It took everything we had to beat them."[26]

What made Stokes's re-election so notable was that he had to contend with the election-day intimidation tactics of the Cleveland Police Department. When black voters went to the polls, they were confronted by white police officers. The rank-and-file of the police department saw election day as an opportunity to remove Stokes from office. Still fuming from the departmental reorganization, the Glenville riot, and the testing scandal, white officers decided to undertake a campaign to prevent blacks from voting.[27]

On the day of the general election several hundred armed off-duty police officers appeared at East Side polls to act as so-called challengers and witnesses. In reality they were acting as intimidators. Not only were they visible at East Side voting locations but some officers went into the voting booth to challenge black voters. Several of Stokes's cabinet members traveled to the sites once they got word of the illegal activity, and all were surprised at what they witnessed. Sidney Spector, one of Stokes's executive assistants, spent the entire day with Police Chief Gerity, canvassing polling places. Their first stop was Perk headquarters, where Spector observed one officer dispatching patrol officers to East Side polling places to intimidate black voters. Although Chief Gerity witnessed this activity, he did nothing. He later told Spector that he was only making sure that the officers were not interfering with the "actual" voting process. Sgt. Richard Barrett, a member of Stokes's security detail, also observed the intimidation: "I talked to the polling officials, the presiding judge and the other ladies who were there, and they were frightened, just totally intimidated. They said that these policemen had been interrogating the citizens who came in to vote and just browbeat them. And they were handling the books, the polling books, which is against the law." Several African American women at the polling precinct informed Barrett that when a polling inspector arrived, they told him of the intimidation and he responded that the police were there for the sole purpose of defeating Stokes and that he was not interested in polling violations. Barrett also heard that police had told members of the black underworld that if they voted, they would be taken to jail.[28]

The carefully planned operation was sponsored by the Committee of the Concerned, under the direction of Richard Vina, a lieutenant. It later came out that Chief Gerity was informed of the entire plan in advance and had given the operation his stamp of approval, with the hope of having a secure position in the department if Stokes lost. The police presence had a severe

effect upon black voter turnout. Black turnout averaged 88 percent of registered voters in the morning hours but dipped to 40 to 50 percent in the late
afternoon when word circulated that armed police were in polling places. As
Arnold Pinkney said, "You have to live in the ghetto to understand the effect
of anybody saying there is a policeman in any place with a gun on him."[29]

The following transcript provides greater detail about the operation:

Q: Is this Larry McManamon?

A: What are you calling for?

Q: I was told to call this number and ask for Larry McManamon. I am a West
Sider who lives next door to a policeman and we were told to call this number to help get Mayor Stokes out of office and my husband and I am interested in helping.

A: Oh yes. Go to the Polish Women's Federation Hall at 7526 Broadway. There
are several police officers and they can help you.

Q: Who should I see out there?

A: Ask for either Terry O'Donnell or Lieutenant Richard Vina. The people out
there will know what you want and they will direct you to these people. They
will give you pamphlets, challenger forms, witness forms, etc. and then you
go out to a ward or precinct. They'll explain everything to you out there. Just
ask Dick Vina.

Q: Is Terry O'Donnell a fireman or policeman, too?

A: No, he is just someone who works on our committee. We need all the help
we can get so come on out.

Q: Thank you.

Clearly, Lieutenant Vina and the rank-and-file of the police department were
determined to defeat Stokes by any means at their disposal.[30]

W. O. Walker, the *Call and Post* editor, was disappointed at the election day
actions of white police officers. But instead of lashing out at the police department, he took aim at Stokes for failing to bring the department under
civilian control. He told *Call and Post* readers that Stokes's failure in the area
of police reform was his inability "to take a real hard line to establish civilian control. To the contrary, Stokes has literally bent over backward to restore
both the efficiency and morale of the law and fire enforcement arm of city
government." Walker mentioned the mayor's support for a salary increase
that would make the department the highest-paid police force in the state,
his purchase of new patrol cars, a new police communications system, and
the establishment of a tuition reimbursement program for police. Yet despite
Stokes's support for these measures, the police were still opposed to his leadership, and Walker wanted to know why. "Just what exactly is the real reason
you [the police] are adamantly contributing to an uncivil atmosphere in

which mobsters, muggers, and vice crooks feel free to fleece the inhabitants of the black community, secure in the knowledge that the 'law' is too busy resisting to do much about it?" Despite the continued open rebellion of the police, Stokes remained confident that he could reform the department. However, he had begun to realize that he needed to be much more aggressive in his efforts. As he began his second term in office, he would suffer further disappointments at the hands of the police department.[31]

8. The General

DESPITE THE SCANDALS and controversies of his earlier efforts, Stokes remained determined to play a visible role in the affairs of the police department. Shortly after his inauguration, Operation Black Unity demanded the removal of Chief Gerity in December 1969. In a lengthy press release the coalition made a strong appeal for his dismissal by arguing that he had not been responsive to the needs of the black community. OBU prefaced its remarks by reminding the public that the black community favored strong law enforcement, having strongly supported increased pay for fire and police personnel. However, in return for this support, a mayoral assistant reported, "the firefighters and policemen have shown contempt for the black community and the administration at city hall in a way that can only be interpreted as an adamant rejection of a black mayor as their boss." OBU representatives claimed that Gerity and the white rank-and-file were attempting to use the police department as a political force in the community by creating an elite "SS Guard." They labeled Gerity's conduct "blatant insubordination to proper authority." Stokes agreed.[1]

Weeks later Stokes informed Gerity that if "drastic improvements" were not forthcoming, he would take "whatever action is necessary." Stokes reminded Gerity of the support that his office had provided the police department: "Every request we've got, we've come to you and they were granted. . . . There is no conceivable way that a city with more police in 1969 than in 1968 should have a 100% increase in crime." As pressure mounted, Gerity announced several reforms: fast-tracking two hundred police cadets through the academy, an anticrime drive that canceled all days off for captains and other administrative personnel, eliminating nonessential police services, and shifting patrol car assignments to concentrate on high crime areas. Although Stokes appreciated Gerity's reorganization strategy, it was not enough to save his job. By all accounts Stokes had already decided to replace him.[2]

When Safety Director Joseph McManamon resigned for health reasons in December 1969, Stokes saw it as a good opportunity to find a new police chief as well. Rather than conduct two simultaneous searches, Stokes decided to first appoint a safety director, who would then play a role in selecting a new chief. After days of evaluating candidates, Stokes decided to offer the position to retired Lt. Gen. Benjamin O. Davis Jr., the first black general in the U.S. Air Force and the man who had organized and led the famed Tuskegee Airmen in World War II. "A military man! A general! Black or not the people would have to respect him. And, being black, he would have to be the kind of man who would agree with what I wanted to do," Stokes recalled. The mayor felt certain that Davis's military background would give him a built-in respect from white police officers. Because Davis had attended high school in Cleveland, he knew the historic relationship of the police department and the black community. After several telephone conversations with the general, Stokes traveled to Tampa, Florida, to make the offer, probably some time in December. Stokes described the bitter conflicts between city hall and the police department. The mayor said that Davis was enthusiastic and recollected that Davis told him: "'Had a situation like that in the army, knew how to handle it. Don't worry. Glad to come. We'll take care of it, Mr. Mayor. Great admirer of yours. Delighted to handle this for you. I understand it. Something has to be done we will do it.'" On the way back to Cleveland, Stokes was euphoric: "I was on cloud nine. I had them now. That damn Police Department wouldn't have a chance." Davis agreed to start as safety director on January 31, 1970, the date of his retirement from the military.[3]

At a news conference announcing Davis's appointment, Stokes told reporters that he expected the general to restore discipline and a "military-like" operation to the police department. "The operation of vital functions of law enforcement must not be on the basis of personalities, our primary concern is that this city have maximum protection from law enforcement forces," declared Stokes. Stokes was confident that he had the perfect person for the job. "He is a doer, not a talker; he honestly wants to do something to curb the crime rate in Cleveland, not sit around and discuss it, as many people do."

The black community shared Stokes's optimism. To celebrate Davis's arrival as the city's first black safety director, thirteen hundred people packed the grand ballroom of the Statler Hilton Hotel for the swearing-in ceremony sponsored by the Greater Cleveland Growth Association. Stokes pledged his complete support: "No one is going to be able to go around or in anyway subvert the primary and individual authority of General Davis." After taking the oath of office, Davis appeared ready to tackle the job: "This is the greatest job that I could have chosen anywhere in the world. The thing that gave me the challenge and desire to come here was the obvious philosophy of Mayor Stokes to be the mayor of the best city in the world . . . and to produce the best living conditions that all of you will be proud of."[4]

Next, Stokes turned his attention to finding his third police chief in two years. His first choice was thirty-seven-year-old James Ahern of New Haven, Connecticut, who was considered one of the top law enforcement officials in the country. He agreed to interview for the position privately because he did not was to compromise his situation in New Haven. However, while Ahern was dining in Cleveland days later, a *Cleveland Press* reporter identified him, and his name was plastered across the front page of the next day's paper. As a result, Ahern asked Stokes to remove his name from consideration. Ahern was clearly the man Stokes wanted, but media exposure negated any possibility of his coming. "A lousy newspaper article and we lost the chance of getting the best police chief in the country," Stokes remarked.[5]

Within days William Ellenburg of Grosse Pointe, Michigan, emerged as the leading candidate after receiving a strong recommendation from Detroit mayor Jerome Cavanaugh. After Richard Peters, a Stokes assistant, investigated Ellenburg's background, the mayor and General Davis decided to appoint him in early February. Only hours after Ellenburg accepted the job, the *Cleveland Press* reported the claim of a lawyer who was a convicted felon— that Ellenburg had been involved in an illegal abortion clinic while he served in the Detroit Police Department. The man accused Ellenburg and two other officers of accepting payoffs. The allegations, which were based on testimony in a court case, created a firestorm of controversy in the Cleveland media. "ELLENBURG ACCEPTED PAYOFFS, DETROIT LAWYER SAYS," read the headline in the *Plain Dealer*. Other local papers refused to print the allegations because they felt that the charges were unsubstantiated and the source lacked credibility.[6]

In an effort to quell the controversy, Stokes called a press conference for February 2. He opened his remarks by stating that he was shocked, because he had done a thorough background check: "We talked with police officers who had worked with him. We discussed his qualifications with as many and as wide a range of persons as possible. We sought the advice of Detroit businessmen and civic leaders, all the people with whom we spoke praised Mr. Ellenburg as a fine policeman and a good citizen." Nonetheless, Stokes accepted full responsibility: "As mayor of the city I am immediately responsible for the appointments. . . . I am not going to fire him on the basis of a story that for the moment at least has no more substantiation than one dope addict's allegation and is more than six years old." Although Stokes said the background check had been thorough, reporters checking with the FBI, the Internal Revenue Service, the Michigan State Police, and the Michigan Attorney General's Office learned that the mayor's office had never contacted them about Ellenburg. A Stokes aide defended the decision by saying, "We did not feel that we would have learned anything we did not find out from those we did check with." The next day Stokes went to Detroit to conduct his own investigation. As he left the plane, local reporters wanted to know why Stokes was so passionate about appointing Ellenburg. "The problem of a police chief is the biggest problem I have as mayor," Stokes replied. "I picked my man and I am responsible for picking him. Certain charges have been levied against him and I have decided to come to Detroit, to the source, and investigate these charges. . . . No one could investigate them as I can . . . and when I am through, I will go to the people of Cleveland and report what I have found."[7]

Ellenburg at first denied the allegations and expressed a commitment to carry out the job. "If given a chance, a fair chance by all facets of the society of the city of Cleveland, I can do the job here. If I am going to be constantly picked at and referred to, et cetera, it's going to be difficult." But when he arrived in Cleveland in early February, Ellenburg informed Stokes that he would resign. "I could have gone anywhere in the United States," Ellenburg said, "and this story never would have broken. But you happen to be a black mayor and you appointed me. I have known about this story for the longest time, it never meant a damn thing to anybody, but I don't think you can survive with me here." The next day, just ten days after being sworn in, Ellenburg announced his resignation publicly: "I came here because I believed I could help build the finest department in the country. The events of the past few days have convinced me that it will be extremely difficult for me to reach that goal under the cloud created by the charges now circulating. I wish to repeat that I categorically deny the allegations made against me. I realize, however, that these charges . . . until cleared . . . would serious impair my effectiveness."[8]

Stokes accepted the resignation, although he declared that his own investigation in Detroit had uncovered nothing but rumors, allegations, and innuendo. However, the pressure from the local press was too much for Ellenburg to overcome. Stokes would later call the media treatment of the allegations "one of the greatest journalistic disservices done during my four years as mayor." Stokes then appointed Cleveland Police Inspector Lewis Coffey to head the police department. Coffey became his fourth police chief in just twenty-eight months. The Ellenburg controversy negated any chance that Stokes's second term would be free of scandal and embarrassment. Although the claims about Ellenburg were never proved, many of Stokes's critics and supporters were disappointed at the administration's lackadaisical attitude toward background checks. This convinced many Cleveland residents that Stokes was unfit to govern. Thomas Vail, editor and publisher of the *Plain Dealer,* summed up much of the city's opinion when he wrote: "Time is running out, the people of Cleveland will not stand for another fiasco in public safety."[9]

Although Davis received a warm reception from the black community, his attitude toward law enforcement reflected his determination to maintain the status quo. Thomas Monahan, a Stokes appointee who worked with Davis, recalled that he recognized Davis's conservative bias within days of his arrival. According to Monahan, the general expressed grave concern about the lack of machine guns and other high-powered weapons for police. When Monahan explained that Stokes did not want the police to carry such equipment, Davis replied, "What the police want, they will get." This conversation convinced Monahan that Davis wanted "to be a good guy with the troops." Monahan judged rightly: Many of Davis's subsequent administrative decisions would favor police personnel at the expense of the black community.[10]

Shortly after taking office, Davis praised the SWAT team for breaking up a black power rally at Cuyahoga Community College. In April 1970 his department neglected to investigate the near-fatal beating in Little Italy of an exchange student from Africa. Later that month he ordered thirty thousand dumdum bullets, which have hollow points and expand more than usual upon impact, and announced the department's purchase of an armored tank, "called a rescue vehicle." He also, it was later discovered, gave the police permission to carry their own special weapons—"Since they are going to carry them anyway, why don't we show our appreciation?" he explained. Next, Davis rejected a request from black activists to require officers to have their name sewn onto their uniform. This request was a response to the habit of officers' removing their badges before engaging in misconduct. Davis further incurred the wrath of the black community when he fired veteran black officer Frank Moss, just twenty-three days before his retirement, because of unsubstantiated charges that Moss had filed a false police report. Finally, black officers became disillusioned with the general after he repeatedly refused to meet with the Black Shield, an all-black police organization. Stokes and other community leaders became convinced that Davis was an Uncle Tom.[11]

Although Stokes tolerated Davis's actions in the hope that he would soon assert some leadership, the mayor had little choice but to second-guess his appointment after a police raid on a local Black Panther headquarters. On the afternoon of June 29, 1970, about fifty members of the SWAT team surrounded Panther headquarters to serve warrants and check for weapons. According to police testimony, someone fired on members of the unit as they forced their way into the residence. One officer and one Panther were injured in a shoot-out. Days later three Panthers were charged with attempted murder. Panther members and supporters provided a very different version of what happened. They charged that the police fired first and without provocation. The raid was apparently well planned because on three previous occasions the SWAT team had aimed their guns at the Panther office and had even used a fire ladder to take pictures of the layout.[12]

In the aftermath of the raid many black residents asked Davis to investigate the SWAT team's conduct. He agreed but refused to consider eyewitness accounts because they were not "official." His findings did not come as a surprise to anyone. "I have assured myself that the allegations are without justification," Davis announced. "If we had done what the Chicago police did in their raid of Panther headquarters then . . . the charges would have been justified. But this was a clean operation. It was so straightforward that only routine follow-up is required. There will be no major investigation." Days later community activists called for Davis's resignation.[13]

In contrast, both white and black conservatives liked Davis for his hardline approach to law enforcement. "Jim Stanton loved him, the newspapers loved him, the white community loved him," Stokes recalled. Leo Jackson, the council member from Glenville, thought that Davis "was a man of exceptional personality and strength." The councilman was pleased that Davis had so quickly "achieved a uniform respect among the disparate political forces in City Hall as well as in the white communities." Jackson warned local black nationalists that if they were planning trouble, "they will be dealt with with force and the General will be supported by all decent blacks." Nelson Belcher, a white patrol officer, told a local reporter that "the policemen are behind him [Davis]." Although impressed with Davis's no-nonsense attitude, the officer was more delighted with the way Davis handled the black nationalist community: "He's cracking down on the black nationalists. They don't like him." Publicly, Mayor Stokes pledged his support to Davis as well. "His leadership already has made an impact on crime statistics. . . . But more importantly, it has made an impact on attitudes and response time of policemen. They have great respect for him." Privately, however, Stokes was incensed at Davis's desire to be one of the boys.[14]

Much of the criticism of Davis came from local black nationalists. In their opinion Davis was the personification of a sellout: a high-ranking black man

in the white man's army. A rabble-rouser who called himself Brother Diablo labeled General Davis a "Judas goat," adding, "He whitewashes the racism in the police and fire departments, but under the surface it is as strong
as ever. He is a Negro who knows the system is not working for black people
but nevertheless preaches that it must be maintained." The *Call and Post* also
expressed displeasure with Davis by running blistering attacks against his
policies. Davis was unaccustomed to intense scrutiny. What angered him the
most was that many of his critics were friends of Stokes. Some were even on
the city's payroll. In his autobiography Davis labeled many of his critics "self-
declared racists" and "enemies of law enforcement." The general was particularly upset that certain elements from the black nationalist community
were calling for open warfare with police.[15]

Davis later acknowledged that he had a difficult time making the transition to a civilian position. "Life in the Air Force was much more ordered,
clearly defined, and precisely channeled," he remarked. He went on to say
that life as a safety director was "completely unpredictable," whereas in the
military he dealt with "predictable groups, carefully trained and placed in a
single mold. You knew how they would act."[16]

As criticism of Davis increased, he approached Stokes about his lack of
support in the black community. Davis asked the mayor to sever his ties with
many of the general's critics. When Stokes refused, Davis abruptly resigned
on Tuesday, July 27. His letter of resignation, portions of which were leaked
to the press, devastated the mayor—Davis said he was resigning because the
police department was not receiving the support it required and because
Stokes was giving gracious support and "comfort" to the "enemies of law
enforcement." Davis declined to reveal the names of the so-called enemies,
leaving the local media to speculate widely on his allegations.[17]

Stokes called a press conference for the afternoon of July 27 in the hope
that reporters would force Davis to explain more fully the reasons for his
resignation. The following exchange characterized much of the proceedings:

> Q: Could you describe for us the particular type of people with whom he
> might be permissive?
> Davis: No, I really would not, and as a matter of fact, I would prefer not to go
> into any detail with anyone on that particular subject.

Although Davis refused to identify the individuals that Stokes supposedly was
cosseting, the general acknowledged that his relationship with Stokes "was
not to his liking. But again I am a pretty selfish individual, I like things my
way and I define cooperation as things being done my way." Stokes then asked
Chief Coffey to discuss their relationship. "Mayor Stokes told me at the time

that he did not care who I arrested or how I had the law enforced as long as it was done in fair and equitable manner and that all the laws were to be enforced," Coffey said. "I had full authority." Reporters then asked Davis about the "enemies of law enforcement." "The people I'm referring to," he stated emphatically and elliptically, "are not hold-up men. They are not people who sell narcotics. If you are able to think of other enemies of law enforcement around this city perhaps you will be able to discern what I'm speaking of." The press conference came to a close with Davis still refusing to elaborate on the letter.[18]

The following day the headlines in the major dailies read: "MAYOR IS DEALT HIS WORST POLITICAL BLOW, THE MAYOR AND THE GENERAL: A COLLISION OF PHILOSOPHIES, STOKES—MAN IN TROUBLE, A CRITICAL HOUR FOR CLEVELAND." Although the press realized that Davis's allegations were vague and unsubstantiated, the stories beneath the headlines all carried the underlying assumption that Davis's allegations were accurate—largely because Davis was echoing the thoughts of many white police officers and conservatives.

The general's allegations angered Stokes because he had moved to implement some of Davis's recommendations. For instance, county prosecutors were put on twenty-four-hour call, and the prosecutor's office was open on Sundays and holidays. Stokes and Law Director Clarence James were convinced these moves showed their commitment to good law enforcement.[19]

Because the charges left a "cloud over the safety department," Stokes held another press conference on Wednesday, the day the papers broke the story, and challenged Davis to identify the enemies of law enforcement. Moreover, Stokes gave the press a copy of Davis's resignation letter so that reporters and the public could clearly understand the vagueness of the allegations. "You will see it is no more revealing" than the leaked excerpts were, Stokes said. "If the General has charges he wants to level against individuals or organizations, then he should list them himself. I see no reason why there should be any continuing mystery about this." Stokes then issued a challenge to Davis: "It is important, I believe, to this city that the General produce such a list so that the community can evaluate for themselves, first, if in fact [these people] are enemies, and secondly, if in fact my administration has aided them."

On Thursday Stokes called his third press conference in as many days and asked Davis to attend. The general refused. At this point Stokes knew exactly who Davis was referring to—"those who work within the system but disagree with it." Stokes added, "I have no problems with his charge that I give them support and comfort." Despite Stokes's pleas, Davis still refused to identify the alleged enemies. When a local reporter informed Davis of the mayor's remarks, he retorted, "I just don't have anything more to say. I'm not going to refuse, but I'm just not going to get into a public debate with the mayor. I don't have anything more to say."[20]

The next day Stokes released the names of the so-called enemies of law enforcement. The list shocked the local media. Equally surprised were the individuals on the "enemies list": the Cleveland Council of Churches, the *Call and Post,* the Friendly Inn Settlement House, local black nationalists Harllel Jones and Baxter Hill, Rev. Arthur LeMon, and the Black Panthers. Stokes told reporters that Davis wanted him to silence these individuals and organizations by "cutting off city money and firing them from city jobs." For instance, Davis asked Stokes to use his influence with the executive committee of the Welfare Federation to get the funding of the Cleveland Council of Churches cut as a means of silencing the Metropolitan Affairs Commission, "a group which has criticized him." Davis later asked Stokes to discontinue funding for the Friendly Inn Settlement, the meeting place of the Black Panthers. Regarding Baxter Hill, the general wanted him "contained." Stokes also spoke of Davis's attitude toward Arthur LeMon, director of the Community Relations Board. Davis said LeMon was "mixed up" with many of the safety director's opponents, including Operation Black Unity. Finally, Stokes recalled that Davis had criticized the *Call and Post* for undermining his effectiveness and had expressed his belief that the editors of the paper "condoned violence."[21]

On an hourlong television special devoted to the controversy, several individuals on the enemies list spoke about their relationship with Davis. Charles Loeb, managing editor of the *Call and Post,* said, "Our criticism of the General was that he was not quite knowledgeable enough of this community to be an effective safety director. . . . We examined him and found him not to our liking." LeMon told the audience that the friction between him and Davis developed when Davis failed to meet with the militant factions of the black community. Although Davis initially agreed to open a dialogue, "he failed to follow through." Harllel Jones argued that Davis considered the Afro-Set an enemy because it was "attempting to police black neighborhoods." Jones also said that he had often confronted Davis about police harassment of members of the Afro-Set, but the general never sought to resolve the situation. Later that week, Dave Phoenix, head of Friendly Inn Settlement, told a reporter that Davis's allegations represented an "attack on me and the board and staff and all those who attend our center. . . . We let them [Black Panthers] meet here just like other groups, including the Society for the Blind and the Cleveland Schools. They are public meetings. I feel that we have a very cooperative relationship with the police. We are a community service center, not a center for militant activity." Baxter Hill argued that Davis was purely one dimensional:

"My only comment is that General Davis always has been a good general and nothing else."

Despite the general's refusal to discuss or elaborate on his allegations and the context provided by the television special, Davis's charges further polarized the black community. Black conservatives joined their white brethren in bellowing that they were more convinced than ever that Stokes was an opponent of law enforcement, whereas liberals were certain that Davis was a sellout.[22]

"It is a tragedy that the General's charges are true," said Dr. Kenneth Clement, the mayor's now-estranged former campaign director. Thomas Guthrie, a columnist for the *Plain Dealer,* told readers, "Ben Davis was another who had the courage to tell the mayor when he thought he was wrong." Meanwhile, some political analysts began to raise questions about the mayor's low tolerance of subordinates who disagreed with his policies. The *Plain Dealer* exploited this idea with a front-page story headlined "TWENTY KEY STOKES' AIDES DEPART IN THREE YEARS," implying broadly that although some of Stokes's aides had resigned to take other positions, others, such as Clement and the former law director Paul White, had left after disagreements with the mayor.[23]

But supporters of the administration—both locally and nationally—flooded the mayor's office with letters of encouragement. The long-time school activist Daisy Craggett believed that Davis was "a military brain-washed man," who by virtue of his military achievements demanded "total and irrevocable and unquestionable obedience and control." Several of Davis's critics pointed to his military background to explain his actions; others mentioned his inability to deal with lower-income blacks as the chief reason for his "downfall." A writer from Phoenix, Arizona, advised Stokes not to "despair because there were a lot of white men trapped in black skin." A writer named Margaret Patton opined that the army and private school training kept "silver-spoon" Davis shielded from the "ghetto walls of his country." Clevelander Charles Underwood saw Davis's resignation in broader terms: "General Davis, like the Clements and [Leo] Jacksons of our race, simply have not come of age. They are allowing themselves to be used as a tool to divide us, black man against black man, moderate against militant, etc."[24] Editors at the *Florida Sentinel-Bulletin* feared that Davis's charges of corruption could prove devastating for black political aspirations: "Since this is a moment in history in which black mayors must be above suspicion, Benjamin O. Davis, Jr., has done the black race a disservice by refusing to name the 'enemies of law enforcement.'"

Stokes privately wrote thank-you letters expressing his opinion of Davis. In a letter to Julian Bond, the Georgia legislator, Stokes wrote: "Thank you for your thoughtfulness in sending me the Atlanta Enquirer editorial regarding General Davis, we've been dealing with people like him throughout our fight for freedom. We have and will continue to overcome all they represent." Stokes would later characterize the Davis controversy as "the greatest debacle of my career." It also represented his last attempt at reforming the police department.[25]

By appointing Davis to head the safety forces, Stokes had hoped to improve the tenuous relationship between city hall and the city's police force. The black community had welcomed Davis with great fanfare, somewhat optimistic that Davis would use his position to bring the Cleveland Police Department under civilian control. By seeking support from the white rank-and-file, Davis was following an example set by his father, the first black general in the army, who was famous for his statement to black troops: "I may be your color, but I am not your kind." Although Stokes realized that the appointment of Davis was a calculated risk, he was desperate. The mayor was still determined to reform the police department, which made Davis attractive—who better to do the job than a military man well respected in law enforcement circles? However, Davis was not the man for Stokes. The mayor needed someone familiar with all elements of the black community and not afraid to sit down and talk with the militant factions within the city. Moreover, Davis was unaccustomed to taking orders and never understood that Stokes was his boss and that his decisions should reflect the mayor's wishes. However, Davis's accommodationist attitude was well known in black military circles, but Stokes failed to have his staff run a solid background check on Davis before offering him the job of safety director. But Stokes's continued failures to reform the police department were not the only front on which he was waging war; his battles with city council continued to escalate.

9. Council Wars

STOKES'S INABILITY to gain control of the city council during his first term convinced him that he would certainly face another two years of hostility from the Stanton bloc. He concluded that with Stanton still council president, he would be able to make only minimal reforms. The only way to lessen the council's resistance was to have a more sympathetic council president. During the postelection reorganization of the city council in the fall of 1969, Stokes attempted to engineer the ouster of his chief nemesis.[1]

As Stokes maneuvered behind the scenes, he realized that winning this war would take every bit of his skill and no small amount of luck. He hoped to gain the support of all eleven black council members, along with that of the six Republicans, which would give him enough votes to remove Stanton. When he learned that five of the city's black council members had pledged their support to Stanton, he quickly abandoned his plan. Their support of Stanton reflected their conservative nature, but in some cases their choice was driven by jealousy of Stokes or loyalty to the county Democratic machine.[2]

Stokes knew that Stanton would learn what he had tried to do and would retaliate. In an apparent attempt to avoid a showdown, Stokes publicly congratulated the council president on his caucus victory, a symbolic overture that the mayor stood ready to work "with council in the overall improvement and betterment of Cleveland as a city." And just weeks after the mayor abandoned his coup attempt, he got a major piece of legislation signed into law.[3]

During the first week of December 1969 the city council passed an equal opportunity law. Labeled "the most sweeping in the country" by its supporters, the ordinance required that all city contractors hire workers without regard to race, color, religion, or gender. The law also banned discrimination in promotions and training, and it held employers responsible for the hiring policies of subcontractors. Compliance officers would enforce the law by examining personnel and financial records, and guilty parties would forfeit their eligibility to receive city contracts. Although Stokes and Clarence James, his law director, drafted the bill shortly after Stokes's 1967 inauguration, Bertram Gardner, director of the Community Relations Board, advised them not to present it to the council. "He [Gardner] did not think Cleveland was ready for it," James later recalled. What surprised many observers was Stanton's willingness to support the bill, which turned out to have been a quid pro quo for Stokes's agreement to support a zoning change in Stanton's ward.[4]

The passage of the equal employment ordinance was only one part of Stokes's strategy to increase the economic base of the black community. He also used the power of his office to help black business owners secure loans from local banks. At a private dinner early in 1969 the mayor told area bankers that their stringent loan policies stifled the growth of black capitalism. Although Stokes recognized that potential black business owners lacked the experience and capital to qualify for a traditional loan, he asked the bankers to relax their policies. The bankers were sympathetic, but they made no commitment to honor Stokes's request. The next morning Stokes instructed Phil Dearborn, the city's finance director, to withdraw the city's deposits from local banks. "Phil put the plan into motion, and it took only a couple of days before the bankers called and asked if we could have another meeting," Stokes recalled with satisfaction. During the next two and a half years, local banks lent more than $6 million to black-owned businesses.[5]

When these businesses opened, the mayor wasted little time in awarding them lucrative city contracts. As the chairman of the Board of Control, he did not hesitate to funnel a large percentage of city contracts into the hands of black business owners. "I deliberately included the black businessmen in every aspect of the award and hiring process, just as they had been deliberately excluded before," he said. When white businessmen realized that Stokes was using the power of his office to help black contractors, they were enraged. Rumors circulated that Stokes illegally awarded contracts to black firms. Despite the outrage from white businesses, Stokes continued to use city contracts as a vehicle for growing black capitalism.[6]

The mayor-council tensions of his second term became heightened in the spring of 1970 when Leo Jackson, the council member from Glenville who was a Stanton ally, threatened to cut the budget of the Community Relations Board in an effort to remove Baxter Hill from its board. Rev. Arthur LeMon, the newly appointed community relations director, considered Hill a valuable asset because he served as an unofficial liaison between ghetto youth and city hall. Jackson's anger stemmed from Hill's persistent criticism of him— Hill often referred to Jackson as an Uncle Tom and a "white nigger." Although Jackson had at one time spoken out against racism and the status quo, he rarely supported the mayor.

Jackson was also angry that Stokes had used city money to send Hill to a black nationalist rally in New Jersey. Jackson could not imagine why a member of the Community Relations Board would be sent to a nationalist meeting at the city's expense. Then it occurred to Jackson to ask how Hill could legally sit on the board, because members were required to have a college degree and Hill did not. Jackson's questions infuriated the mayor's supporters. "Hill speaks the language of the people who live in the ghetto. . . . He is able to translate their needs and demands into terms legislators and administrators can understand," fumed Robert McCall, another council member. "There is no degree for that. . . . The biggest problem in the black community is the lack of adequate communication. . . . They listen to Hill." Stokes confirmed his support for Hill and told reporters that if Hill were removed from the Community Relations Board, he would create another position for Hill. "He is able to reach the alienated . . . that makes him a very valuable man. I stand absolutely behind him. If he doesn't meet Civil Service requirements for a permanent appointment to his present position, another job classification may have to be created for him."

Meanwhile, Jackson made it clear that he would substantially reduce the budget of the Community Relations Board unless Hill was removed. In response, Stokes transferred Hill to a position that did not carry strict educational requirements. However, Hill still fulfilled his role as the voice of the administration in the ghetto. Jackson's inability to see beyond his personal issues with Hill was completely human. But his failure to understand Hill's importance was just another illustration of how Jackson had lost touch with the voters in his ward.[7]

The spring of 1970 also found Stokes and Stanton engaged in another bitter dispute about the location of public housing. In late 1969 Irving Kriegsfeld, director of the Cuyahoga Metropolitan Housing Authority (CMHA), had proceeded with plans to build two public housing complexes on the West Side. Unlike the Lee-Seville housing project, these developments did not need the approval of city council because all the necessary infrastructure improvements were already in place.

To express their displeasure with CMHA's housing proposal, white conservatives staged a series of protests at city hall and at project construction sites in the summer of 1970. Although one unit was earmarked as housing for the elderly, Stanton and council member Richard Harmody exploited the racial fears of homeowners by telling them that the projects would destroy their community. The opposition to the proposed Green Valley and Lorain Square housing developments marked Stokes's second major battle to place public housing units outside low-income areas, and he was growing frustrated. "There's probably no city in America that has fought against public housing for the poor and elderly so desperately as has Cleveland. . . . I have done everything I can to get housing for this city, but there are elements in Cleveland that will stop at nothing to thwart our efforts," Stokes fumed. "When people say they don't mind low-cost housing for the elderly but are opposed to housing for these families . . . these families are black families. People know that older black people have become conditioned to all of the evil aspects of our society and won't move to the west side because of the struggle. . . . But a woman wants to take her children where they have a chance." Stokes then attacked the white liberals who supported his Lee-Seville proposal but who opposed Green Valley and Lorain Square: "We are now seeing what happens when you peel back the veneer, when you make people follow up on what they've been saying in their churches and councils. Now we're calling their word and trying to build low-cost housing on the west side without regards to race, creed, color, and the people are silent."[8]

Stokes was primarily referring to the Greater Cleveland Growth Association, the city's chamber of commerce, which, he told reporters, "had failed to come to grips with the gut issues of the central city." Stokes called its silence on the issue of scattered-site public housing "appalling." William Adams II, president of the association, denied the mayor's accusations: "I resent the implication that the growth association is dodging risks in dealing with the pressing urban problems of the entire Greater Cleveland area." Adams then suggested that he and Stokes hold off-the-record meetings to discuss the breakdown in communication between city hall and the business community because public finger pointing wouldn't solve anything.[9]

As he battled for the housing units through the summer, Stokes failed to understand why people who had once been poor refused to help the less fortunate. Nevertheless, he pledged to keep fighting for housing for the working poor. "One bad thing about people is they forget the times when they were poor and didn't have much," he said. "I am determined to give every person I touch a chance to have the things I didn't have. That's why I am going to continue to fight the people in this city who are opposed to low-income housing."[10]

When Stokes pledged to fight for Green Valley and Lorain Square, Stanton countered by bringing the entire legislative process to a stop. Stanton believed that the mayor's desire to build public housing over the objections of area homeowners typified the breakdown in communication between the city council and the mayor's office. "Until there is an understanding, department by department, on council's complaints and until the administration puts forth a program agreed to by council, the legislative branch is out of business," Stanton had declared in June. The mayor was not intimidated, firing back: "If one man can bring the whole legislative process to a halt, the whole city is in poor condition. He is hurting all the citizens of the entire city." Days later Stokes announced that his city council supporters and his cabinet members would not take part in any Democratic caucus; that made them "independent Democrats" with no allegiance to the local party. Stanton carried out his threat at the next council session on June 15 by calling for adjournment twelve minutes into the meeting. After ramming through several minor resolutions, the council ended its session without undertaking any significant legislative activity. What made this session so vital was that the agenda included several important measures pertaining to housing, recreation, urban renewal, water pollution, gun control, and safety. Days after the brief council session Stokes reminded Stanton that the bills were "necessary for the life of our city, and the needs of human beings young and old."[11]

Pressed by the white business establishment, Stanton agreed to lift the ban on legislative activity. At the second-to-last council session of the year, Stanton argued for a measure requiring council approval for any public housing project sponsored by the housing authority. When the bill went down to defeat, Stanton quickly adjourned the meeting, without bringing to a vote several vital pieces of legislation. The legislative logjam was broken the next week when Stanton chaired a four-hour marathon session in which the council acted on two hundred pieces of legislation. But Stokes was unable to secure passage of a cooperation agreement between city council and the housing authority that would have authorized construction of an additional thirty-seven hundred units (the Green Valley and Lorain Square projects). Without the agreement, the agency had no authority to undertake new construction. The council's refusal to approve the agreement also jeopardized federal funding because HUD was considering decertifying the city's "workable program," a document necessary for obtaining most federal funds. Before the vote Stokes informed the council that unless it passed the measure, the city was in danger of losing $72 million. "If we lose $72 million, well, let's lose it," said Harmody. The session ended without an agreement.[12]

Months later Stanton and Anthony Garofoli, the council member from Ward 19, teamed up to oust Kriegsfeld from the housing authority. According to the housing authority's by-laws, the mayor could appoint two members, and the county commissioners, probate judges, and the court of common pleas could each make one appointment. In the fall of 1970 the board consisted of Stokes appointees Alfred Soltz and Louise Hall, along with Miles Moran, Lois Filipic, and A. I. Davey. Davey, who had been appointed by the Cuyahoga County Commission, submitted his resignation in October. Stanton (who by now was running for Congress) and Garofoli began looking for a replacement to recommend to the Democratic county commissioners. They came up with Robert Sweeney, a former Democratic member of Congress, who was duly named to the seat by the county commissioners.

Once Sweeney was sworn in, Garofoli instructed him to engineer Kriegsfeld's dismissal. "Your first act is to have a motion on the floor to fire Irving Kriegsfeld and if you don't fire him, I'll get your ass outta there," Garofoli told him. "I stacked the board against him [Kriegsfeld]," Garofoli later boasted. Sweeney did as he was told, which wasn't all that difficult because some board members already were unhappy with Kriegsfeld. The vote was 3-1, with one abstention. Board member Filipic explained the firing: "I feel that in recent months there has been a contentious attitude toward much of the community, which, if continued, could lead to the ultimate phasing out of public housing in this area." Kriegsfeld's only comment that day was "no comment."

Stokes's response was predictable: "It is obvious that the CMHA voted for tradition over today's progress. Their vote clearly indicates a prejudice against the elderly and low-income families. It is a tragic day for housing in Cleveland." When word of the board's actions reached the black community, many leaders and public housing activists expressed similar outrage. Ernest Cooper of the local Urban League chapter remarked that his organization was shocked, while the housing activist Charles Beard commented that the community could not afford to lose the "production and momentum" gained under Kriegsfeld's leadership. Louise Hall, the only black member of the housing authority's board, claimed that "the action was personal and political. No other director has made much progress in his thirty months time." Randall Osburn, who chaired the local branch of the Southern Christian Leadership Conference, was organizing a rent strike by housing authority tenants when Kriegsfeld was fired, and he was furious: "Kriegsfeld was fired because of politics, he dared to give a damn." (The rent strike notwithstanding, Osburn liked Kriegsfeld's approach to public housing and considered Kriegsfeld to be more of an advocate than a landlord.)[13]

In a collective act of protest against the firing of the man under whom the housing authority had built or rehabilitated five thousand housing units in less than three years, the agency's maintenance workers called in sick the next day. Osburn and public housing residents also announced a citywide rent strike. "Tenants are now aware of their rights and we are very upset over the dismissal. . . . We are going to withhold our rent," declared Osburn. Joseph Haggerty, a rent strike organizer and Kriegsfeld supporter who worked for the housing authority, was hoping that 75 percent of the area's ten thousand public housing residents would withhold rent for the month of January. He announced, "I believe that the great majority of tenants from all estates will support a strike." Osburn added, "The strike will go on until the CMHA board resigns and Mr. Kriegsfeld is restored." On a televised news program Osburn asserted that the tenants would support the maintenance workers by placing their rent money in escrow until Kriegsfeld was reinstated and tenants secured representation on the board. Housing authority officials then warned the tenants that unless they paid their rent, they would face eviction. To help forestall eviction the lawyers James Carson and Edward Haggins, along with several staff members from Legal Aid, agreed to represent the tenants. "If CMHA evicts anyone it will have to evict all the dissidents. . . . We have asked our lawyers to insure that any eviction would be a mass eviction," Osburn said. As the "sick-out" and rent strike continued, the protesters took their demonstrations to the authority's headquarters. On Friday, January 15, 1971, hundreds of protesters were arrested after disrupting a board meeting to demand Kriegsfeld's reinstatement. Days later the protest continued at housing authority offices; employees needed a police escort to enter the building's parking lot. On the night of January 19 the protest turned violent when a firebomb was tossed through the front window of the apartment of James Jones Jr., the on-site manager of the housing authority's Outhwaite Estates. Fortunately, no one was injured.[14]

As the rent strike gained momentum, Garofoli—now the city council president because Stanton had been elected to Congress—called on Stokes to end the demonstrations. "No level of government, including the metropolitan housing authority, can operate in an atmosphere of fear, intimidation, and violence," Garofoli noted. "When offices of the board are themselves intimidated, and when staff members are subject to fire bombing and shootings, there is a need for demonstrative and decisive action. . . . The threat on employees and tenants of CMHA should not be allowed to continue." Stokes reminded him that no one was in danger because unruly protesters were being arrested. Common Pleas Court Judge Frank Celebrezze then intervened by issuing a temporary injunction limiting demonstrators to six people at each site, although he did allow peaceful protest at board meetings. As the housing authority and its tenants negotiated, the controversy continued. By mid-March all the striking employees were back on the job, but tenants were still withholding their rent.[15]

The rent strike made the issue of a cooperation agreement between the city and the housing authority more important than ever. In January 1971 Francis Fisher, HUD's regional director, sent a strong warning to Stokes and the city council that they were in jeopardy of losing federal funding because their public housing program did not comply with federal guidelines. Fisher told them to proceed with the Green Valley and Lorain Square developments, facilitate a cooperation agreement between the city and housing authority, and disperse public housing units throughout the city. When the city council remained steadfast in its resistance to the mayor's housing program, Stokes asked Fisher to pull the funding. Days later Fisher cut off all HUD funds for urban renewal, Model Cities programs, demolition, and neighborhood programs. At the time the city had $33.3 million in grants pending before HUD, and grant applications for another $62.5 million were being prepared. HUD's actions and public pressure forced the city council to sign an agreement with the housing authority within ninety days.[16]

Even as the council and city hall battled their way through the Baxter Hill controversy and duked it out over the housing authority's plans to build Green Valley and Lorain Square, the mayor launched a broad-based tax reform campaign in the summer of 1970 to generate more revenue for the city. The city needed additional income because its tax base remained in decline, while the Stokes administration had expanded the city's payroll and had committed to $30 million in wage and benefit increases for municipal employees. Since Stokes had taken office, the city had added 1,091 workers to the city payroll, primarily in the area of public safety. With the increased payroll came drastic budget increases. In 1970, 53.4 percent, or $74.4 million, of the city's budget went to safety, up from $37.9 million in 1967. Police officers accounted for 30 percent of the city's workforce as the Cleveland Police Department increased its police-to-citizen ratio to 3.4 for every 1,000 citizens. These increased safety expenditures, largely a response to cries for law and order, had a devastating effect on city finances. The city was also hit hard by tax sharing. In 1969 the city lost $5.1 million to reciprocity agreements, while suburban areas like Cleveland Heights and Lakewood gained $307,000 and $360,000, respectively. (Under the city's reciprocity agreements with the surrounding suburbs, a nonresident working in the city would pay 75 percent of his income tax to Cleveland and 25 percent to his own community.) Thus because of the structural changes in the economy, the increased city payroll, and tax sharing, the city was facing a financial nightmare. It was Stokes's responsibility to sell the city council and voters on his tax reform package.[17]

When Finance Director Philip Dearborn suggested an increase in the municipal income tax and the repeal of reciprocity credit for nonresident taxpayers, Stokes agreed to support it. He established the Task Force on City Finances and appointed to it a group of black and white bankers, lawyers, and corporate executives. They worked for several months to find ways for the city to obtain the money it needed. Based on the projection that the city needed $133.1 million in revenues to operate, the task force made the following recommendations:

—Allow the 5.8 mill operating levy (property tax) to expire on December 31, 1970
—Increase in the municipal income tax from 1.0 percent to 1.8 percent
—Eliminate tax sharing with the suburbs.

In discussing its rationale for recommending that the city not renew its property tax levy, the task force noted that it would be "unduly burdensome to those on fixed incomes," in particular the elderly and the poor. Although the task force realized that doing this would decrease revenue, it hoped that the additional revenue raised by increasing the city income tax and dropping tax sharing would offset the loss. The task force told residents that the tax increases would fall hardest on suburbanites. Both measures would force those working but not living in the city to support city services. The task force recognized that suburban communities would face financial hardships as a result of the city's moves, but the task force believed that suburban officials could "look to their own internal resources for future financing." The mayor thanked the task force for "analyzing Cleveland's financial crisis and finding the answers to the meeting of that crisis." Stokes believed that the combination of eliminating reciprocity, lowering real-estate taxes, and adopting an income tax as the major base of revenue would work. Although he eagerly accepted these recommendations, he knew that their implementation would entail another battle. Implementing them required city council approval, and then they had to be "approved by the people." But he believed these changes would be well worth the effort, for they "will provide the city with a base of revenue that will ensure the needed income for several years," Stokes said.[18]

Late in July Stokes gave a speech on his tax proposal at the City Club, social home of Cleveland's white business establishment. He led off by labeling the city limits a financial noose that choked residents by inflicting a lopsided tax burden on the poor. In response to suburban criticism of his plans to repeal the reciprocity agreement, Stokes contended: "I am a Clevelander and my responsibility as Mayor is to the people of this city. And I must insist that there be unity in the suburbs, total cooperation, because I cannot in good conscience ask Clevelanders to pay when much wealthier suburbanites refuse." Stokes was willing to keep reciprocity if the suburbs did likewise, but as it stood only a handful of suburbs had agreements with the city, and these did not include the highly industrialized suburbs of Brookpark and Bedford Heights with their rich tax bases. "All people who work in Cleveland will support this city," said Stokes. "Suburbanites must understand that the time has come when they will have to pay their fair share for their use of this city." Stokes referred to the approximately 250,000 people who commuted to the city each day, which meant that the poorer citizens of the city were subsidizing commuters' needs for police protection, street maintenance, and traffic control. "The most taxable people and many of the best tax-paying industries and businesses move outside the city. That has left Cleveland with the least taxable people, the oldest real property, and the costliest slum and welfare problems," he said. He acknowledged that the tax was "regressive, that it hits the little guy the hardest," and he said he was willing to listen to other plans that presented a "fair and equitable alternative." None was offered.[19]

Several of his council critics denied the need for a tax increase, most notably, Dennis Kucinich. Although the young and brash city council member from Ward 7 agreed that ending tax reciprocity was a good idea, he felt that a tax increase was unnecessary. In arguing against the tax, he suggested that the city would be able to meet its financial obligations from the existing 1 percent income tax, thanks to inflation and through the attrition of the city workforce. Other council members such as Lawrence Duggan and Anthony Garofoli agreed. In early August, Stokes took his plans to the council's finance committee, because he needed a two-thirds vote from the city council to get his tax package on the ballot for November. While the council agreed to let the voters decide, the Stanton bloc made no commitment to support the package. "It's the mayor's issue, let him sell it," said one unidentified council member. Labor came out openly against the tax plan. The United Auto Workers and the Cleveland Federation of Labor (CFL), AFL-CIO, believed—incorrectly—that the tax package was nothing but a sneaky way to give big business a tax break at the expense of the working class. "We want no part of this make-believe tax reform," said Robert Weismann of the fifty-thousand-member UAW. "It subsidizes commercial and industrial interests at the expense of wage earners." Although two large labor organizations were pledged to fight the plan, and the city council was disinclined to support the package, Stokes persisted: "The CFL endorsement would have been a big boost. However, this will not deter us in our effort to have the Cleveland voters approve decent wages and a standard of living for the thousands of city employees who have served them so well."[20]

Stokes faced two other major obstacles in his efforts to secure the tax initiative: making residents understand the impending financial crisis and convincing them that the increased income tax would not be a burden. Before the campaign Stokes met with his entire cabinet and other high-ranking city employees to let them know that he expected "full cooperation" from them in working to pass the plan. He instructed them to "develop a campaign package to disseminate clear and understandable facts to all city employees" concerning the tax. Stokes expected all city workers "to be actively involved." Once the drive was underway, "blitz squads" went door-to-door, placards were placed on city buses, and town hall meetings featuring Stokes and his cabinet were held across the city. At the neighborhood gatherings Stokes stressed the decline of the city's tax base, escalating police costs, salary increases, and how his tax increase would be spread among "all people who use the city, based on their income." The tax reform team printed up four-page brochures to make clear how much the tax would affect the average Cleveland resident. Based upon average incomes, a Clevelander earning $9,109 annually would pay $163.91 a year in taxes, up from $91.09, while a Shaker Heights resident grossing $25,758 a year would pay $463.64, up from $257.58. According to the campaign literature, this was a "fair way to tax Clevelanders because it places more of the burden on the people who live in the suburbs and work in Cleveland. Under tax reform suburbanites and business will pay 72 percent of the increased tax." In stressing the need for voter support, Stokes emphasized the repeal of reciprocity effective October 1 and the expiration of the property tax at the end of the year. To allay other fears about the increase, Stokes made it clear that income from Social Security, unemployment, alimony, and old-age pensions was exempt.[21]

One week before the election Stokes held two town hall meetings and appeared on a thirty-minute television special paid for by the Committee on Tax Reform, a group of Stokes supporters. To attract white conservatives Stokes argued that the increased revenues would go toward maintaining law and order. "We must have more police," he said. "This is how we have reduced violent crime by 9% so far, we need more men to prevent crime and to apprehend criminals. That takes money." But this appeal did not generate much support. While everyone expected the Stanton bloc to actively oppose the package, the silence of the Greater Cleveland Growth Association and the Citizens League of Greater Cleveland was shocking. Although both organizations endorsed the tax plan, neither actively campaigned for it. Their refusal to actively support the plan caused the Committee for Tax Reform to fall short of its fund-raising goal of $50,000. The growth association had had little trouble raising money in past campaigns. It seems clear that Stanton and Garofoli had orchestrated the decision not to actively support the tax. They were trying to force Stokes into governing a bankrupt city. According to William O. Walker of the *Call and Post*, their strategy was to ignore the issue, then support a smaller tax increase at a later time to provide just enough money "to keep policemen on the street and the garbage trucks running. But not enough to get at the real problems that plague the city." Walker also suggested that Stanton and Garofoli's plan was to keep services minimal and phase out the city's low-income housing programs and enforcement of equal opportunity laws, all under the guise of fiscal conservatism.[22]

The strategy worked; the "Stokes tax" failed 106,410 to 76,277. The tax plan basically came down to a referendum on Stokes: the black East Side voted for the tax plan; the white West Side did not. Stokes placed the blame for its failure squarely on the shoulders of the Cleveland City Council: "The failure by council to support the increase represents an abdication of its responsibilities and duties. They reviewed the budget three times and still decided to place the increase on the ballot. They were therefore unjustified in not supporting the tax." Speaking at the tax reform committee's headquarters as the disappointing election results were announced, Stokes labeled the defeat "a great blow for the city" while adding that the anticipated cutback measures "will have to be done." Stokes then lashed out at the lack of support he received from his own friends on the council, calling their effort atrocious. He charged, "Even with the councilmen who expressed support for the issue, I have yet to see more than four of them out working for it." Even in defeat, though, Stokes claimed a moral victory, believing that the failed campaign gave him an opportunity "to educate our public about the present status and financial needs of the city."[23]

At a news conference the next day Stokes noted that the city's anticipated $27 million shortfall would mean a 3,200-person reduction in the city's 12,000-plus work force. He pledged to close the police academy and lay off cadets, to place a freeze on hiring by the safety department, and to cancel all winter recreation activities. He also announced a 50 percent reduction in the activities of the health center, the layoffs of 50 percent of all maintenance employees, and the closing of all urban renewal offices. "There will be no new programs of any kind," Stokes said. After hearing of the planned cutbacks, Garofoli and Robert Weismann, the UAW leader, went on the defensive. "It seems to me a fifteen percent cutback in the workforce is not warranted," said Garofoli. "Now is not the time to point the finger of blame or to panic by answering with unwarranted and unreasonable cuts in service. Council provided a budget to meet the needs of 1970 and, I can assure you, will meet its responsibilities in 1971." Kucinich agreed: "The people of Cleveland have made an intelligent decision in asking a tighter fiscal policy for our city. . . . It will be up to city council to reassess the spending policies of the administration and to

suggest budget adjustments." By announcing the drastic cuts, Stokes was trying not only to meet the city's financial needs but to embarrass those who
asserted that the city did not need to increase the tax. However, when the cuts
were announced, the city council was already making plans to call a special
election for a referendum on a smaller tax increase.[24]

The plain and simple fact was that the Garofoli clique was aware of the
need for a tax increase back in November yet had failed to campaign for it.
This caused Stokes to wonder whether race was more important than the
general welfare of the city. By choosing to play the politics of race over the
politics of fiscal practicality, Stokes's city council opponents jeopardized the
city's financial stability.

Stokes was further disappointed when Common Pleas Court Judge George
McMonagle refused to permit the city to end reciprocity. McMonagle found
that under the existing agreement Cleveland should have notified suburban
governments before February 20, 1970, of its plans to end tax sharing, a ruling that cost the city an additional $6 million in revenue because it had not
met that deadline. Stokes also suffered another defeat on election day when
voters approved a charter amendment that gave the city council the authority to name two members of the Board of Control (which awarded city contracts), which had historically been made up of the mayor's cabinet. The basis
for this legislation was Garofoli's displeasure with Stokes's awarding contracts
to black firms. The effective opposition mounted by the anti-Stokes forces
on the city council, combined with the lack of support from the city's labor,
business, and welfare sectors, was a sure sign that the Stokes phenomenon
was wearing off. Whereas Stokes probably expected his opponents on the
council to actively oppose him, the lack of support that he received from the
other segments of society was a clear sign that Cleveland was ready to end
the Stokes experiment.

The smaller tax increase championed by the city council at the behest of
Garofoli called for a 0.6 percent increase in the city income tax, which meant
that the tax would rise to 1.6 percent, instead of the 1.8 percent that Stokes
wanted. Although race politics had prevented him from campaigning for the
Stokes tax plan, Garofoli nevertheless realized that the city had a critical need
for additional revenue. After the city council agreed to the referendum, to
be held later that spring, Garofoli worked for passage of this tax increase. The
new council president called the special election "a day of testing for our city
of Cleveland." He later added that the election "will decide whether the public is willing to pay a small additional municipal income tax . . . to maintain
basic city services at acceptable levels." To placate fears that he himself once
raised concerning fiscal mismanagement by the administration, Garofoli

promised not to let the increased revenues go for "frivolities and foolishness." Stokes assisted Garofoli in asking voters to approve the issue and disregard personalities. "This is not a matter of Carl Stokes versus any other individual or faction. This is not a matter of testing any individual's strength or council's collective strength," he declared. Rather, "it is a question of whether or not Cleveland will survive as a city." Despite their appeals voters rejected the plan 62,639 to 54,649. As usual, the black wards voted for the tax plan, while the anti-Stokes wards voted against it. Stokes was clearly at a loss: "I blame everyone in the city of Cleveland." Garofoli, obviously embarrassed at his own inability to deliver the vote, stated simply, "The will of the people of Cleveland has been expressed. They have chosen a reduction in city spending and as a result a reduction in city services." Many political observers added that the defeated tax levy was a "plebiscite on the mayor's popularity," because by now it was clear that voters were voting more against Stokes than against the tax. Others agreed that, as one public official put it, by making race the unstated but central issue, "it was a split vote against the black mayor . . . that's the only way I know how to put it."[25]

With the city in the midst of a financial nightmare, Stokes called for more citizen participation in local government. "Although the loss of the tax issue certainly was a vital blow," Stokes told his constituents, "we aren't wallowing in despair. Citizens are going to have to go back to doing for themselves many of the things that their government has been doing for them." After telling approximately one thousand businessmen, industrialists, and civic leaders at the annual Future of Cleveland Luncheon on February 3, 1971, that "your city isn't dead," he affirmed that "it's time for a do-it-yourself course in many areas." Later at a televised news conference Stokes announced a plan of volunteerism: "What we are hoping for is a renaissance of volunteerism in Cleveland, a growth and strengthening of a 'do-it-ourselves' spirit, which will create a kind of Cleveland Peace Corps . . . of Very Involved Persons."[26]

With the second tax failure Stokes was forced to lay off 1,725 employees, including 193 police officers; 146 public health doctors, dentists, nurses, health center aides, and health technicians; 67 waste collectors; 79 housing inspectors; and 386 recreation employees. In addition, the city closed three of its seven health centers, along with twenty-six year-round recreation centers.

After forcing Stokes into governing a financially strapped city, Garofoli went for the jugular as city council meetings turned into a virtual battlefield between the administration and city council. Throughout the Stokes era the Monday night sessions always presented an opportunity for Stokes's critics to use the administration as the scapegoat for the city's problems. Because the weekly meetings were broadcast live on educational television, thousands of residents used the council sessions to assess the Stokes administration. Under Stanton and Garofoli the weekly meetings turned into an ugly example of the political process. During Stokes's first term Stanton would often gavel down his opponents or unplug their microphones as they were speaking. Nor was it rare for Stanton to quickly adjourn a meeting, all in an apparent attempt to demonstrate his power over the mayor. After Stanton's election to Congress, Garofoli continued in the footsteps of his predecessor and mentor.

In February 1971 Ralph Tyler, director of the service department, and Walter Burks, director of city personnel, came under attack from the old Stanton bloc. The council members ridiculed Tyler because of the city's inability to clear the major thoroughfares during a major snowstorm, and they summoned Burks to the council chambers because he had supposedly placed a city employee on the wrong department's payroll.[27]

The attacks continued at the next council session when Councilman Francis Gaul accused Thomas Stallworth, the African American commissioner of markets, weights, measures, of "malfeasance, misfeasance, nonfeasance" of duty. Stokes was livid, declaring, "That kind of language is uncalled for." Gaul stated that his conclusions were based on a personal investigation of two grocery stores in his ward. According to Gaul, he and an off-duty inspector from Stallworth's division went to the area stores and found that both were selling many short-weighted meat packages. Stokes then asserted that Gaul had violated the council's courtesy rule, which stated that council members could not personally insult other members on the floor (Stokes was referring to Stallworth). This caused Harmody to yell, "Point of order! . . . It is not the place of the mayor to bring this point before council." Garofoli agreed that Stokes had no jurisdiction to raise questions of impropriety. Stokes responded, "I'm not calling names Mr. President, but the issue I am raising is that we are here voluntarily in the interests of the affairs of the city, and our appearance here will not continue through these base personal attacks. As long as we are here, we are entitled to each and every privilege and protection of the rules according to council." Garofoli then reminded him that council rules applied only to council members. Stokes was further enraged. "What you have said is that the same standard will not be afforded to the administration. I must insist that the privileges and protections be equal. You have made it quite clear, and I am going to instruct my cabinet members to remove themselves from council chambers, and we will not return until the same standards are extended to both branches of government. I don't want to get caught up on rules—I'm just asking for respect," Stokes shouted as he and his cabinet exited the council chambers. Local journalists remarked that the walkout marked one of the only times that a mayor has staged a walkout from the council.[28]

Stokes supporters characterized the Gaul attack as racist, and they supported the mayor's decision to boycott the meetings. Virgil Brown, a Republican member of the council, labeled the council's actions "a terrible disgraceful performance" while expressing his concern about "the open racism being heard on council floor." Councilman James Bell noted that he had not heard or seen anything "like the kind of tactics that have been tolerated in council during the past several years in a deliberate attempt to make the city's first black administration under a black man look bad." Kellogg, another Republican, probably placed the entire episode into context when he stated: "I can't recall any mayor who has had to put up with the kind of disrespect and sniping that has been accorded Mayor Stokes and his cabinet by city council." After the walkout Stokes and Garofoli held several unproductive meetings, and for the remainder of his tenure Stokes and his cabinet did not attend the Monday night council sessions. Instead, he launched his own weekly televised news conference. "In a half hour of television, I could get out what I wanted in my own words."[29]

The mayor's continuing battles with city council convinced him that seeking another term would be futile. Even if he did manage to win re-election, he concluded that he would be unable to implement major reforms. But Stokes understood that the climate throughout the country was not conducive to reform. Nixon and white conservatism were in vogue. The decision not to seek a third term was not a difficult one.

At a dinner party on April 16, 1971, Stokes announced to fifty of his close friends and advisers that he would vacate the mayor's office in November. Stokes then went to Channel 5 to tape a public announcement. "I have decided not to seek a third term as Mayor of the City of Cleveland," said Stokes, who went on to say that his fourteen-year political career had been devoted to "bringing more citizens into the governmental process" and to bringing "out into the open the real issues and problems confronting our urban society." He then closed his remarks by commenting that he wanted to devote more of his time to expanding his efforts "to assist others, particularly the locked-in minority groups to better understand their role in government and politics."[30]

Once the decision reached his political foes, they expressed shock, surprise, or joy. When Garofoli was notified, he said he had no comment other than that he was shocked. Others, like the black conservative Jack Oliver and council member Theodore Silwa, commented that they did not think Stokes was serious. "We just have to wait and see what the mayor really wants," said Oliver. "I won't believe it until I see it," echoed Silwa, "because I'm used to the mayor making remarks and then they don't come to pass." The black business owner William Seawright, a one-time Stokes supporter, saw the announcement as "an old political trick. He wants to stir the black community into an emotional pitch to create a draft movement. This is not good for the city, not good for the country." Other council members were elated that Stokes was not running again. Joseph Lombardo confidently predicted that Stokes's exit would "clear the way for a mayor that will be good for all the people of the city," and Joseph Kowalski felt that Stokes's decision "will be beneficial to him personally and to the city." Others, such as Michael Zone, believed that Stokes's decision was part of a long-term plan to leave the city in horrible condition. "The city is in a terrible financial situation, and for him to leave at this time . . . I don't know . . . I think he should have stayed around and not walked away from the people. It's unfair. He's polarized the city." Andrew Bass, the city council's budget analyst, was equally critical, saying, "He gets us in trouble and then he runs away." Geraldine Williams, who was still bitter about her dismissal in 1968, was pleased that her estranged friend was not seeking a third term: "He left a lot of people out on a limb, including his councilmen. It will take a long time to pull the black community together again. Who wants this city after the mess Carl got it in?"[31]

Members of the black working class, who had considered Stokes's four-year tenure as a logical extension of their continuing battle for equality, were disappointed but supportive of the mayor's decision to bow out. Many of those polled said that they had grown tired of seeing Stokes attacked. An unidentified Cedar Avenue man blamed Stokes's decision on "the racist councilmen and the envious blacks who know they couldn't do as well as the mayor." He also predicted that black municipal employees would be laid off and the "cops will be turned loose." Another unidentified black resident believed that "if blacks and whites had gotten behind him from the start, he could have done something." Nonie Fuller, a Glenville housewife, was "glad he's not running. His own people criticized him too much. I thought he was an excellent mayor, but let somebody else have those headaches. He can use the rest." Frank Gorman of East 119th Street concurred: "I agree with the mayor's decision. He was not getting a fair deal from city council at all. He should have quit a long time ago. Let the next mayor see what he can accomplish under those circumstances."

Lowell Bradley, a machine operator, argued that Stokes's decision was best and that "he might have done a better job if the people had only given him full support. For black people things will get a lot worse without him." Bradley Wilkinson, a Greenlawn Avenue resident, echoed Bradley's prediction: "He [Stokes] kept things calm during his term, and he tried to do what he could for people in need. Now you can expect things to get heated in some areas." Although many of the respondents agreed with Stokes's decision, others said they felt hurt. Fredericka Bradshaw of East 140th Street thought Stokes had failed to "give himself enough time to accomplish all he set out to do." Bradford Tabor was equally disappointed: "Mayor Stokes made a bad decision. He should run again. The city needs him. Cleveland was nowhere before he took office and now it will become a nowhere place when he leaves."[32]

The mayor's decision not to seek a third term sent shock waves throughout the political community as politicians began to consider the ramifications. Because Stokes had unified the black community, many of his supporters did not want to lose this hard-fought momentum. Paul T. Haggard, a black member of the council, was certain that "we ain't going back to business as usual now that Stokes is leaving." Virgil Brown said, "The black community has seen what political power means. We will come up with a candidate who will be responsive and a voice for disadvantaged people." Rev. Don Jacobs complemented Brown's comments by assuring a local reporter that the black community would be "working hard for the next few days to build for the future." Gladstone Chandler, the city manager of East Cleveland, said that it would be a shame if the next mayor was not black. But others were not confident that they could field another successful black mayoral candidate right away. Rev. Emmanuel S. Branch did not know of a likely candidate, while Rev. Jonathan Ealy was unequally certain whether the black community could make a "smooth transition" to another candidate. Carrie Cain, another council member, felt that the mayor's departure presented an opportunity for the community to mature: "There is only one Carl Stokes, now the rest of the leadership must take a stronger stand." After pondering the political effects of Stokes's announcement, Forbes stated eloquently, "There is no more Mayor Stokes."[33]

Although he was a lame-duck mayor with seven months remaining in office, Stokes continued to battle for the needs of the black poor. In the aftermath of the failed tax increase, Stokes continued to argue that suburbanites drained the city's resources while showing utter disregard for conditions within the inner city. One of the chief perpetrators of the suburban dollar drain was the Northeast Ohio Areawide Coordinating Agency (NOACA), a regional planning body. Formed in 1966 to review areawide federal grants in a seven-county section of northeastern Ohio, NOACA held a powerful position because any government seeking federal dollars needed its approval. The forty-nine-member board consisted of county commissioners and city representatives from the area. But although the city of Cleveland had 25 percent of the population in the seven-county area, it held only three seats on the NOACA board. In essence, officials from outside the city were ruling on Cleveland's grant requests.[34]

Stokes at first failed to notice the city's underrepresentation on NOACA. But with the arrival of the fiscally conservative Nixon administration, Stokes began to pay closer attention to the affairs of the regional body. At a meeting in March 1969 the mayor's representative appealed to the board's steering committee to reapportion the body to make it reflect the seven-county population. He requested that NOACA take the initiative but remarked that the city was prepared to make recommendations.

In December 1969 the suburb-dominated agency angered Stokes when it approved a path for the planned Interstate 290, which would run from East 55th Street through the eastern suburbs of Shaker Heights, Cleveland Heights, and Beachwood. Stokes and the city council objected to the proposed highway because it would displace twelve hundred low-income families. Stokes and his advisers, particularly Norman Krumholz, chair of the city planning commission, argued that the highway would destroy neighborhoods, reduce the supply of affordable housing, increase residential segregation, and cause additional fiscal problems for the financially strapped city government. In opposing the highway Stokes was going up against powerful interests, such as the state highway department and the county engineers office. To satisfy the needs of the city and its constituents, Stokes and Krumholz drafted an alternate route for the highway, which would have displaced only 164 families. Despite the city's objections and its subsequent alternate route proposal, NOACA went ahead with its original plan. That was when Stokes realized that he needed to get serious about gaining more representation on the board.[35]

He filed suit in federal court claiming that NOACA violated the city's right to proportional representation under the one-man, one-vote rule. The mayor argued that NOACA's voting structure was contrary to and in violation of the Constitution. He further stated that because the city did not have fair representation, "the non-urban communities" were voting on the city's grant requests. Stokes then alerted Samuel Jackson, an assistant HUD secretary and the highest-ranking African American in the agency, to the controversy.[36]

Stokes protested NOACA's actions by withholding the city's yearly contribution, causing the agency to suspend Cleveland's voting privileges. City officials and agency representatives met throughout the summer of 1970 to try to reach an agreement. The city brought a number of plans to the table. The first proposal suggested a smaller four-county organization, with the city of Cleveland having 8 of the 27 votes. The second plan called for Cleveland to have 3 votes on a body of 15. After much debate the NOACA negotiating committee agreed to the 15-member body with one representative from each of the seven counties, three from Cleveland, three from Cuyahoga County, one from the city of Akron, and one from Summit County. Despite the tentative agreement, the NOACA review committee unanimously rejected it. It did so on the ground that "if a change is to be made, representation should be on a county, or district basis, and that no individual political subdivision should be designated direct representation." NOACA officials further argued that they had erred in giving "direct representation" (they meant proportional) to Cleveland and Akron, "since board members had always acted in the best interests of the entire area." Last, the review committee also rejected an alternative proposal that would have given Cleveland 8 votes on a 52-member body. This rejection shocked Stokes and other city officials because Cleveland would still have only 15 percent representation. In the midst of the crisis Irving Korningsberg, the chair of NOACA, summed up his body's attitude toward the idea of representation: "NOACA was formed to establish a coordinating body for the governments in the seven-county area. It was not established for the purpose of forming a new government. Accordingly, the concept of one-man one-vote is out of order in an organization of existing governments. I feel NOACA is doing the job it set out to do, and that it has excellent representation." Korningsberg's comments did not come as a surprise to Stokes. What puzzled him was that the NOACA board members had had the audacity to suggest that they were acting in the best interests of the city when they had just killed a resolution encouraging local communities to provide public housing and had delayed support for equal employment opportunity legislation.[37]

The denial of the city's reapportionment plan gave Stokes the impetus to take the matter to Jackson at HUD. In their discussions the mayor told Jackson how NOACA acted against the best interests of the city. In response to these complaints Jackson pressured NOACA to reorganize its board. Weeks later NOACA submitted a revised membership plan giving Cleveland 8 votes on a 52-person board. Stokes felt that although the plan was "clearly a step in that right direction, it still has many deficiencies from the standpoint of equity." The mayor's foremost concern was that the city was still underrepresented. Stokes wondered how it was that each representative from rural Geauga County could represent 15,654 people, while each Cleveland representative spoke for 94,000 residents. This was clear and blatant racial discrimination. Stokes was shocked to learn that Jackson had sided with NOACA. He told Stokes that the regional board's proposal met federal requirements. Nonetheless, Stokes still refused to pay the city's yearly dues, jeopardizing the city's eligibility for funding. As expected, the city was automatically expelled from the board on May 5, 1971. However, the expulsion of Cleveland from the regional agency was simply a pressure tactic, because under HUD guidelines the central city had to be a participating member in order for NOACA to receive any money. By expelling Cleveland, NOACA tried to force Stokes into accepting unfair representation. Shortly after the city's expulsion NOACA announced that it would charge Cleveland 1 percent of all project costs, and the board rejected Cleveland's police cadet program.[38]

On June 11 Stokes wrote HUD Secretary George Romney expressing his dissatisfaction with Jackson's support for NOACA. Stokes stressed that NOACA had blatantly ignored HUD's own guidelines relative to citizen participation, equal employment, and open space grants for low-income people. In closing, Stokes argued, "it is our conviction that by continuing to certify NOACA, HUD and other federal agencies are turning their backs on their own regulations and supporting an unjust and intolerable solution." Romney agreed and four days later temporarily decertified NOACA. The move by HUD froze approximately $14 million and jeopardized an additional $248 million in pending grants. Nonetheless, Stokes filed a lengthy complaint with the U.S. Civil Rights Commission and with HUD requesting that they make the decertification permanent and establish a new organization "that will meet regional needs as well as the needs of Cleveland's residents." The impetus for this complaint was an ordinance passed by the Cleveland City Council that authorized Stokes to pay the city's 1971 dues to NOACA. The controversy remained in a stalemate through the end of the summer because neither Stokes nor NOACA was willing to compromise. NOACA officials made it known that they were waiting for Stokes to leave office in November. With millions of dollars at stake Gov. John Gilligan stepped in to mediate. Ultimately, Stokes, NOACA, and HUD agreed to let the Ohio State Department of Development act as an interim areawide planning agency.[39]

The battle against NOACA further convinced Stokes that the United States needed a multifaceted approach to solve the problems of its cities. As the nation's leading urban politician, Stokes was active in the U.S. Conference of Mayors, and in 1970 he was named president-elect of the National League of Cities. He used his popularity to organize several highly publicized meetings with the Nixon administration and other mayors to discuss urban problems. Stokes articulated many of his ideas in a lengthy piece entitled, "Saving the Cities," which appeared in the January 1971 edition of *Playboy.*

The mayor was convinced that the problems of the cities—housing, unemployment, poor schools, pollution, and transportation—"were unprecedented in the history of organized society." As such they were so widely "cussed and discussed, analyzed and penalized" that any urban manager "would be able to list them in his sleep and give you a dollar figure for solving or alleviating each specific problem in his own city." But Stokes was optimistic that they could be solved: "There is nothing fundamentally wrong with America's cities that money can't cure." The cities needed billions to "mount the programs, to staff the projects, to reverse the decay, to counterattack, to change and improve. If only there were the funds." Fiscal conservatives suggested that no money was available to aid the cities, but Stokes was convinced otherwise. "There are the funds," he declared. "They have been poured down the open sewer" of Vietnam. Stokes then attacked the vast U.S. defense budget and space program, which he felt took millions away from the people who needed the money, poor urbanites. But Stokes realized that what was really needed was the "resolve to reorder national priorities."[40]

"Part of the urban problem," said Stokes, "is that state government is tragically archaic" and unresponsive to the needs of the cities. Stokes stressed that the structure of state government "has impeded efforts to meet the urban crisis." In Stokes's opinion state legislatures had no "delivery system to respond to the problems of the urban centers and no built-in motivation for it." He was speaking in particular of the reapportionment practices that left many state legislatures dominated by rural and suburban interests. "The one-man, one-vote ruling gave great hope to mayors of big cities that we would be delivered from rural domination at the statehouse," Stokes told *Playboy*'s readers. "But it came too late. The population has shifted from the city proper to the suburbs and exurbs; thus even with reapportionment, central cities are far from adequately represented in the state legislatures." This posed a serious barrier because the suburban legislator "has no more concern for the ghetto than did the farmer whose seat he took." Because cities tended to have such inadequate representation in state legislatures, Stokes was not a strong supporter of federal-state revenue-sharing proposals. He figured that if the state received additional money under such a plan, it was highly unlikely that the inner cities would receive any of it. Rather, he proposed federal-to-city revenue sharing.[41]

Stokes also proposed the elimination of state government, which he would replace with a reconstituted Congress that would consist of an "upper House composed of 100 representatives from the 50 largest metropolitan areas and one at large." In the place of a state government "I would substitute regional government," which could more efficiently handle the problems of the central city. Although Stokes knew that this proposal would never be implemented, he hoped that the federal government would recognize that 70 percent of the U.S. population lived in cities. What the country really needed was not a "southern strategy" but an "urban strategy" that preserved and strengthened the democratic process, especially for those who were "locked in the ghettos of our big cities."[42]

In closing, Stokes argued that U.S. cities represented a tremendous investment of time, energy, talent, ingenuity, hope, and human resources, "that they cannot and must not be written off." As an example of what a city could do if given the resources and vision, Stokes pointed to his Cleveland: Now! program, which he felt was successful "in reordering priorities to put first things first." He suggested that the Nixon administration and Congress implement a similar program, "'The Cities: Now!'"[43]

With much of his urban agenda blocked by the city council and other governmental bodies, Stokes devoted much of his remaining time in office to strengthening the all-black Twenty-first District Democratic Caucus, an independent political party.

10. The Twenty-first District Caucus

STOKES SAW THE RESISTANCE from the city council as representative of a larger issue: the failure of the Cuyahoga County Democrats to reward black voters for their decades of allegiance. Although black Clevelanders had functioned as an essential part of the county Democratic Party since the 1930s, it refused to share power with its black constituents. In fact, blacks were never elected or appointed to positions within the organization and were denied substantive patronage benefits. The party usually was supportive only of black candidates running for city council from all-black wards. In an effort to alter this dysfunctional relationship, Stokes decided to spearhead the formation of the all-black Twenty-first District Democratic Caucus to unify the city's black politicians, to institutionalize his power base, and to make the Cuyahoga County Democratic Party responsive to black interests and concerns. On a more personal level Stokes was eager to create a political organization that would rival that of the county Democrats who provided the most resistance to his agenda in the city council. Within weeks four hundred to five hundred people, and anyone else "who loved the Stokes boys," paid the $2 membership fee. The caucus quickly emerged as one of the most powerful political organizations in the county.[1]

It launched its first challenge to the county Democrats in May 1970 when it made three demands: 20 percent membership on the county executive committee, a black appointee to the elections board, and another black appointee to the position of either chairman, secretary, treasurer, or vice chairman of the party. Unless these demands were met, caucus leaders warned, black Democrats would leave the party en masse: "If we cannot have a voice in the Democratic Party, maybe it is time the black people determined they do not belong to either party. Maybe it is time we traded off with both political parties."[2]

When the caucus first presented these demands, Democrats responded by saying it could name the secretary of the county organization. The caucus then selected council member George Forbes for the post, but the county Democrats rejected him because he was Stokes's main liaison to the black community and because of his reputation as especially militant. The county Democrats then decided instead to create three vice chairmanships, with one specifically designated for an African American. Although the caucus initially objected, its members eventually agreed to the proposal. However, instead of letting the caucus make the appointment, the county leaders said, "We'll pick the black person."[3]

The county Democrats nominated Stokes's executive assistant, Arnold Pinkney, and U.S. Representative Louis Stokes. Both declined. The caucus then renominated Forbes for a vice chairmanship of the county Democratic organization and put out a statement: "The Twenty-First District Caucus has unanimously endorsed George Forbes as its nominee for vice chairman of the central and executive committees. We will not accept any other nominee." In a move engineered by Stanton, the party flatly rejected Forbes and nominated instead Ken Clement, Stokes's estranged campaign director. When caucus members learned that Clement was the nominee and that Forbes had been rejected, more than four hundred caucus members boycotted the county Democratic Party convention later that day. In fact, newspapers reported that only two black elected officials participated in the convention.[4]

Stokes explained the reasons for the boycott: "My concern is to see to it that the party comes out truly representative, reflecting the minority ethnic groups, and that young people have a clear voice in the need for reform, they have put up a slate representing their wishes and not the desires of others." When the county Democrats inducted the new officers, the caucus announced that it was leaving the county organization. "We will evaluate candidates for ourselves and select the ones we want and reject the ones we do not want," Pinkney said. Breaking away from the party meant that "we would be free agents, and nonpartisan, supporting candidates of either party, depending upon what their election meant to the black community," Carl Stokes said. A caucus press release stated the group's position succinctly: "The old, traditional and historical practices of those who resist change and perpetuate the status quo of having a Negro fight another Negro is over. George Forbes and no other member of the caucus is fighting or contesting another Negro for the position created by the Democratic party for a Negro. The caucus rejects this as being contemptuous of the 400,000 people black and white who live and vote in the 21st Congressional District and are represented in the 21st District caucus."[5]

Stokes labeled the actions of the county Democrats an affront. He then went on to remark that the failure of party leaders to consult him was insulting. "So far as I am concerned nobody asked me and I was not included in the original talks that were held to make up the structure adopted by the convention." Stokes then wondered why the Democrats would expect him to continue to support the party. "They can't exclude the mayor of the largest city from their talks in the development of the party, then expect him to ratify their talks and actions."[6]

Days later Stokes announced that he would not support any Democratic organizational activity, that he was declining a position on the new Democratic County Executive Committee and withdrawing from his seat on the Central Committee. Stokes argued that the newly formed executive committee structure did not adequately represent black interests, largely because four of the five seats were held by suburban whites. When reporters asked Stokes about Clement's appointment, the mayor told them that because Clement was not a member of the caucus, his appointment was meaningless. Stokes also told the reporters that his displeasure was not directed toward party chair Joseph Bartunek but at Stanton, who had engineered the chicanery. Despite his disappointment, Stokes assured his supporters that he was still a Democrat—"All this means is that I will not take any role in the Democratic party. Joe Bartunek and I can talk any time. I am still a Democrat." At a caucus meeting attended by six hundred people, Pinkney, the vice chair, echoed Stokes's comments: "We are not out of the Democratic party, we are temporarily out of the county Democratic party."[7]

The caucus then voted not to have any contact with the county organization or any of its officials until after the November 1970 general election. Caucus members also agreed to run their own slate of candidates and endorse others, to conduct a voter registration and education campaign, and to open a permanent office in order to demonstrate to white Democrats that "what the caucus is about is not just rhetoric." Last, they prohibited Democratic ward leaders and precinct committee members from cooperating with the county organization.[8]

As expected, the local press criticized Stokes for leading the caucus out of the county organization. A *Cleveland Press* editorial labeled it a "sorry day" for the Democratic spirit and for partisan politics. The writer believed that "such separatism" would be a divisive, destructive force in the community. Although the writer agreed that the caucus had legitimate grievances against the party, "this did not justify breaking away from the party. Losing one battle is poor reason to pick up one's marbles and go off and play a separate game, especially to the extent of dividing the party along racial lines."[9]

In July 1970 Bartunek made an effort to end the controversy by offering Stokes a vice chairmanship on the executive committee. Stokes refused the offer, and the caucus continued with its plans to run candidates against white Democrats in the fall elections. The caucus opened a headquarters in August, dropped the word *Democratic* from its title, and by September was making endorsements across party lines. With a paid membership of seven hundred to one thousand, the Twenty-first District Caucus began "to take on the characteristics of a powerful urban machine."[10]

The caucus announced its list of endorsed candidates in front of a standing room–only crowd at the organization's headquarters. The caucus used as its criterion for endorsement "who will be most responsive to the needs of the people. Party labels, political popularity and race have been set aside as considerations." On the list were several dyed-in-the-wool Republicans, including Seth Taft, who was engaged in a close race for county commissioner against Frank M. Gorman, a Democrat. In fact, Louis Stokes made it clear that Taft deserved special mention: "This individual is a man we urge all citizens of Cuyahoga County to elect to the office of County Commissioner." Noticeably absent from the coveted endorsement list of thirteen Republicans and nine Democrats was the name of Leo Jackson, the conservative council member who was seeking a municipal judgeship. The caucus had made it clear that it would use the November 1970 elections as a test of its political strength.[11]

Gorman was not surprised that he did not get the caucus endorsement because he "figured my GOP opponent would bid very high for this support and pay a dear price. I wonder what was promised the Caucus?" Garofoli told reporters that Stokes and the caucus had endorsed GOP candidates in exchange for an appointee to the housing authority board. Their remarks illustrated the concern held by white Democrats, that black voters could not think for themselves. The *Call and Post* writer Charles H. Loeb understood the significance of the decision of the caucus to declare its independence of the Democratic Party: "No more blind loyalty, no more alliances of conveniences, no more encouragement of weak-kneed 'brothers' because they are 'brothers,' and no more supine capitulation to the powerful County Democratic bosses who have held the whip hand over Cleveland for more than a half-century, and the black vote in its hip-pocket."[12]

As the caucus sent blitz squads door-to-door to marshal its forces against the county Democrats, a group of Democrats formed the all-white Twenty-first Congressional Democratic Caucus in an obvious attempt to confuse black voters and lessen the effectiveness of the Twenty-first District Caucus. In fact, Stokes and other district caucus leaders had to call a press conference to distance themselves from the competing organization after the latter advertised an "old-time political rally."[13]

Because the district caucus had specifically designated the county commissioner's race as a litmus test of its effectiveness, it waged an all-out effort to elect Taft. Pinkney recalled that "we carried the man [Taft] all around the city, door-to-door." On election day Taft received a whopping 48 percent of the black vote, defeating the shocked Gorman.[14]

Although the district caucus took credit for beating Gorman, Bartunek attempted to downplay its influence. "The people in that district, like any other voters, look at the newspapers, the political parties and the candidates, then make up their minds." In other races the district caucus's endorsement had little effect on the outcome. But it still represented a giant step for the future of black politics. After the general election the *Cleveland Press*'s political writer, George Anthony Moore, summed up what the district caucus was all about: "The initial performance of the Twenty-First District Caucus had the effect of a drop of water on a huge shoulder. . . . If we look into the future that small drop will turn into a steady flow and the impact of the Twenty-First District Caucus will be that of a thundering waterfall on the political life of this city."[15]

In the aftermath of the 1970 elections the district caucus was convinced that it occupied a strategic position in county politics and expressed little desire to mend relations with white Democrats. For instance, Stokes called a boycott by all district caucus–supported black legislators when white Democrats held a Democratic caucus in their effort to elect state representative Anthony J. Russo as minority leader of the Ohio House of Representatives. As Stokes emerged as a modern-day political boss, county Democrats were livid. "Carl Stokes is desperately and effectively preventing any white legislator in Cuyahoga County from seeking leadership in the Ohio House under terms he has dictated," Bartunek said. "His stand will polarize the legislators and his interference will hurt the people of Cuyahoga County." After years of waiting to become party chair, Bartunek was growing frustrated that the Stokes's caucus was disrupting many of his political power plays.[16]

In an act of retaliation U.S. Representative Charles A. Vanik, a Cleveland area Democrat, reneged on a commitment to nominate Louis Stokes for a seat on the powerful House Appropriations Committee. Although Vanik had approached Stokes in the summer of 1970 about filling the vacancy, the actions of the district caucus convinced him to re-evaluate. One rumor in black political circles was that Vanik was angry because the district caucus had supported his opponent, which Vanik believed had forced him to spend an additional $25,000 on his campaign. Another rumor was that Vanik was equally disappointed at the actions of the district caucus in general. "I have told Louis Stokes that I will not nominate him," Vanik said. "I had intended to nominate him." When Louis Stokes received word that Vanik had broken his commitment, he accused him of "denying the black people an opportunity to have a man on the committee." Carl Stokes saw Vanik's actions as part of a wider pattern of white Democrats' refusing "to recognize qualified black leadership." The mayor was further convinced that Vanik's actions meant that the caucus would never rejoin the Cuyahoga County Democratic Party. Vanik later nominated Louis Stokes to the committee after Democratic House leaders told him that bringing local party conflicts to Washington was inappropriate.[17]

When Carl Stokes announced his plans not to seek a third term as mayor, Bartunek saw an opportunity to bring the district caucus back into the party. But his hopes for a quick end to the controversy were squashed after a meeting with Louis Stokes in the spring of 1971. He refused to withdraw any of the caucus's original demands. "If meaningful changes are made and the blacks can see that it is to their advantage to return to the party, it could be done," Louis Stokes allowed.[18]

Within a week a vacancy occurred on the county elections board. Louis Stokes and other caucus officials watched closely. "Here is an opportunity for Bartunek to show good faith toward the caucus and get the caucus back into the party," Louis Stokes said. "He could offer some black person this position." Days later, however, Bartunek made it clear that he wanted the office. Louis Stokes was disappointed but not surprised: "They talk about bringing us together, then when they have the opportunity for unity they ignore us. It's the same old 'white-only policy.'"[19]

The dispute spilled over into the Ohio Democratic Convention in June 1971, when Mayor Stokes staged a dramatic walkout in an effort to get his brother seated as a delegate. In fact, the mayor was seated only after he made a personal request in front of the credentials committee. Bartunek refused to seat Louis Stokes. "I don't believe they can support Republicans on the local level, then profess to be Democrats on a state and national level," Bartunek fumed. He later told reporters that Louis Stokes was trying to be a "power-broker" between Republicans and Democrats. The county chair continued his attacks on the Stokes brothers when he called a press conference to proclaim that district caucus members were not Democrats. The mayor found Bartunek's edict comical: "Who endowed him with the right to determine who is or is not a Democrat? It's almost laughable. Bosses belong to the years long past. It's the people who decide now." Bartunek's actions and comments inspired the district caucus to take on the county Democrats in the upcoming mayoral campaign.[20]

Back in May, Arnold Pinkney, the former mayoral assistant who was now the school board president, had announced his candidacy for mayor. In early August he received the endorsement of the district caucus. Pinkney was a logical candidate to succeed Stokes. He had been active in several of the mayor's political campaigns, and during Stokes's second term he emerged as the mayor's chief lieutenant, before budget constraints forced his layoff. Stokes decided that Pinkney should run as an independent, largely in the hope that a three-candidate race would split the white vote in the general election and hand city hall to Pinkney. Stokes understood that if the district caucus wanted to remain effective, it needed to capture city hall.[21]

Before embarking on a three-week trip to Europe that August, Stokes gave Pinkney his personal endorsement in front of a crowd of several hundred at the Cleveland Hotel Sheraton. "I am for Pinkney because he is the most qualified. . . . He makes decisions without regard to politics," said Stokes. "He walked with me when some would not walk with me. He walked with me when nobody believed a black man could be elected to office." But Stokes warned the crowd that Pinkney would face adversity: "Pinkney is going to need a great deal of support and understanding. He is following in the pattern of a man who created issues in this town. Just because this man is a Negro, he will have to pay the price for some of my failures and receive some of the hostilities felt toward me." In closing his brief remarks, Stokes concluded that Pinkney was the man for the office because city hall was "not the place for scalawags and Toms" but for someone who had a commitment to the black community.[22] But Pinkney, running as he was as an independent, had to wait out primary season before mounting a full-bore assault on his opponents.

Meanwhile, the Stanton wing of the county Democratic Party endorsed Garofoli, and with their backing he figured to coast into city hall. Stokes countered with an aggressive, complicated, and risky strategy to defeat Garofoli and his pals: Stokes endorsed James Carney, a liberal, young, white, millionaire real estate developer, in the Democratic primary. When Pinkney and George Forbes noticed that black voters were wearing and distributing "Carney for Mayor" buttons, they realized how risky Stokes's strategy was, but they deferred to the mayor. "I didn't have anything to do with that strategy," Pinkney recalled. "It was not a caucus decision, it was strictly Carl's." Although they objected to it, they could not convince Stokes to change his strategy: "He went ahead anyway" with his plans to mount an all-out effort to defeat Garofoli, Pinkney said. "I needed his base so I went along with it."[23]

On the eve of the primary election Louis Stokes emphasized why defeating Garofoli was so important: "I don't know how you can tell people who cannot eat or walk on Murray Hill [Little Italy] that you want to be their mayor." While the district caucus was openly calling for Garofoli's defeat, it also came out against several black council members, including Warren Gilliam, Clarence Thompson, and Mary Yates. In essence, the district caucus was acting like a full-scale political machine.[24]

The efforts of the Twenty-first District Caucus made national headlines on primary day in 1971 when James Carney won the Democratic nomination by an astounding 14,000 votes. Carney's margin of victory came in the black community, where he received 53,000 votes, which represented more than 95 percent of the black vote. Further, the district caucus's candidates in the council races defeated all three conservative incumbents. Afterward, supporters converged on the Lancer restaurant for an all-night celebration. Fleet Slaughter, owner of the Lancer, declared that "this vote lets the white voters know how far out of touch they are with the black community and its new political awareness." Attorney Stanley Tolliver was really surprised at what the district caucus, and particularly the Stokes brothers, had pulled off: "Admittedly I didn't believe it would happen . . . but the Stokes brothers delivered the black vote."[25]

Carl Stokes told reporters that by defeating Garofoli, the "city had shown it wants to avoid the divisive, corrosive, degrading campaign that it would have had if the other candidate [Garofoli] had been nominated." Carl Stokes also told the crowd that he was glad that his black council foes had been defeated: "Those in council who have for so long been against forward movement and who would continue plantation politics have been reduced to the anonymity they richly deserve." But the best comments of the evening came from an unidentified supporter who stated, "Black voters didn't know their own power while they were voting yesterday. . . . Cleveland's black community has finally come of age as a voting instrument." Pinkney saw a larger issue in the results: "It shows that people in the district follow the leadership of their elected officials. It means that any person running for office in the city is going to have to relate the concerns and programs of the Caucus, and the same goes for the county." Carl Stokes had finally achieved a victory over Stanton and the county Democrats. Now Stokes prepared to pass the mantle of executive power on to Arnold Pinkney.[26]

After the primary the local and national press heralded Carl Stokes as the boss of the nation's most powerful black political machine. The primary results showed that the community had made the transition from personalized to institutionalized power. The idea that the Stokes machine had defeated the Democratic nominee astounded political experts. As Carl Stokes traveled throughout the country, he gloated about his ability to deliver the black vote. He was often heard to remark that he was the boss of the greatest black political organization in the nation's history and that he alone controlled Cleveland politics.

As the general election approached, Pinkney received several endorsements, including the support of the *Cleveland Plain Dealer.* Based largely upon Pinkney's service on the school board, the editor of the *Plain Dealer* had "no hesitation in recommending Pinkney for election as mayor." The readers of the *Plain Dealer* were told that Pinkney had the "drive and diplomacy" needed to improve the city. The editors also suggested that Pinkney would work for the "common good" to overcome hostilities. In closing, the editorial said: "He is not a confrontational politician. He has established a record of cooperation, compromise, and statesmanship on the school board, while dealing with the most sensitive needs of the city." Carl Stokes was elated upon hearing of the endorsement. "It is only natural to endorse Pinkney," he said, because Pinkney "had been an integral part of the Stokes administration." Stokes further remarked that the influential endorsement represented an "implicit endorsement of the Stokes policies and programs over the last four years." But Carl Stokes made it clear that Pinkney would not be a puppet. "Pinkney will not be another Stokes, but will build an administration in his own image. . . . He has different strengths from me and he doesn't suffer from many of my weaknesses." Although Pinkney was running on Stokes's popularity, he appreciated that Stokes "did all he could for me without overshadowing me."[27]

The district caucus sponsored marches, rallies, and festivals for Pinkney. In the week before the election Jesse Jackson and Aretha Franklin came to Cleveland to help Pinkney. But it was too late. The mayor had miscalculated his ability to appoint a successor. The strategy of supporting two candidates backfired. Pinkney remembered that "it created so much confusion in the minds of black people . . . they didn't know where Stokes stood." Black voters were not able to make the transition from Carney to Pinkney during the three-week interval. One politician remarked that Stokes "thought he could turn-on and turn-off the black community like a faucet." On election day Republican Ralph Perk, the man Carl Stokes had defeated two years earlier, coasted to a 15,000-vote victory over Pinkney as he took advantage of a split black vote. Pinkney lost because he captured only 75 percent of the black vote. "We've lost the battle," Carl Stokes told a shocked crowd at Pinkney's downtown headquarters, "but not the war." Because Carl Stokes personified the district caucus, the defeat was both personal and professional for him. With the district caucus unable to control city hall, the election signaled not the ascendance but the decline of black political power in Cleveland. Although Stokes tried to appear optimistic about the future of the district caucus, he understood that he was the caucus. His risky campaign strategy meant that he would not be leaving an institutionalized base of power as his legacy.[28]

Although Stokes was unsuccessful in passing the reins of power to Pinkney, the formation of the district caucus added another and important dimension to the Stokes legacy. For a brief time it served as a local model of black political independence and power, the first of its kind in the history of black America.

Out of office, Carl Stokes actively toured the country on the lecture circuit. But he played only a minor role at the 1972 Black National Political Convention in Gary, Indiana, largely because he was without a base of power. As the 1972 presidential elections approached, he turned down several requests to enter the race. He reiterated to his supporters that being mayor of a city presented the best opportunity to affect people's lives.

In the spring of 1972 Carl Stokes officially retired from Cleveland politics when he became an anchorman on WNBC-TV in New York City, NBC's flagship station. Management saw Stokes as a gimmick to increase ratings. "And it worked," Stokes said. "But not for long. The black viewers did tune-in that first month to see the new black anchorman. But once they saw he was just a different face in the same old tired program format, their racial duty done, they turned back to the other stations whose total news program they enjoyed more." After eighteen months as an anchor, he was relegated to roving reporter.[29]

When Stokes left for New York that spring, district caucus leaders took steps to end the feud with county Democrats. Party officials agreed to give African Americans equitable representation throughout the party structure. A power struggle soon developed, however, between Forbes and Louis Stokes regarding the appointment of a district caucus member to a party co-chairmanship. To prevent further disunity, Forbes, Pinkney, and Louis Stokes decided to divide leadership responsibilities. Forbes was given the party co-chairmanship, Pinkney was named executive director of the caucus, and Stokes would have no Democratic challengers as he sought re-election to his congressional seat.[30]

The truce was brief. A new round of internal bickering developed when the district caucus endorsed Albert Porter instead of Ralph Tyler, a black Republican and one-time Stokes cabinet member, for county engineer. Louis

Stokes said he was opposed to the endorsement because Porter was a racist, while Pinkney and Forbes said that they were obligated to support the Democrat. The controversy came to an end when Louis Stokes, "taking advantage of his authority as chairman of the caucus," pushed through a controversial amendment giving him 100 percent administrative authority. This convinced Forbes, Pinkney, and other black elected officials to end their affiliation with the district caucus.[31] By 1973 the caucus no longer was an instrument of black political power.

Carl Stokes returned to Cleveland in 1980 with the hope of re-entering politics. He worked as a labor lawyer before re-entering public life as a municipal judge in 1983. His election to a judgeship marked another first: He became the only black man to serve in all three branches of government. Stokes made front-page headlines in 1988 when he was accused of stealing a $2.39 screwdriver from a local hardware store. Although his failure to pay for the tool was an honest mistake—he absentmindedly walked out of the store with the item in his hand—the local media gave it extensive coverage. Charges were not filed after he paid $50 in restitution to the store. A similar incident occurred six months later when he was accused of stealing a bag of dog food from a suburban grocery store. He eventually was acquitted of the charge. The local media made a spectacle of the former mayor as "talk shows abounded with analyses of experts and non-experts on kleptomania, early Alzheimer's, and senility," he recalled. His legal problems effectively ended any talk of his making another run at city hall.[32]

In 1994 President Bill Clinton appointed Carl Stokes ambassador to the Seychelle Islands, a tiny country in the Indian Ocean. It was seen as a fitting tribute and a crowning achievement to his career. In June 1995 Stokes was diagnosed with esophageal cancer. After treatments failed, he died on April 3, 1996, at the age of sixty-eight. Days later, as the lengthy funeral procession left the downtown Cleveland Music Hall and headed to Lakeview Cemetery, an unidentified African American man gave Stokes the ultimate farewell: the black power salute.

The decline of the caucus and Stokes's departure from local politics "changed the fundamental goal of black politics from community uplift to self-aggrandizement," according to the political scientist William E. Nelson. George Forbes personified this new style of black politics during his sixteen-year reign as president of the Cleveland City Council (1973–89) and while serving a brief stint as co-chair of the Cuyahoga County Democratic Party. Although Forbes emerged by the early 1980s as Cleveland's black political boss, his stature garnered few benefits for the African American community. Instead of using his position to redevelop Cleveland's decaying inner city, Forbes chose to focus on projects that favored the city's business community. For instance, he cultivated strong ties with the business elite at the expense of the city's black poor by using his clout as council president to push through several controversial redevelopment packages that gave big business a wealth of incentives and benefits. The most controversial aspect of these packages was tax abatement, a policy that exempts businesses from paying income and property taxes. In fact, when the urban populist mayor Dennis Kucinich (1977–79) attempted to take tax incentives away from the business sector, Forbes emerged as one of his chief opponents. Despite his questionable record as city council president, Forbes was able to maintain the posture of a militant black politician by occasionally speaking out against police brutality, housing discrimination, and employment bias. Forbes became so entrenched as Cleveland's black political boss that he remained in power until 1989.[33]

That year Forbes was toppled as Cleveland's black political boss by Michael R. White, a thirty-seven-year-old Cleveland native and state senator, who defied the odds and beat Forbes in the mayoral election. Throughout his three terms (1989–2001) in office, downtown development occupied much of White's legislative agenda, which came at the expense of neighborhood revitalization. He led the fight for such publicly subsidized developments as Gund Arena, Jacobs Field, the Rock and Roll Hall of Fame, Cleveland Browns Stadium, and downtown buildings. Many of his critics argued that his administration catered more to visitors than to city residents. Although corporate revitalization did capture much of his attention, White initiated a housing boom in the inner city, assumed control of the troubled Cleveland public schools, and continued the Stokes legacy by increasing minority and female participation in city government. However, Cleveland is still plagued many of the problems that Stokes inherited more than three decades ago: population decline, high unemployment, working-class flight to the suburbs, loss of industry, poor schools, and, of course, racial discrimination. Although the power of the vote is still emphasized as a tool of black liberation, many of Cleveland's black residents have grown rather cynical about the political process and suspicious of black politicians in general.

Conclusion

WHEN CARL STOKES became the first black mayor of a major American city in 1967, black Clevelanders expected him to revitalize their neighborhoods, provide more low- to moderate-income housing, end police brutality, create a plethora of social welfare programs, and devise endless economic opportunities. As a veteran of the civil rights movement, Stokes agreed that his primary responsibility as mayor was to elevate the social and economic conditions of black residents. Second, Stokes also understood that as the first black mayor of a large city, he was a symbol of pride and that as such he represented to a large extent the aspirations and hopes of all African Americans. More bluntly, he was supposed to prove to all whites that an African American was capable of governing. Stokes eagerly embraced these twin mandates, and in the process he wanted to set an example for other black mayors to follow.

Upon taking office, Stokes immediately took steps to restore the city's federal funding. He also reorganized the Cleveland Police Department, kept the peace after Martin Luther King's assassination, secured a much-needed tax increase, and launched Cleveland: Now! a $1.5 billion urban redevelopment package designed to address virtually every facet of the city's problems: housing, employment, health and welfare, neighborhood rehabilitation, economic revitalization, and city planning. Unfortunately, much of his early success was quickly forgotten when a gun battle erupted between Ahmed Evans's Republic of New Libya and members of the Cleveland Police Department on the evening of July 23, 1968. From that point on, Stokes was unable to fulfill his legislative plans.

He had inherited a dying city. A declining tax base, conservative federal and state governments, a continual influx of poor citizens, and white residential and commercial flight made it difficult to find the revenue for implementing many of his reforms. Although Stokes was able to rely upon large-scale federal support for Cleveland: Now! his major redevelopment package, once the conservative administration of Richard Nixon came into office, Stokes had to seek alternate sources of funding. Consequently, when Stokes failed to secure vital tax increases in 1970 and 1971, he was forced to lay off several hundred workers and discontinue vital social programs. Further, once the Cleveland business community made it clear that it would no longer support Stokes's legislative agenda, Stokes was forced to govern a city with virtually no money.

Black middle-class resistance also posed a problem for Stokes. Although Cleveland's black middle class represented a good portion of his political base, its resistance to his housing proposal and disapproval of his relationship with local black nationalists cost him a great deal of political capital. When Lee-Seville residents blocked his housing plans for low-income single-family units in their community, Stokes was virtually blindsided. He could not understand why Cleveland's black middle class objected to a revolutionary housing package designed to improve the lives of the black poor. Further, Stokes found it hard to comprehend why many of these same homeowners, who had probably been the victims of housing discrimination themselves, were eager to adopt the attitudes of conservative white homeowners. This black-on-black conflict convinced Stokes that in some ways, the attitudes of black middle-class homeowners did not differ a great deal from that of their white counterparts.

Nor did he have carte blanche from the black elite, which was quite unhappy when Stokes made it clear that the city's black nationalist community would have a voice in his administration. This was especially shocking to the city's black clergy, who had assumed that Stokes would continue their pattern of ignoring the concerns of the black nationalist community. Although the black middle class supported Stokes's efforts to use nationalists to control black frustration after Martin Luther King's assassination, middle-class blacks were critical, as were whites, of the Stokes administration's decision to give Ahmed Evans a Cleveland: Now! grant. Despite their disapproval, Stokes maintained his commitment to the nationalist community when he supported the David Hill–led boycott of McDonald's franchises. Again, Stokes could not understand why conservative black leaders in the city not only refused to support the economic boycott but even attempted to kill the effort by splitting Operation Black Unity, the coalition of civil rights organizations. Attacks from the black middle class gave white conservatives a broader platform from which to attack the mayor.

Race, however, was the primary obstacle that Stokes confronted throughout his historic mayoral career. His inability to reform the racist Cleveland Police Department and his inability to gain control over the antiblack Cleveland City Council during his brief four-year tenure hamstrung most of his plans. When Stokes entered office, he inherited a city polarized by decades of unresolved racial conflict. For many black residents the virtually all-white police department was the source of much frustration. Stokes's first attempt at reorganizing the police in early 1968 was met with resistance when white officers responded with the blue flu. From that point on the relationship between Stokes and the department worsened. The mayor's decision to pull police out of Glenville during the rebellion, the police testing scandal, and his numerous reorganization efforts enraged white officers who believed that Stokes had no right to interfere in their affairs. Thus they took whatever opportunity they could find to block Stokes's reform efforts. When they orchestrated a plan to keep blacks from voting in the 1969 election, they made their hatred of Stokes plain to everyone.

If the police department represented one set of racial obstacles, Stokes's inability to control the Cleveland City Council was another. Throughout his tenure Stokes and the city council were constantly at odds. The Cuyahoga County Democratic Party's rejection of Stokes's candidacy spilled over into the city council chambers. Stokes's reform agenda, his determination to reward his black constituents, and the voting bloc they represented posed a threat to city council president Jim Stanton's control of city politics. Even during the so-called honeymoon period, Stokes used favor swapping to capture the support of Stanton and his lieutenants. The Stanton-led city council became even more determined to curb the mayor's initiatives after the Evans fiasco and effectively blocked Stokes's attempts at scattered-site public housing, called for the indictment of Stokes's civil service commissioners, mobilized against his tax proposal, questioned his executive appointments, accused him of fiscal mismanagement, and made it virtually impossible for him to pass any meaningful legislation.

But Stokes remained convinced that being mayor of a city offered the best opportunity to improve people's lives. In an interview shortly before he announced his decision not to seek a third term, he said, "I don't happen to believe that there is any office higher than mayor of a large city other than the Presidency of the United States. There is no office which allows you to have the immediate impact upon people and the unparalleled opportunity to take your own philosophy and act on it." He did just that.

Stokes built more than five thousand units of public housing, whereas Cleveland had built only about sixty-seven hundred units in the previous three decades. His push to build public housing was critical for alleviating the city's housing shortage and providing much-needed quality housing for the city's black poor. Although Stokes was largely unsuccessful in placing low-income housing in middle-class areas, he placed the issue of scattered-site public housing on the urban agenda. Stokes also implemented an aggressive affirmative action program that increased contracting opportunities for black-owned firms that had historically been excluded from securing work with the city. Moreover, he used the leverage of the city's deposits to encourage banks to aggressively support black businesses through favorable loan policies and programs. Another major accomplishment of the Stokes administration was that he hired or promoted black men and women into management positions at city hall. In all he promoted 274 minorities to supervisory positions in city government that had a combined salary of more than $3 million. The majority of his executive appointments were historic: first black law director; first black chief police prosecutor; first black safety director; first black city treasurer. He appointed the city's first black women commissioners, and he appointed many women to the city's various boards and commissions. He also brought hundreds of African Americans into unskilled positions.

Another of Stokes's major political accomplishments was the formation of the all-black Twenty-first District Caucus, which rivaled the Cuyahoga County Democratic Party and quickly emerged as one of the most powerful urban political machines in the country. Stokes realized that to a large extent black political power in Cleveland was personal and not institutional. He understood the importance of creating an all-black political organization that would continue the momentum that his election created long after he left office. By establishing the Twenty-first District Caucus, Stokes hoped to keep Cleveland City Hall in black hands and challenge the county Democrats while providing an organizational model for African Americans in other cities. Although the effectiveness of the caucus was short lived, it foretold the possibilities of institutionalized black political power.

But as spectacular as his successes were his failures. Scandals stemming from the appointments of Geraldine Williams, Daniel Ellenburg, and Benjamin O. Davis; the civil service commission police testing fiasco; and the revelation that Ahmed Evans had used Cleveland: Now! money to buy weapons for the Glenville rebellion were public relations nightmares for the nation's first big-city black mayor. These scandals could perhaps have been avoided if Stokes had conducted in-depth background checks, more closely supervised his appointments, and had better follow-up procedures in place for agencies and groups receiving grant money. For instance, black military personnel knew how conservative Davis was and that he considered himself a military man first and a black man second. He never had intended to reform the city's police force, at least not in the ways that Stokes had imagined. Why Stokes failed to talk to black military officials is puzzling. As his political blunders piled up, Stokes lost much of his white support.

Stokes's confrontational and aggressive style of leadership also worked to his detriment at times. His determination and passion to enhance the lives of the black poor and working class were not leavened with an inclination to engage in negotiation and politicking. Stokes was so focused on his political agenda that whites considered him too black, too insensitive to business interests, and believed that he polarized the races instead of being a bridge builder. His in-your-face style of leadership worked as long as it helped maintain racial peace, but when he proved unable to keep a lid on black unrest, his approach became unattractive. As the public perception of his administration grew increasingly negative, particularly in the aftermath of Glenville, his delicate coalition of poor and working-class blacks, white liberals, and the business community became fractured. Nonetheless, Stokes continued to govern as he had during his first eight months in office. But perhaps Stokes's inability to alter his confrontational leadership style is an example both of his stubbornness and of his unwavering commitment to the needs of his black constituents. Stokes may well have believed that changing his approach would be tantamount to selling out his constituents. Because Stokes knew the complex nature of race and politics, he refused to sacrifice his principles for political expediency. Rather, in standing for principle he became engaged in one political skirmish after another.

In many ways Stokes's successes and failures inaugurated a basic pattern subsequently followed by other aggressive black mayors such as Richard Hatcher of Gary, Ernest Morial of New Orleans, Maynard Jackson of Atlanta, and Harold Washington of Chicago, all of whom experienced similar successes and failures. For instance, Jackson implemented an aggressive affirmative action program that required that 25 percent of all city contracts go to black-owned firms. Consequently, black firms in Atlanta secured contracts worth more than $36 million during the expansion of Atlanta's airport in 1977. Like Stokes, Jackson threatened to withdraw city money from white-owned banks that refused to invest money in African American communities and those that had a poor record of promoting minorities and women to executive positions. The majority of black mayors have also followed Stokes's example by using strict affirmative action mandates to bring African Americans into the mainstream of municipal government through executive appointments, appointments to boards and commissions, and municipal employment. Unlike their predecessors, black mayors made the recruitment of African American employees a priority.[1]

The ability to mobilize fiscal resources is another legacy of the Stokes administration. By using his cordial relationship with federal officials, Stokes was able to raise millions of dollars for a plethora of social welfare programs. Similarly, Richard Hatcher also tapped into federal funds for the creation of low-cost housing and job training for Gary's black poor. Further, Coleman Young of Detroit used his relationship with Jimmy Carter and the Michigan governor to support his broad-based economic development plan.[2]

Nor have subsequent black mayors presided over cities in their heyday. As Hatcher and Morial, along with Kenneth Gibson of Newark and Philadelphia's W. Wilson Goode, can attest, the majority of black mayors have inherited dying cities created by white flight, deindustrialization, and the large influx of poor citizens. Nonetheless, their constituents expected unlimited job opportunities and neighborhood revitalization. Similarly, local business leaders wanted economic development proposals that centered on downtown development and playgrounds for the wealthy, such as stadiums, arenas, and entertainment districts. As Stokes realized, it is virtually impossible to accomplish both objectives.[3]

Black mayors who followed Stokes also encountered legislative hostility from their city councils. For instance, during Harold Washington's first term as mayor of Chicago he was unable to pass any meaningful legislation because his chief nemesis, Alderman Edward R. Vrdolyak, and his twenty-nine white supporters on the council, commonly known as the "Vrdolyak 29," controlled the city council. They blocked Washington-sponsored legislation, held up his confirmations and appointments, and basically thwarted his broad-based reform agenda. Likewise, during his second term Ernest Morial battled the "Gang of Five," which dominated the seven-person New Orleans city council. Further, following the pleas of their black constituents, subsequent black mayors have also attempted to reform their cities' police departments. Both Morial and Jackson succeeded in getting more blacks on the police force, but like Stokes they were unsuccessful in bringing the forces under their control.[4]

Finally, as Stokes learned, black mayors cannot always count on their black constituents to support them, come what may. Gary's black middle class attacked Richard Hatcher when he launched SOUL Inc., a $250,000 project to reach out to local gangs. Similarly, black residents lambasted Philadelphia's W. Wilson Goode when his appointees made the controversial decision to bomb the MOVE house in May 1985. In less tragic fashion Morial faced consistent criticism from the two most prominent black political groups in New Orleans when he fired their political appointees in favor of more qualified black professionals.[5]

Unfortunately, since Stokes left office in 1971, black mayors have made no serious effort to institutionalize their power. Although Stokes was unable to pass the mantle of power to another African American, for a time the Twenty-first District Caucus was one of the most effective political organizations in urban America. Stokes followed the tradition of white ethnic mayors by using his control of the executive branch to influence all phases of the policy-making process. The failure by black mayors to institutionalize their power has resulted in the loss of political momentum in several key cities. For example, the failure of Harold Washington to build such an organization in Chicago before his death allowed the Daley machine to once again assert its vise-grip control over the city's political system.[6]

Although Stokes pioneered the aggressive style of black mayoral leadership, second- and third-generation black mayors stunted the momentum of black political power by taking a more accommodationist approach. Some, such as Tom Bradley of Los Angeles, Sydney Barthelemy of New Orleans, Richard Arrington of Birmingham, Atlanta's Andrew Young, and Wilson Goode of Philadelphia, adopted less racially confrontational and aggressive attitudes toward urban governance. They eagerly embraced corporate needs, downtown interests, and pro-growth economic strategies over neighborhood and community interests. Consequently, their respective agendas were not based on championing the social, political, and economic needs of the black community.[7]

This corporate-centered governance has created a great deal of political apathy in black urban communities. The election of a black mayor once created hope and optimism. Today, the candidacy of an African American does not necessarily translate into excitement. In fact, it no longer arouses much interest. Several factors explain this phenomenon. First, black voters are not necessarily convinced that a black candidate will represent their interests. Second, African Americans are cognizant of the limits of black political power. Third, many African Americans realize that the problems associated with black urban life cannot be solved by city hall. Finally, black voters are also understanding that the vote has in many ways been overemphasized as a tool for black liberation.

What, then, is the Stokes legacy? First, he created a positive national image that allowed African Americans in other cities to elect black mayors of their own, and he raised the aspirations of black politicians while instilling confidence in black voters who believed that political power was the next stage of the civil rights movement. When he entered office, he had to overcome fears, doubts, and suspicions: Could an African American effectively manage a city? But through his example, he opened up the way for other black mayors to fulfill the expectations that his election created. Second, Stokes defined the agenda of "the black mayor" by making black issues a priority. Although African Americans in Cleveland and throughout urban America had actively participated in the political process, white politicians rarely addressed their concerns. Third, Stokes personified urban change by consistently discussing the urban crisis. Stokes did not use his platform for self-promotion or self-aggrandizement but as a vehicle for discussing the problems of the cities. Finally, Stokes was a symbol of pride and inspiration to millions of black people. When he came into office at the height of the black power era, Stokes was a deft and charismatic politician, and he allowed black people to discover dignity and power in the color of their skin.

Notes

Introduction

1. Richard Hatcher was elected mayor of Gary, Indiana, in 1967, the same year that Stokes became mayor of Cleveland. Although they were elected on the same day, Stokes is often credited as the first black mayor of a major city because of Gary's relatively small population. That was also the year that President Lyndon B. Johnson appointed Walter Washington mayor of Washington, D.C. For more on the mayoral victories of 1967, see Chuck Stone, *Black Political Power in America,* and Hadden, Masotti, and Thiessen, "Making of the Negro Mayors."

2. For excellent statistical data on the population shifts during the second great migration, see Holt and Brown, "Black Population in Selected Cities," p. 222.

3. The housing crisis in Cleveland was typical of other northern cities. See Hirsch, *Making the Second Ghetto,* and "Massive Resistance in the Urban North"; and Sugrue, *Origins of the Urban Crisis,* and "Crabgrass-Roots Politics."

4. For a good case study of employment discrimination during the second great migration, see Sugrue, *Origins of the Urban Crisis.*

5. For a good overview of the school crisis that affected many northern cities, see Taylor, *Knocking at Our Own Door.*

6. For a vivid description of police-community relations in the urban north, see U.S. Commission on Civil Rights, *Hearing.*

7. Malcolm X, *Malcolm X Speaks,* pp. 23–44.

Chapter 1: Cleveland Boy

1. Carl B. Stokes, "Draft of Autobiography," Feb. 1972, p. 1, Container 64, Folder 1209, Carl Burton Stokes Papers (hereafter, Stokes Papers), Western Reserve Historical Society, Cleveland, Ohio.

2. Ibid., p. 2.

3. Stokes, "Draft of Autobiography." For further information on black Cleveland's early

history, see Kusmer, *Ghetto Takes Shape;* Campbell and Edward Miggins, *Birth of Modern Cleveland;* Russell H. Davis, *Memorable Negroes in Cleveland's Past;* R. H. Davis, *Black Americans in Cleveland.*

4. Stokes, "Draft of Autobiography," p. 2.

5. Ibid., p. 5; Kusmer, "Black Cleveland."

6. Stokes, "Draft of Autobiography," p. 16; Stokes, *Promises of Power,* p. 24.

7. Stokes, "Draft of Autobiography," pp. 13, 15; Stokes interview, 1967, Schomburg Center for Research in Black Culture, Harlem, N.Y. The Great Depression had a devastating effect on Cleveland's economy. Six months after the crash, forty-one thousand residents were out of work. One year later that number had swelled to 100,000. African Americans felt the full brunt of the economic collapse. Although black workers constituted only 10 percent of the city's workforce, they were 27 percent of the total unemployed during the depths of the depression. In fact, approximately 50 percent of all black workers were unemployed during the depression, and in the Central area roughly 90 percent of eligible workers could not secure employment. Labor unions' discriminatory practices contributed to the high rate of unemployment. For a broader look at how the depression affected the city's black inhabitants, see Wye, "Midwest Ghetto" and "At the Leading Edge."

8. Stokes, "Draft of Autobiography," p. 6.

9. Ibid., p. 7.

10. Ibid., pp. 14–15.

11. Ibid., p. 9.

12. Ibid., pp. 12–13.

13. Stokes, *Promises of Power,* pp. 24–25; Wye, "Midwest Ghetto," p. 79; Wye, "New Deal and the Negro Community," p. 622. Outhwaite was an outgrowth of the New Deal. As housing conditions continued to deteriorate in the midst of the depression, the U.S. Housing Authority built seven housing projects in Cleveland. Part of the construction boom was to offset a disastrous slum clearance program that displaced thousands of Central residents, forcing them to relocate to existing overcrowded and slum areas.

14. Stokes, "Draft of Autobiography," pp. 6–8; Stokes, "2nd Draft of Autobiography," Feb. 1972, Container 64, Folder 1209, Stokes Papers; William Harris, interview by Richard Murway, Cleveland, Container 6, Folder 100, Stokes Papers.

15. Stokes, "2nd Draft," pp. 9–11.

16. Ibid.

17. Stokes interview.

18. Stokes, "3rd Draft of Autobiography," July 1972, p. 28, Container 64, Folder 1210, Stokes Papers.

19. Ibid., pp. 2–4.

20. Ibid., pp. 25–26.

21. Ibid., pp. 40, 43, 46, 47.

22. Ibid., pp. 16–17.

23. Ibid.

24. Stokes, *Promises of Power,* p. 28. For an in-depth study of black Cleveland after World War II, see Jirran, "Cleveland and the Negro Following World War II."

25. Stokes, *Promises of Power,* p. 29.

26. Ibid., pp. 29–30. Canady was a legend at West Virginia State. Robert Williams, the

former head of the NAACP chapter in Monroe, North Carolina, who gained headlines in the 1950s by advocating armed violence against whites, recalled that Canady was one of several professors at the school who helped shape the racial consciousness of the student body. Williams recalled that West Virginia State College "was one of the most militant schools. I didn't exactly understand what was going on, but I could see that they had [black] nationalist tendencies" (Tyson, *Radio Free Dixie*, p. 65).

27. Stokes, *Promises of Power*, p. 19.

28. Stokes, "3rd Draft," p. 4. For more on Holly and the Future Outlook League, his protest organization, see Phillips, *Alabama North*.

29. Stokes interview; Stokes, *Promises of Power*, p. 31.

30. Stokes, *Promises of Power*, pp. 33–34, 37.

31. Ibid., p. 38; Stokes interview.

32. Stokes interview; Stokes, *Promises of Power*, pp. 32, 39; *Newsweek*, 26 May 1969.

33. Stokes, *Promises of Power*, pp. 39–40.

34. Ibid., p. 44.

35. Cooper, *Negro in Cleveland*, p. 12.

36. Swanstrom, *Crisis of Growth Politics*, p. 52.

37. Ibid.

38. Nelson and Meranto, *Electing Black Mayors*, p. 77.

39. U.S. Commission on Civil Rights, *Hearing*.

40. Cooper, *Negro in Cleveland*.

41. Ibid.

42. Ibid.

43. "Campaign Flyer," 1955, Alexander H. Martin Files, Cleveland Press Archives, Cleveland State University, Cleveland, Ohio; *Cleveland Plain Dealer*, 27 Sept. 1955, 1 Oct. 1955; *Cleveland Press*, 30 Sept. 1955, 23 Sept. 1955.

44. *Cleveland Plain Dealer*, 23 Sept. 1955.

45. *Cleveland Press*, 24 Aug. 1955.

46. *Call and Post*, 2 Nov. 1957, 9 Nov. 1957, 16 Nov. 1957.

47. *Cleveland Press*, 10 Sept. 1957, 27 July 1951, 2 Nov. 1957; *Call and Post*, 11 Jan. 1958, 18 Jan. 1958. For more on Stokes's record as a campaign manager, see Lowell Henry Papers, Western Reserve Historical Society.

48. *Call and Post*, 11 Jan. 1958.

49. *Cleveland Press*, 4 June 1959; *Cleveland Plain Dealer*, 25 Aug. 1958, 16 Jan. 1959. As the second great migration continued to enlarge the city's population, black residents faced obstacles in housing, employment, police-community relations, and in education. Although his congregation was largely middle class, McKinney was outspoken on civil rights issues. One of his more memorable sermons was titled "Why This Concentration of Crime in the Negro District," delivered on August 23, 1942. In the sermon he placed blame for Central's slum conditions on white public officials (Container 5, Folder 1, Rev. Wade H. McKinney Papers, Western Reserve Historical Society). In the mid-1940s the city took a proactive measure when it asked McKinney and Holly to spearhead the formation of the Cleveland Community Relations Board to promote peaceful race relations in the city. In fact, this represented the first time that a U.S. city had "legally attempted to solve its racial problems," according to the city's Community Relations

Board (*Call and Post,* 14 Apr. 1945; Cleveland Community Relations Board, *To Promote Amicable Relations,* p. 1). For good primary sources that chronicle the city's racial problems during the 1940s and 1950s, see the Cleveland Mayoral Papers, which contain the files of the Community Relations Board; the Cleveland Urban League Papers; the Cleveland NAACP Papers; the papers of a local Urban League official, Clifford E. Minton; and the papers of Anthony J. Celebrezze, especially Container 1, Folders 7–14, all at the Western Reserve Historical Society.

50. Campbell, "Cleveland," p. 117.

51. Powell is quoted in Ralph, *Northern Protest,* p. 35. For a good narrative on the history of the Cleveland NAACP, see Harold H. Davis, "Cleveland in 1912–1961: An Account of the Cleveland Branch of the NAACP," n.d., Container 9, Folder 140, Russell H. Davis Papers, Western Reserve Historical Society, and Woody L. Taylor, "History of the Cleveland Branch of the NAACP," n.d., Container 54, Folder 4, Cleveland NAACP Papers, Western Reserve Historical Society. Russell H. Davis also provides a good narrative of black political life in Cleveland (Container 9, Folder 131, Davis Papers).

Chapter 2: The Making of a Mayor

1. Stokes, *Promises of Power,* p. 47.

2. Ibid., pp. 48–49; "Stokes Campaign Letter," undated draft, Container 1, Folder 1, Stokes Papers.

3. *Call and Post,* 9 Apr. 1960, 23 Apr. 1960, 30 Apr. 1960, 25 June 1960, 24 Sept. 1960; Miscellaneous Campaign Literature, 1960, Container 1, Folder 1, Stokes Papers.

4. Stokes, *Promises of Power,* pp. 54–55.

5. Ibid., pp. 52, 57–61. *Call and Post,* 4 May 1960, 11 May 1960, 25 June 1960, 8 Aug. 1960, 24 Sept. 1960; "Legal Brief," n.d., Container 1, Folder 1, Stokes Papers. Although Stokes felt that he was cheated in the election, he was nonetheless inspired because the recount controversy gave him a great deal of name recognition throughout the city.

6. "Newsletter of Representative Carl B. Stokes," 15 Mar. 1963, 20 Apr. 1963, 5 June 1963, 25 June 1963, Container 1, Folder 1, Stokes Papers; Stokes, *Promises of Power,* p. 64.

7. *Call and Post,* 14 Dec. 1963, 16 May 1964, 4 Apr. 1964; "Newsletter of Representative Carl B. Stokes," 15 Mar. 1963, 20 Apr. 1963.

8. *Call and Post,* 15 Aug. 1964.

9. Cooper, *Negro in Cleveland; Newsweek,* 26 May 1969.

10. U.S. Commission on Civil Rights, *Hearing,* p. 274; *Call and Post,* 12 Feb. 1949; Jirran, "Cleveland and the Negro Following World War II," p. 275.

11. Civil Rights Commission, *Hearing,* p. 274.

12. "School Housing Report," Jan. 1961, Cleveland Public Schools Memorandum, Container 28, Folder 4, Cleveland NAACP Papers, Western Reserve Historical Society. School overcrowding was an issue that plagued many large school districts in the Midwest and Northeast. For a good overview of the situation in the New York City schools, see Taylor, *Knocking at Our Own Door.*

13. Relay Parents to School Board, 23 Oct. 1961, Container 28, Folder 2, NAACP Papers.

14. "Transcript of meeting between the Cleveland School Board and the United Freedom Movement," Sept. 1963, Container 25, Folder 5, NAACP Papers.

15. Kenneth Rose, "Politics of Social Reform," pp. 84–85.

16. For an in-depth discussion of the history of the Cleveland NAACP, see Russell H. Davis, "An Account of the Cleveland Branch of the National Association for the Advancement of Colored People," 1973, Container 9, Folder 140, Russell H. Davis Papers, Western Reserve Historical Society.

17. Nelson and Meranto, *Electing Black Mayors*, p. 86; K. Rose, "Politics of Social Reform," pp. 45–50. For more on Cleveland CORE see Meier and Rudwick, *CORE;* and an interview with Cleveland CORE chair Ruth Turner that can be found in Warren, *Who Speaks for the Negro?* pp. 380–90.

18. "Transcript of Meeting between the Cleveland School Board and the United Freedom Movement"; "Education Resolution of the United Freedom Movement to the Board of Education," n.d., Container 28, Folder 2, NAACP Papers; *Cleveland Press,* 21 Aug. 1963.

19. For more on this civic tradition see Campbell, "Cleveland."

20. *Cleveland Plain Dealer,* 27 Sept. 1963.

21. "The UFM v. the Cleveland School Board: An Interpretation Paper," n.d., Container 36, Folder 5, Cleveland Urban League Papers, Western Reserve Historical Society.

22. *Call and Post,* 25 Jan. 1964, 1 Feb. 1964, 8 Feb. 1964; K. Rose, "Politics of Social Reform," p. 89.

23. *Call and Post,* 1 Feb. 1964.

24. *Call and Post,* 8 Feb. 1964.

25. Ibid.

26. Donald Jacobs to Mayor Ralph Locher, Feb. 1964, and Anonymous to Mayor Ralph Locher, Feb. 1964, both in Container 19, Folder 1, Ralph Locher Papers, Western Reserve Historical Society; *Cleveland Press,* 31 Jan. 1964; *Call and Post,* 8 Feb. 1964. Conservatives praised Locher for his refusal to get involved in the controversy. See Container 19, Folder 1, Locher Papers.

27. *Call and Post,* 15 Feb. 1964.

28. *Cleveland Press,* 3 Mar. 1964; *Call and Post,* 7 Mar. 1964; *Cleveland Plain Dealer,* 29 Feb. 1964.

29. *Cleveland Plain Dealer,* 18 Mar. 1964.

30. *Call and Post,* 11 Apr. 1964.

31. Ibid.

32. *Cleveland Press,* 3 Mar. 1964; "The UFM v. the Cleveland School Board"; *Call and Post,* 11 Apr. 1964; "Cleveland Civil Rights Report," 30 June 1964, Container 39, Folder 4, Urban League Papers.

33. *Call and Post,* 18 Apr. 1964; *Cleveland Plain Dealer,* 12 Apr. 1964; "The UFM v. the Cleveland School Board."

34. *Call and Post,* 25 Apr. 1964; *Informer,* 25 Apr. 1964, Container 1, Folder 2, Bruce Klunder Papers, Western Reserve Historical Society.

35. *Informer,* 25 Apr. 1964, Klunder Papers; *Call and Post,* 25 Apr. 1964.

36. K. Rose, "Politics of Social Reform," pp. 95–96; Brisker, "Black Power and Black Leaders," pp. 171–74.

37. *Call and Post,* 25 Apr. 1964.

38. *Call and Post,* 16 May 1964.

39. Stokes, *Promises of Power*, pp. 67, 69; Chatterjee, *Local Leadership in Black Communities*, p. 118.

40. Stokes, *Promises of Power*, p. 71; *Call and Post*, 21 Nov. 1964, 28 Nov. 1964, 13 Mar. 1965.

41. *Call and Post*, 15 May 1965, 22 May 1965; Stokes, *Promises of Power*, p. 84; Nelson and Meranto, *Electing Black Mayors*, p. 90; Dr. Kenneth Clement, interview by John Britton, 6 June 1968, Ralph J. Bunche Oral History Collection (hereafter Bunche Papers), RJB#191, Moorland-Spingarn Research Center, Howard University.

42. *Call and Post*, 17 Apr. 1965.

43. Nelson and Meranto, *Electing Black Mayors*, p. 91.

44. *Call and Post*, 20 Mar. 1965.

45. *Cleveland Plain Dealer*, 14 May 1965; "Speech Announcing Candidacy for Mayor," 1 Oct. 1965, Container 2, Folder 39, Stokes Papers.

46. *Call and Post*, 29 May 1965.

47. Nelson and Meranto, *Electing Black Mayors*, pp. 98–100.

48. *Call and Post*, 17 July 1965; "Speech by Carl B. Stokes," 1 Oct. 1965, Container 2, Folder 39, Stokes Papers; Nelson and Meranto, *Electing Black Mayors*, pp. 93–95.

49. *Call and Post*, 25 Sept. 1965.

50. *Call and Post*, 9 Oct. 1965, 30 Oct. 1965, 18 Dec. 1965. Stanton and Porter also used the party's newsletter to work against Stokes. See "Cuyahoga Democratic Executive Committee Newsletter," 13 Oct. 1965, 21 Oct. 1965, 23 Oct. 1965, 27 Oct. 1965, 28 Oct. 1965, Container 5, Folder 75, Stokes Papers; Nelson and Meranto, *Electing Black Mayors*, p. 100. Porter carried out his threats to Democratic ward leaders and committeemen who failed to support Locher. Weeks after the election Porter and Stanton wasted little time in removing them from their ward posts.

51. *Cleveland Plain Dealer*, 12 Oct. 1965; *Call and Post*, 23 Oct. 1965; Carl Stokes to Councilman Charlie Carr, 26 May 1965, Container 3, Folder 41, Stokes Papers.

52. *Call and Post*, 19 June 1965.

53. Nelson and Meranto, *Electing Black Mayors*, p. 100; Clement interview.

54. "Speech Before the City Club of Cleveland," 22 Oct. 1965, Container 2, Folder 39, Stokes Papers; *New York Times*, 27 Oct. 1965.

55. *Call and Post*, 30 Oct. 1965.

56. "Voting Returns," fall 1965, Cleveland Board of Elections; *Call and Post*, 13 Nov. 1965, 6 Nov. 1967, 13 Nov. 1967, 20 Nov. 1967, 27 Nov. 1967; Nelson and Meranto, *Electing Black Mayors*, pp. 103–4; Stokes, *Promises of Power*, p. 92; Elmer J. Whiting, CPA, to Stokes, 12 Nov. 1965, Container 3, Folder 42, Stokes Papers. For a detailed eyewitness account of voter fraud, see Jerry Hamilton to Stokes, 5 Nov. 1965, Container 3, Folder 41, Stokes Papers. For a ward-by-ward breakdown of the election results, see "City of Cleveland: 1965 Mayoral Election," Container 6, Folder 89, Stokes Papers.

57. Civil Rights Commission, *Hearing*, pp. 514–15, 607, and Civil Rights Commission, Ohio Advisory Committee, Cleveland Subcommittee, *Cleveland's Unfinished Business*. Actually, the Civil Rights Commission investigated the state of police-community relations in Cleveland in 1961 and determined that the police department had one of the worst records in the nation in terms of police brutality and discrimination. For more on that report see *Call and Post*, 25 Nov. 1961. Further evidence of Stokes's national popularity came

weeks later when he was a keynote speaker at the 57th Annual Convention of the NAACP in Los Angeles. For a full text of his speech see Container 1, Folder 7, Stokes Papers.

58. Civil Rights Commission, *Hearing,* pp. 513–15. For the full transcript of the hearings on police-community relations, see pp. 511–607; Lackritz, "Hough Riots," p. 56.

59. Civil Rights Commission, *Hearing,* p. 621.

60. Lackritz, "Hough Riots," pp. 38–39. Earl Selby and Robert Strother, "Cleveland in Crisis: An Urban Renewal Tragedy," undated and untitled magazine article in Container 28, Folder 499, Stokes Papers; Civil Rights Commission, *Hearing,* pp. 18–230, 648–712.

61. Lackritz, "Hough Riots," pp. 37–39.

62. Ibid., pp. 44–45.

63. Ibid.

64. Ibid., p. 45.

65. *Call and Post,* 9 July 1966; Lackritz, "Hough Riots," p. 46.

66. Cleveland Citizens Committee, "Hough Grand Jury Report," 31, 33, 37, 113; *Call and Post,* 19 July 1966. The "Hough Grand Jury Report" was a transcript of the hearings held by CORE and the Cleveland Citizens Committee in the aftermath of the Hough Riots. These hearings and the report had no connection to the Cuyahoga County Grand Jury. For a study of the Hough riots in a comparative context, see Upton, "Urban Violence."

67. *Cleveland Press,* 19 July 1966; Lackritz, "Hough Riots," p. 8.

68. Lackritz, "Hough Riots," p. 8; *Cleveland Press,* 19 July 1966, 20 July 1966; *Cleveland Plain Dealer,* 20 July 1966.

69. Lackritz, "Hough Riots," p. 14; *Cleveland Press,* 22 July 1966; *Cleveland Plain Dealer,* 23 July 1966.

70. Cuyahoga County Grand Jury, "Report of the Special Grand Jury Relating to the Hough Riots," 1966, pp. 1, 4–7, 12–14, 17.

71. *Call and Post,* 13 Aug. 1966, 20 Aug. 1966.

72. Cleveland Citizens Committee, "Hough Grand Jury Report," testimony of Henry Townes, Diana Townes, and a Mr. Hewey, pp. 11–18, 87–88.

73. Ibid., testimony of Mr. Lewis, pp. 108–10.

74. Ibid., testimony of Edward Adams, pp. 19–25; Bertha Pollard, pp. 25–31, Geneva Burns, pp. 37–41, and Wallace Kelley, pp. 64–68.

75. Ibid., testimony of Harllel Jones, p. 106; Bertha Pollard, p. 30.

76. Congress of Racial Equality and Cleveland Citizens Committee, "Final Report of the Citizens Panel on the Hough/Superior Disturbances," 1968, pp. 1–2.

77. *Cleveland Plain Dealer,* 18 Aug. 1966; *Cleveland Press,* 18 Aug. 1966, 19 Aug. 1966.

78. *Call and Post,* 3 Sept. 1966.

79. *Cleveland Press,* 19 Aug. 1966.

80. *Cleveland Press,* 9 Sept. 1966.

81. *Cleveland Press,* 19 Sept. 1966.

82. Lackritz, "Hough Riots," p. 68.

83. *Call and Post,* 19 Oct. 1966, 29 Oct. 1966; *Cleveland Press,* 22 Oct. 1966.

84. *Cleveland Press,* 24 Nov. 1966, 24 Jan. 1967, 21 Feb. 1967, 10 Mar. 1967, 29 Mar. 1967, 8 June 1967; *Cleveland Plain Dealer,* 23 Apr. 1967; *Call and Post,* 25 Feb. 1967; Chatterjee, "Local Leadership in Black Communities," p. 122.

85. Selby and Strother, "Cleveland in Crisis"; *New York Times,* 21 May 1967; Nelson and Meranto, *Electing Black Mayors,* pp. 110–11; Robert Weaver to Ralph Locher, 16 Jan. 1967, Container 69, Folder 1309, Locher Papers.

86. *Cleveland Plain Dealer,* 17 June 1967; Nelson and Meranto, *Electing Black Mayors,* pp. 114–15; "Statement by State Representative Carl B. Stokes at Cuyahoga County Board of Elections," 5 July 1967, Container 51, Folder 955, Stokes Papers; "Statement by State Representative Carl B. Stokes," re: Law and Order, 15 June 1967, Container 51, Folder 955, Stokes Papers.

87. "Al Ostrow Campaign Strategy for Carl Stokes," 18 June 1967, Container 1, Folder 9, Stokes Papers. The Ostrow plan was detailed and explicit (Nelson and Meranto, *Electing Black Mayors,* pp. 116–17; Clement interview).

88. *Point of View,* 26 June 1968. Once the program was in operation, Besse convinced local journalists not to publicize it, feeling that it would give activists a tremendous amount of power. One community leader characterized the program as an idea "to pay people who ordinarily could be pretty mad" (Bartimole, "Keeping the Lid On," p. 102). One business participant who contributed to the effort labeled it "a bold gutsy approach to the problems" (Ancusto Butler, interview by John Britton, 14 Nov. 1967, RJB#83, Bunche Papers). For more on the importance of a peaceful summer, see "The Question in the Ghetto: Can Cleveland Escape Burning," untitled and undated magazine article in possession of the author.

89. Nelson and Meranto, *Electing Black Mayors,* pp. 120–21.

90. Stokes, *Promises of Power,* pp. 100–103; Nelson and Meranto, *Electing Black Mayors,* p. 123; Clement interview. Despite its fears of what the influx of civil rights workers might spark, the Stokes campaign could not underestimate the indispensable support it received from civil rights organizations.

91. Memorandum from "Save Our Homes Committee," n.d., Container 4, Folder 67, Stokes Papers; "Important Notice," n.d., from anonymous writer, Container 4, Folder 67, Stokes Papers.

92. "Cuyahoga County Democratic Newsletter," 26 Sept. 1967, 28 Sept. 1967, 29 Sept. 1967, Container 4, Folder 67, Stokes Papers; "Cuyahoga County Democratic Newsletter," 22 Sept. 1967, 30 Sept. 1967, 2 Oct. 1967, Container 15, Folder 4, Locher Papers. The "Cleveland Democrat" was published on the eve of the primary. I do not know whether the Stokes campaign published any subsequent brochures under that title after his primary victory (Container 1, Folder 10, Stokes Papers).

93. Nelson and Meranto, *Electing Black Mayors,* pp. 133–34.

94. Stokes to Locher, 4 Sept. 1967, 5 Sept. 1967, 7 Sept. 1967, 8 Sept. 1967, 20 Sept. 1967, Container 4, Folder 66, Stokes Papers.

95. *Cleveland Plain Dealer,* 27 Sept. 1967.

96. *Cleveland Plain Dealer,* 2 Oct. 1967; *Call and Post,* 30 Sept. 1967.

97. "Voting Returns," Board of Elections; Nelson and Meranto, *Electing Black Mayors,* pp. 139–40, 143–44. Martin Luther King issued a press release on the day after Stokes's primary victory, stressing that it was a result of a coalition of "Negro and White voters and reminds us that when black and white together, we shall overcome." For a full text of King's statement, see Container 4, Folder 66, Stokes Papers.

98. Nelson and Meranto, *Electing Black Mayors,* pp. 144–47.

99. *Cleveland Plain Dealer,* 11 Oct. 1967; Nelson and Meranto, *Electing Black Mayors,* pp. 150–51, 155.

100. "Transcript of 1st debate between Carl Stokes and Seth Taft," 16 Oct. 1967, Container 2, Folder 40, Stokes Papers.

101. Ibid., pp. 287–93; Nelson and Meranto, *Electing Black Mayors,* pp. 153–55; *Cleveland Plain Dealer,* 19 Oct. 1967; "The Making of a Mayor," *Cleveland Plain Dealer,* 10 Dec. 1967; "Transcript of 2nd debate between Carl Stokes and Seth Taft," 28 Oct. 1967, Container 2, Folder 40, Stokes Papers. For the content of the final two debates between the candidates, see Container 2, Folder 40, Stokes Papers.

102. *Cleveland Plain Dealer,* 22 Oct. 67; "Flyer," n.d., Container 3, Folder 46, Stokes Papers; Nelson and Meranto, *Electing Black Mayors,* p. 150.

103. *Cleveland Press,* 24 Oct. 1967; *Cleveland Plain Dealer,* 30 Oct. 1967.

104. *Cleveland Plain Dealer,* 26 Oct. 1967; Nelson and Meranto, *Electing Black Mayors,* pp. 157–58.

105. *Cleveland Press,* 8 Nov. 1967; *Cleveland Plain Dealer,* 8 Nov. 1967; Nelson and Meranto, *Electing Black Mayors,* p. 161.

Chapter 3: Cleveland: Now!

1. *Cleveland Plain Dealer,* 9 Nov. 1967; *Cleveland Press,* 9 Nov. 1967.

2. Stokes, *Promises of Power,* pp. 108–9.

3. Ibid., pp. 111–12.

4. Ibid., p. 113.

5. "Data on Mayor Stokes's Cabinet," 14 Mar. 1968, Container 51, Folder 956, Stokes Papers; "Announcement of LeMon appointment," 26 Mar. 1968, Container 51, Folder 596, Stokes Papers; "Resume of Arthur LeMon," Container 51, Folder 596, Stokes Papers; Benjamin Stefanski Jr., interview by Richard Murway, Cleveland, Ohio, 1971, Container 7, Folder 106, Stokes Papers; Dr. Frank Ellis, interview by Richard Murway, Cleveland, Ohio, 1971, Container 6, Folder 98, Stokes Papers; Stokes, *Promises of Power,* p. 111; *Call and Post,* 30 Dec. 1967, 18 May 1968; Stanley Tolliver, interview by author, Cleveland, 4 Nov. 1997; "Employment Survey, City of Cleveland," September 1969, Container 88, Folder 1744, Stokes Papers; *Cleveland Press,* 20 Nov. 1967.

6. *Cleveland Plain Dealer,* 21 Nov. 1967, 27 Dec. 1967; *Cleveland Press,* 28 Nov. 1967, 6 Dec. 1967; *Business Week,* 21 Sept. 1968; *Industry Week,* 16 Aug. 1971; Statement by Mayor Carl B. Stokes, 15 Dec. 1967, Container 69, Folder 1309, Stokes Papers.

7. *Cleveland Press,* 28 Nov. 1967. Stein also served as Stokes's attorney during the recount controversy in 1960.

8. *Cleveland Press,* 21 Nov. 1967, 22 Nov. 1967, 25 Nov. 1967, 26 Nov. 1967, 27 Nov. 1967, 29 Nov. 1967; *Cleveland Plain Dealer,* 26 Nov. 1967.

9. *Cleveland Plain Dealer,* 6 Dec. 1967; *Cleveland Press,* 5 Dec. 1967.

10. *Cleveland Press,* 4 Dec. 1967, 6 Dec. 1967.

11. *Cleveland Press,* 30 Apr. 1959, 18 Sept. 1965, 27 Nov. 1963, 30 Nov. 1963; *Cleveland Plain Dealer,* 12 Jan. 1964. Days after Stokes's election he convened a meeting with Stanton and twenty-two other council members; Stanton assured Stokes that he would not interfere with the mayor's agenda (*Cleveland Plain Dealer,* 10 Nov. 1967).

12. *Cleveland Press,* 16 Jan. 1968, 15 Jan. 1968; *Cleveland Plain Dealer,* 9 Jan. 1968; Richard Murway, interview by Murway, Cleveland, Ohio, 1971, Container 7, Folder 104, Stokes Papers.

13. *Cleveland Press,* 17 Jan. 1968; *Cleveland Plain Dealer,* 18 Jan. 1968; *Call and Post,* 20 Jan. 1968; "Statement by Mayor Stokes," 17 Jan. 1968, Container 51, Folder 956, Stokes Papers; Walter Burks, interview by Richard Murway, Cleveland, Ohio, 1971, Container 6, Folder 97, Stokes Papers; Murway interview.

14. *Call and Post,* 27 Jan. 1968. Williams's supporters sent Stokes a barrage of letters expressing their displeasure with his decision to fire her. See Container 17, Folders 300–301, Stokes Papers.

15. Ibid.

16. Stokes, *Promises of Power,* pp. 170–71.

17. *Call and Post,* 9 Nov. 1967; *Cleveland Press,* 14 Nov. 1967; black police to Stokes, undated memo, Container 84, Folder 1663, Stokes Papers. In late December about twenty representatives from several Black Power groups met with McManamon and Blackwell to discuss their plans for police department staffing. Both assured the nationalists that they would not condone police brutality and that they were willing to meet in the future if necessary. A member of the Community Relations Board stressed to McManamon and Blackwell that "the militant group has some native intelligence and that they are capable of leading people the wrong way and that they are not exactly 'dummies'" (Minutes of the Community Relations Board," 14 Dec. 1967, Container 88, Folder 1746, Stokes Papers).

18. Stokes, *Promises of Power,* p. 176; Thomas Monahan, interview by Richard Murway, Cleveland, Ohio, 1971, Container 7, Folder 104, Stokes Papers; Joseph McManamon, interview by Richard Murway, Cleveland, Ohio, 1971, Container 7, Folder 103, Stokes Papers; Chief Michael Blackwell to CPD Personnel, re: "Transfers," 30 Nov. 1967, Container 82, Folder 1589, Stokes Papers; McManamon to Stokes, 8 May 1968, Container 82, Folder 1589, Stokes Papers; Inspector Steve Szereto to Chief Michael Blackwell, re: "Transfers," 8 May 1968, Container 82, Folder 1589, Stokes Papers; *Cleveland Plain Dealer,* 26 Jan. 1968; *Cleveland Press,* 29 Jan. 1968.

19. Monahan interview.

20. *Cleveland Press,* 5 Dec. 1967; *Cleveland Plain Dealer,* 7 Dec. 1967; "Crime Comparison," December 1967–January 1968, Container 51, Folder 956, Stokes Papers; McManamon interview. Some members of the police department wanted the police chief's job to be placed under civil service rather than being an appointed position (*Cleveland Plain Dealer,* 23 Jan. 1968).

21. Earl Selby and Robert Strother, "Cleveland in Crisis: An Urban Renewal Tragedy," undated and untitled magazine article in Container 28, Folder 499, Stokes Papers.

22. Ibid.; U.S. Commission on Civil Rights, *Hearing.*

23. Edward J. Logue to Carl B. Stokes, "Early Action Program," 12 Dec. 1967, Container 69, Folder 1309, Stokes Papers.

24. Ibid.; Paul Unger and Urban Renewal Task Force to Carl Stokes, re: "Logue Proposal," 26 Dec. 1967, Container 69, Folder 1309, Stokes Papers; Paul Unger and Urban Renewal Task Force to Carl Stokes, re: "Logue Proposal," 4 Jan. 1968, Container 69, Folder 1309, Stokes Papers.

25. Carl Stokes to Robert Weaver, 7 Feb. 1968, re: "Progress on Sixteen Points," Con-

tainer 69, Folder 1309, Stokes Papers; "Additional Urban Renewal Actions by Cleveland City Administration," 2 July 1968, Container 69, Folder 1309, Stokes Papers; "A Growing Cleveland," Speech by Stokes to University-Euclid Citizens Advisory Council, 16 Feb. 1968, Stokes Papers.

26. *Cleveland Press,* 20 Feb. 1968; *Cleveland Plain Dealer,* 20 Feb. 1968; *Call and Post,* 24 Feb. 1968; "Data on Mayor Stokes's Cabinet"; "Speech by Mayor Carl B. Stokes to the Housing Sub-Committee," 20 Mar. 1968, Container 51, Folder 956, Stokes Papers.

27. *Cleveland Press,* 21 Feb. 1968.

28. *Cleveland Press,* 1 Mar. 1968, 4 Mar. 1968, 9 Mar. 1968; *Cleveland Plain Dealer,* 2 Mar. 1968, 5 Mar. 1968; 10 Mar. 1968; *Call and Post,* 9 Mar. 1968.

29. *Call and Post,* 9 Mar. 1968.

30. *Cleveland Press,* 5 Mar. 1968; Stokes, *Promises of Power,* p. 115.

31. *Cleveland Plain Dealer,* 5 Apr. 1968, 9 Apr. 1968; *Cleveland Press,* 5 Apr. 1968; *New York Times,* 5 Apr. 1968, 7 Apr. 1968, 9 Apr. 1968.

32. "Statement by Mayor Carl B. Stokes," 4 Apr. 1968, Container 51, Folder 957, Stokes Papers; Minutes of the Community Relations Board, Executive Board Meeting, 11 Apr. 1968, Container 88, Folder 1745, Stokes Papers.

33. *Cleveland Plain Dealer,* 9 Apr. 1968; Neil J. Carruthers to Stokes, and A. I. Davey to Stokes, both dated 8 Apr. 1968, Container 23, Folder 404, Stokes Papers. For more letters of support see Container 23, Folders 403–6, Stokes Papers.

34. "Statement by Carl Stokes" regarding Black Tuesday, n.d., Container 52, Folder 983, Stokes Papers; Stokes to all City Employees, 8 Apr. 1968, Container 27, Folder 487, Stokes Papers; Don Bean, interview by Richard Murway, Cleveland, Ohio, 1971, Container 6, Folder 97, Stokes Papers; *Cleveland Plain Dealer,* 9 Apr. 1968; *Cleveland Press,* 8 Apr. 1968.

35. *Cleveland Plain Dealer,* 5 May 1968.

36. Cleveland: Now! "What Cleveland: Now Is All About," n.d., Container 1, Folder 5, Cleveland: Now! Papers, Western Reserve Historical Society; E. E. Hargett to Daniel B. Wiles, Greater Cleveland Growth Association Memorandum, 11 Nov. 1968, Container 1, Folder 5, Cleveland: Now! Papers.

37. Cleveland: Now! "What Cleveland: Now Is All About"; Cleveland: Now! "Fact Sheet," 1 May 1968, in author's possession; *Business Week,* 21 Sept. 1968.

38. Stokes, *Promises of Power,* p. 130. Toward the end of his tenure Stokes still believed that business support was essential for redeveloping a dying city (*Industry Week,* 16 Aug. 1971).

39. *Cleveland Plain Dealer,* 2 May 1968.

40. Ibid.; *Cleveland Press,* 2 May 1968; Greater Cleveland Growth Association, "Cleveland Now Salaried and Hourly Employees Campaign," 6 May 1968, Container 1, Folder 5, Cleveland: Now! Papers.

41. *Cleveland Press,* 2 May 1968; *Cleveland Plain Dealer,* 2 May 1968.

42. *Cleveland Plain Dealer,* 2 May 1968; *Cleveland Press,* 1 May 1968.

43. *Cleveland Press,* 1 May 1968. Blaha's concerns were valid. Several Cleveland: Now! promotional items encouraged citizens to "support the increased income tax" (Container 1, Folder 5, Cleveland: Now! Papers).

44. Memo: Greater Cleveland Growth Association, re: "Employees Campaign," 6 May 1968, Container 1, Folder 5, Cleveland: Now! Papers; *Call and Post,* 19 May 1968; *Cleveland Press,* 15 May 1968; *Cleveland Plain Dealer,* 16 May 1968.

45. *Cleveland Plain Dealer,* 14 May 1968; Seymour Slain, coordinator of Mayor's Youth Council, to Carl B. Stokes, re: "Summer Programs," 29 Apr. 1968, Container 39, Folder 723, Stokes Papers.

46. "Statement by Mayor Carl B. Stokes," 8 May 1968, Container 51, Folder 957, Stokes Papers; *Cleveland Plain Dealer,* 28 Feb. 1968, 27 Feb. 1968, 4 May 1968, 16 May 1968; *Cleveland Press,* 14 May 1968.

47. *Call and Post,* 1 June 1968.

48. *Call and Post,* 8 June 1968; *Cleveland Press,* 11 June 1968, 17 June 1968.

49. Nelson and Meranto, *Electing Black Mayors,* p. 343.

50. *Call and Post,* 18 May 68.

Chapter 4: Glenville

1. Stokes, *Promises of Power,* p. 175. By 1967 the local black nationalist community was gaining influence. In fact, Charles Rawlings of the Greater Cleveland Council of Churches told one interviewer that "the Negro is utterly terrified of them" (Charles Rawlings, interview by Vincent Brown, 17 Nov. 1967, RJB#81, Bunche Papers). Community activists like Philip Mason generally believed that Stokes "was in contact with militant people." Mason also felt that the nationalist community understood that its tactics had to be different now that Stokes was in office: "Their confrontation with the power structure must be a different kind of one—cannot be the same confrontation that you would have if it was Mayor Locher. It has to be a very sophisticated one" (Philip Mason, interview by John Britton, 13 Nov. 1967, RJB#82, Bunche Papers).

2. Keagan, *Blacktown, U.S.A.,* p. 322; *Cleveland Press,* 10 Aug. 1968, 12 Aug. 1968.

3. Keagan, *Blacktown, U.S.A.,* pp. 322–23.

4. Ibid., 326–28.

5. Ibid., 323–24.

6. Ibid., 325.

7. "The Facts Behind the Arrest of Ahmed," *Dialogue in Black,* undated newsletter in the William O. Walker Papers, Howard University, Moorland-Spingarn Research Center, Washington, D.C.; *Cleveland Press,* 11, Mar. 1967, 17 Apr. 1967, 21 Apr. 1967; *Cleveland Plain Dealer,* 11 Mar. 1967, 22 Apr. 1967.

8. Rawlings interview; *Call and Post,* 1 June 1968.

9. Sgt. Bosie Mack, interview by Richard Murway, Cleveland, Ohio, 1971, Container 7, Folder 103, Stokes Papers; McManamon interview; *New York Times,* 29 July 1968; *Cleveland Press,* 30 July 1968; *Cleveland Plain Dealer,* 30 July 1968.

10. Mack interview; Joseph McManamon, interview by Richard Murway, Cleveland, Ohio, 1971, Container 7, Folder 103, Stokes Papers; Clarence L. James, interview by Richard Murway, Cleveland, Ohio, 1971, Container 84, Folder 1655, Stokes Papers; Michael Blackwell, interview by Richard Murway, Cleveland, Ohio, 1971, Container 84, Folder 1654, Stokes Papers; press conference on "Glenville Disturbances," 9 Aug. 1968, Container 84, Folder 1663, Stokes Papers; "Chronological Report of Events: Glenville Area Disturbance," n.d., Container 84, Folder 1666, Stokes Papers; Masotti and Corsi, *Shoot-out in Cleveland;* "Questions and Answers by Informant and Chief Blackwell," n.d., Container 82, Folder 1612, Stokes Papers.

11. Mack interview.

12. "Chronological Report"; Mack interview; McManamon interview; Masotti and Corsi, *Shoot-out in Cleveland;* Keagan, *Blacktown, U.S.A.,* pp. 396–414, 317–32.

13. Masotti and Corsi, *Shoot-out in Cleveland,* p. 48; Mack interview.

14. McManamon interview; Masotti and Corsi, *Shoot-out in Cleveland,* pp. 51–53; "Chronological Report"; "Casualty List for July 23, 1968," Container 84, Folder 1663, Stokes Papers; *Cleveland Press,* 2 Aug. 1968.

15. Sworn testimony of Louise Brown, Jean Grisby, Peggy Finley, John Pegues, Arthur Radan, and Trenton Irwin in ACLU of Greater Cleveland, "A Showing of Probable Cause: Documentary Evidence Tending to Show Criminal Activity by Cleveland Police during the Glenville Incident, July 23, 1968, in Support of the Charge That Responsible Local Officials Have Failed to Investigate Where Probable Cause Exists" (hereafter ACLU Report), 1968 transcript, Container 9, Folder 41, Stokes Papers; Mae Mallory, interview by by Malaika Lumumba, RJB#523, Bunche Papers.

16. Testimony of Alfred Reed and Leola Williams, ACLU Report.

17. Testimony of Andrew Wright, Albert Forrest, Sandra Parks, ACLU Report.

18. *Call and Post,* 3 Aug. 1968.

19. Masotti and Corsi, *Shoot-out in Cleveland,* p. 61.

20. Ibid., pp. 56–59. Julius Lester later wrote that "July 23, 1968 will have to go down in the history of the black revolutionary struggle as a day of even more importance than July 25, 1967 (Detroit), and August 11, 1965 (Watts). It was on a Tuesday night, July 23, that a small group of black men set up an ambush for the police in Cleveland. They set it well and carefully" (Lester, *Revolutionary Notes).*

21. Masotti and Corsi, *Shoot-out in Cleveland,* pp. 61–62; "Looting Reports," Memo from the Cleveland Police Department, 24 July 1968, Container 82, Folder 1582, Stokes Papers.

22. "Arrest Record List," Memo from the Cleveland Police Department," n.d., Container 84, Folder 1663, Stokes Papers.

23. Mack interview; McManamon interview; Masotti and Corsi, *Shoot-out in Cleveland,* pp. 65–68; William Silverman, interview by Richard Murway, Cleveland, Ohio, 1971, Container 83, Folder 1636, Stokes Papers; "Chronological Report."

24. "Mayor's Press Meeting—3:00 P.M.," 24 July 1968, Container 51, Folder 957, Stokes Papers; Masotti and Corsi, *Shoot-out in Cleveland,* pp. 67–69; Stokes, *Promises of Power,* pp. 216–17; McManamon interview; Silverman interview; testimony of Walter Beach, ACLU Report; Walter Burks, interview by Richard Murway, Cleveland, Ohio, 1971, Container 83, Folder 1636, Stokes Papers; *Call and Post,* 3 Aug. 1968; *Cleveland Plain Dealer,* 25 July 1968; *Cleveland Press,* 24 July 1968.

25. McManamon interview; Masotti and Corsi, *Shoot-out in Cleveland,* pp. 72–73; "Statement by Carl B. Stokes," news conference, 25 July 1968, Container 84, Folder 1666, Stokes Papers.

26. Masotti and Corsi, *Shoot-out in Cleveland,* pp. 73–74; *Call and Post,* 10 Aug. 1968, 31 Aug. 1968; *Cleveland Plain Dealer,* 25 July 1968, 28 July 1968; *Cleveland Press,* 25 July 1968, 26 July 1968.

27. Stokes, *Promises of Power,* p. 217.

28. Masotti and Corsi, *Shoot-out in Cleveland,* pp. 76–77; McManamon interview; "Glenville Disturbances"; Beach interview; "Statement by Mayor Carl Stokes—News Con-

ference," 25 July 1968, Container 51, Folder 958, Stokes Papers; Stokes, *Promises of Power,* p. 217.

29. Stokes, *Promises of Power,* p. 221.

30. Testimony of Charles Ray and Julius Boros, ACLU Report; Masotti and Corsi, *Shootout in Cleveland,* pp. 78–79.

31. "Proposal for an African Culture Shop," n.d., Container 84, Folder 1665, Stokes Papers; "Status of Funds in Project Afro," 5 Sept. 1968, Container 40, Folder 752, Stokes Papers.

32. "Information Regarding the Glenville Disturbance," n.d., Container 84, Folder 1666, Stokes Papers.

33. Article in *Presbyterian Life Magazine,* date and author unknown, in Container 90, Folder 1778, Stokes Papers, pp. 14–16, 36; J. E. Wilhelm to George Grabner, chairman of Cleveland: Now! 2 Aug. 1968, Container 1, Folder 9, Cleveland: Now! Papers; "Survey," n.d., Container 84, Folder 1664, Stokes Papers; Stokes, *Promises of Power,* p. 224; "How Washington Subsidizes Revolution—Against the U.S.A.!" *Saga Magazine,* n.d., Container 52, Folder 974, Stokes Papers.

34. *Cleveland Plain Dealer,* 20 July 1968; Walter Beach, director of Mayor's Council on Youth Opportunity, to Stokes, 28 June 1968, Container 39, Folder 723, Stokes Papers.

35. Among the more memorable letters are Joseph Kosempa to Carl Stokes, 24 July 1968; Martha Symms to Carl Stokes, 25 July 1968; Charles Coleman to Carl Stokes, 27 July 1968; Anonymous to Carl Stokes, 25 July 68; and Loreen Howard to Carl Stokes, 31 July 1968, all in Container 83, Folder 1636, Stokes Papers. For additional hate mail see Container 27, Folder 479, and Container 83, Folders 1635–36, Stokes Papers.

36. Thomas Hauscher to Stokes, 31 July 68, Container 83, Folder 1636, Stokes Papers; William Castillo to Stokes, 31 July 1968, Container 84, Folder 1644, Stokes Papers; *Cleveland Press,* 31 July 1968; *Cleveland Plain Dealer,* 29 July 1968, 2 Aug. 1968.

37. Throughout the 1968–69 fiscal year Cleveland: Now! disbursed a total of $1.74 million. See "Cleveland Development Foundation–Cleveland: Now! Funded Program Expenditures," 30 June 1969, Container 2, Folder 28, Cleveland: Now! Papers; *Cleveland Press,* 27 Nov. 1969; "Mayor's Council on Youth Opportunities, 1970 Funded Programs," n.d., Container 1, Folder 4, Cleveland: Now! Papers. Stokes made sure that the city's Appalachian whites and Puerto Ricans also received Cleveland: Now! money (Richard Murway, interview by Nonette Freeman, 30 Aug. 1970, RJB#601, Bunche Papers).

38. "Statement by Mayor Carl B. Stokes Regarding Demand for Resignation of the Safety Director Joseph McManamon," n.d., Container 51, Folder 958, Stokes Papers; poster of Stokes and McManamon "Wanted to Answer Questions for the Murder of Three Policemen," 28 Aug. 1968, Container 83, Folder 1636, Stokes Papers; *Cleveland Press,* 2 Aug. 1968. After police were tipped on July 22 that Evans and his followers were in Detroit and Pittsburgh to buy weapons in preparation for a July 23 showdown with police, Stokes's enemies within the department immediately pressed him to permit the arrests of all New Libya members solely on the basis of the tip. He refused. And, despite the tip, many in the rank-and-file did not know the New Libya members were armed: Some white officers failed to pass the information along because they wanted a showdown.

The FOP circulated another poster showing Stokes walking with black nationalists during the Hough Anniversary Parade with the headline "wanted for police brutality—

POLICE BRUTALITY IS BEING BRUTAL TO THE POLICE ESPECIALLY BY THE SAFETY DIRECTOR" (Container 83, Folder 1636, Stokes Papers; notes from an FOP meeting, 12 Aug. 1968, Container 82, Folder 1612, Stokes Papers).

39. *Cleveland Press*, 5 Aug. 1968, 8 Aug. 1968.

40. *Call and Post*, 3 Aug. 1968.

41. *Cleveland Plain Dealer*, 13 May 1969; Keagan, *Blacktown, U.S.A.*, p. 331. Evans was supported at the trial by the July 23 Defense Committee, a group of fellow black nationalists who held demonstrations outside the courthouse. He was also honored during the "Week of Political Prisoner Rally" held in Cleveland in early May 1969. For a fuller description of the activities sponsored by the nationalist community during Evans's trial, see Container 84, Folder 1666, Stokes Papers.

42. *Cleveland Press*, 10 Sept. 1968, 18 Sept. 1968.

43. *Cleveland Press*, 20 Sept. 1968; *Cleveland Plain Dealer*, 20 Sept. 1968.

44. *Cleveland Press*, 25 Sept. 1968, 26 Sept. 1968; *Cleveland Plain Dealer*, 27 Sept. 1968.

45. *Cleveland Plain Dealer*, 26 Sept. 1968; Stokes, *Promises of Power*, p. 158.

46. *Cleveland Plain Dealer*, 30 Sept. 1968.

47. *Cleveland Plain Dealer*, 1 Oct. 1968.

48. *Cleveland Plain Dealer*, 2 Oct. 1968.

49. Stokes, *Promises of Power*, p. 158.

50. Masotti and Corsi, *Shoot-out in Cleveland*, pp. 86–87; Stokes, *Promises of Power*, pp. 159, 164.

51. "News Conference," 16 Oct. 1968, Container 51, Folder 960, Stokes Papers.

52. *Call and Post*, 12 Oct. 1968, 26 Oct. 1968; *Cleveland Plain Dealer*, 9 Oct. 1968; Stokes, *Promises of Power*, p. 179.

53. *Cleveland Press*, 12 Oct. 68.

54. Viehe, "Carl B. Stokes."

Chapter 5: Lee-Seville

1. For good background information on the community, see *Cleveland Press*, 2 Aug. 1962, 3 Aug. 1962.

2. John Pilch, Dept. of Properties, Parks and Recreation, to Stokes, 7 Jan. 1969, Container 88, Folder 1730, Stokes Papers; "Chronology of Events Concerning Lee-Seville," n.d., Container 32, Folder 578, Stokes Papers.

3. Stokes to Francis Fisher, HUD regional administrator, 9 May 1968, Container 68, Folder 1299, Stokes Papers; Stokes to Paul Unger, Urban Renewal Task Force, re: "Lee-Seville Public Housing," 4 Mar. 1968, Container 88, Folder 1734, Stokes Papers; Howard B. Cain, Cleveland Chapter, American Institute of Architects, to Stokes, 24 July 1968, Container 88, Folder 1734, Stokes Papers; "Cleveland's New Look in Public Housing," n.d., Container 88, Folder 1735, Stokes Papers; "Fact Sheet: CMHA Housing in Lee-Seville," 31 Dec. 1968, Container 88, Folder 1736, Stokes Papers; "Statement by Mayor Carl B. Stokes: Appointment of Irving Kriegsfeld to the City Planning Commission," 21 June 1968, Container 51, Folder 957, Stokes Papers.

4. *Cleveland Press*, 24 May 1968, 27 May 1968, 29 May 1968; Irving Kriegsfeld to Clarence Thompson, 11 June 1968, Container 88, Folder 1730, Stokes Papers.

5. *Cleveland Press,* 3 July 1968, 8 July 1968, 9 July 1968, 10 July 1968, 16 July 1968; *Cleveland Plain Dealer,* 19 July 1968; "Chronology of Events Concerning Lee-Seville"; Linwood J. Smith to Carl B. Stokes, 30 Sept. 1968, Container 88, Folder 1734, Stokes Papers.

6. *Call and Post,* 13 July 1968.

7. *Call and Post,* 20 July 1968.

8. Sidney Spector, administrative assistant to the mayor, to Director Ralph Tyler, Utilities Dept., 19 Aug. 1968, Container 88, Folder 1734, Stokes Papers; Spector to McManamon, safety director, 20 Aug. 1968, Container 88, Folder 1734, Stokes Papers; Spector to Edward Baugh, director of public properties, 20 Aug. 1968, Container 88, Folder 1734, Stokes Papers; Spector to Richard Green, community development director, 20 Aug. 1968, Container 88, Folder 1734, Stokes Papers; Linwood Smith, administrative assistant, community development, to Carl B. Stokes, 30 Sept. 1968, Container 88, Folder 1734, Stokes Papers; McManamon to Stokes, 7 Jan. 1969, Container 88, Folder 1734, Stokes Papers.

9. *Call and Post,* 21 Sept. 1968.

10. *Call and Post,* 28 Sept. 1968.

11. *Call and Post,* 12 Oct. 1968.

12. Ibid.

13. "Quotes on Lee-Seville Housing Proposal," n.d., Container 84, Folder 1735, Stokes Papers; *Call and Post,* 12 Oct. 1968.

14. *Southeast Newsletter,* May 1969, Container 88, Folder 1735, Stokes Papers; Harold D. Brittain to Clarence Thompson, 8 Jan. 1969, Container 88, Folder 1734, Stokes Papers.

15. *New York Times,* 5 Sept. 1968; *Cleveland Plain Dealer,* 7 Jan. 1969, *Cleveland Press,* 7 Jan. 1969.

16. *Call and Post,* 2 Nov. 1968, 11 Jan. 1969, 31 May 1969; Arthur LeMon to Stokes, 27 Jan. 1969, Container 88, Folder 1734, Stokes Papers; *Cleveland Press,* 27 Jan. 1969; "Chronology of Events Concerning Lee-Seville"; Kenneth Johnson, the Lee-Seville-Miles Economic Development Corporation, to Stokes, 31 Dec. 1968, Container 88, Folder 1735, Stokes Papers; *Cleveland Plain Dealer,* 31 Jan. 1969; *Cleveland Press,* 27 Jan. 1969.

17. *Cleveland Press,* 31 Jan. 1969, 1 Feb. 1969, 4 Feb. 1969, 7 Feb. 1969, 10 Feb. 1969; *Cleveland Plain Dealer,* 31 Jan. 1969, 1 Feb. 1969, 4 Feb. 1969.

18. *Call and Post,* 8 Feb. 1969; *Cleveland Plain Dealer,* 8 Feb. 1969; "Statement by Mayor Carl B. Stokes," 31 Jan. 1969, Container 88, Folder 1734, Stokes Papers.

19. *Call and Post,* 24 May 1969.

20. "Housing in Lee-Seville: Facts You Should Know," n.d., Container 88, Folder 1735, Stokes Papers; "Statement of the Lee-Seville Homeowners Improvement Association," n.d., Container 32, Folder 579, Stokes Papers.

21. "Statement of the Lee-Seville Homeowners Improvement Association"; *Cleveland Press,* 13 Feb. 1969; *Cleveland Plain Dealer,* 14 Feb. 1969.

22. "Statement of the Lee-Seville Homeowners Improvement Association."

23. Ibid.

24. Ibid.; *Southeast Newsletter,* May 1969, Container 88, Folder 1735, Stokes Papers.

25. *Cleveland Press,* 12 Mar. 1969, 1 Apr. 1969, 3 Apr. 1969; *Cleveland Plain Dealer,* 5 Apr. 1969.

26. *Call and Post,* 18 Apr. 1969.

27. "Affidavits filed by those in opposition to Lee-Seville Housing," in the Fifth District Court of the United States, 26 Apr. 1969, Container 32, Folder 579, Stokes Papers; *Call and Post*, 10 May 1969; *Cleveland Plain Dealer*, 2 Apr. 1969, 19 Apr. 1969, 1 May 1969, 13 May 1969; *Cleveland Press*, 1 May 1969, 12 May 1969.

28. *Call and Post*, 24 May 1969.

29. *Cleveland Press*, 29 May 1969, 30 May 1969; *Cleveland Plain Dealer*, 29 May 1969.

30. *Call and Post*, 24 May 1969.

31. *Call and Post*, 17 May 1969.

32. *Cleveland Press*, 3 June 1969; *Call and Post*, 7 June 1969.

33. The Task Force to Save Public Housing, "City Wide Lee-Seville Housing Rally," n.d., Container 88, Folder 1735, Stokes Papers; "WGAR Sidney Andorn Commentary," 3 June 1969, Container 88, Folder 1735, Stokes Papers.

34. *Call and Post*, 14 June 1969; *Cleveland Press*, 2 June 1969, 13 June 1969; *Cleveland Plain Dealer*, 5 June 1969.

35. *Call and Post*, 21 June 1969.

Chapter 6: Police Reform and Black Capitalism

1. *Call and Post*, 10 Apr. 1965.

2. "Announcement of appointments to Civil Service Commission," 15 Jan. 1968, Container 51, Folder 956, Stokes Papers.

3. *Call and Post*, 17 Sept. 1968, 14 Sept. 1968; "Police Recruitment Program," n.d., Container 3, Folder 45, Stokes Papers; "Greater Cleveland Growth Association Memo, re: NAACP Request for $13,900," 20 Sept. 1968, Container 3, Folder 45, Stokes Papers; Stokes to Daniel Wiles, Greater Cleveland Growth Association, 10 Sept. 1968, Container 3, Folder 45, Stokes Papers; *Cleveland Plain Dealer*, 6 Oct. 1968; Marvin Chernoff, interview by Richard Murway, Cleveland, Ohio, 1971, Container 6, Folder 97, Stokes Papers.

4. Chernoff interview.

5. *Cleveland Plain Dealer*, 3 Oct. 1968.

6. Cuyahoga Grand Jury, "Apr. 1969 Term, to the Honorable George J. McMonagle, Presiding Judge, Apr. 1969 Term, from Joseph Nook, Foreman" (hereafter, "1969 Report") Container 87, Folder 1721, Stokes Papers; Zannes, *Checkmate in Cleveland*, pp. 148–57; *Cleveland Plain Dealer*, 3 Oct. 1968; Stokes, *Promises of Power*, p. 232.

7. Stokes to County Prosecutor John Corrigan, 18 Mar. 1969, Container 88, Folder 1727, Stokes Papers; "Statement by Mayor Carl Stokes," 14 Mar. 1969, Container 88, Folder 1727, Stokes Papers; Clarence James to Charles Butts, 19 Mar. 1969, Container 88, Folder 1730, Stokes Papers.

8. *Cleveland Press*, 21 Apr. 1969, 18 Apr. 1969; *Call and Post*, 26 Apr. 1969.

9. *Cleveland Press*, 5 May 1969, 5 June 1969; Stokes, *Promises of Power*, p. 233.

10. *Cleveland Press*, 13 June 1969, 16 June 1969.

11. *Call and Post*, 5 July 1969; Stokes, *Promises of Power*, p. 233.

12. Cuyahoga County Grand Jury, "1969 Report"; *Call and Post*, 20 Sept. 1969; *Cleveland Press*, 13 Sept. 1969.

13. Stokes, *Promises of Power*, pp. 233, 235.

14. Ibid., pp. 233–34.

15. Ibid., p. 235; Stokes to Corrigan, 11 Mar. 1970, Container 31, Folder 567, Stokes Papers.

16. Stokes, *Promises of Power,* p. 235.

17. *Point of View,* 19 Mar. 1970.

18. Keagan, *Blacktown, U.S.A.,* pp. 278–95; *Cleveland Press,* 30 May 1964, 14 July 1969; *Cleveland Plain Dealer,* 31 May 1964, 16 July 1969.

19. Keagan, *Blacktown, U.S.A.,* pp. 285–89. Hill not only preached the gospel of black economics but he practiced it as well. He operated a small food store on East 105th Street, and on July 9, 1968, he submitted to Cleveland: Now! an application entitled "A Proposal for Economic Development and Community Development" for a $75,000 grant. The application was denied. (See Container 76, Folder 1463, Stokes Papers.)

20. Keagan, *Blacktown, U.S.A.,* pp. 285–89.

21. *Washington Post,* 25 Aug. 1969.

22. "McDonald's Chronology," n.d., Container 32, Folder 583, Stokes Papers; Edward Bood to Operation Black Unity, 3 July 1969, Container 32, Folder 583, Stokes Papers; Harllel Jones, interview by author, Cleveland, Ohio, 25 Feb. 1998; *Washington Post,* 25 Aug. 1969; *Call and Post,* 12 July 1969.

23. *Cleveland Press,* 8 July 1968, 9 July 1968, 11 July 1968; *Cleveland Plain Dealer,* 11 July 1969; "McDonald's Chronology."

24. "Operation Black Unity—Position Paper," 24 July 1969, Container 33, Folder 608, Stokes Papers.

25. Bood to Operation Black Unity.

26. *Cleveland Plain Dealer,* 11 July 1969, 12 July 1969, 13 July 1969, 14 July 1969, 15 July 1969, 16 July 1969, 17 July 1969; *Cleveland Press,* 14 June 1969; Jones interview. On the directive sent by McDonald's to inner-city franchisees, see untitled and undated magazine article in Container 1, Folder 3, Operation Black Unity Papers (hereafter OBU Papers), Western Reserve Historical Society.

27. *Cleveland Plain Dealer,* 11 July 1969, 12 July 1969, 18 July 1969; *Cleveland Press,* 12 July 1969, 17 July 1969; Bood to Operation Black Unity; *Call and Post,* 19 July 1969; Rev. Jonathan Ealy, interview by Nonette Freeman, 5 Aug. 1970, RJB#596, Bunche Papers.

28. *Cleveland Plain Dealer,* 15 July 1969; *Cleveland Press,* 15 July 1969.

29. *Cleveland Plain Dealer,* 16 July 1969; *Cleveland Press,* 18 July 1969; *Black Voices: Organ of Black Information Service,* undated special issue in Container 1, Folder 3, OBU Papers.

30. "OBU—Position Paper."

31. Ibid.; *Cleveland Press,* 17 July 1969; *Cleveland Plain Dealer,* 18 July 1969.

32. "OBU—Position Paper."

33. Ibid.; *Cleveland Plain Dealer,* 26 July 1969.

34. "OBU—Position Paper"; telegram from McDonald's to Operation Black Unity, 26 Sept. 1969, Container 1, Folder 2, OBU Papers.

35. *Call and Post,* 9 Aug. 1969, 16 Aug. 1969.

36. *Black Voices;* telegram from McDonald's to Rev. Donald G. Jacobs, 6 Aug. 1969, Container 1, Folder 2, OBU Papers; *Cleveland Plain Dealer,* 8 Aug. 1969.

37. Edward Bood to Operation Black Unity, 31 July 1969, Container 1, Folder 2, OBU Papers; *Washington Post,* 25 Aug. 1969.

38. *Call and Post,* 9 Aug. 1969, 16 Aug. 1969, 23 Aug. 1969, 30 Aug. 1969; *Cleveland Press,*

20 Aug. 1969, 28 Aug. 1969; *Cleveland Plain Dealer,* 20 Aug. 1969. Although OBU had no interest in receiving donations, McDonald's had long contributed to the NAACP and the United Negro College Fund. See letter from Walker Williams to Philip Mason, 12 Aug. 1969, Container 1, Folder 2, OBU Papers.

39. *Call and Post,* 13 Sept. 1969.

40. *Cleveland Press,* 4 Sept. 1969, 5 Sept. 1969, 8 Sept. 1969, 29 Sept. 1969; Operation Black Unity press release, n.d., Container 1, Folder 3, OBU Papers; *Washington Post,* 25 Aug. 1969.

41. *Cleveland Press,* 26 Sept. 1969, 29 Sept. 1969; James C. Davis to Stanley Tolliver, 4 Dec. 1969, Container 1, Folder 2, OBU Papers.

42. Operation Black Unity press release, 30 Jan. 1970, Container 1, Folder 2, OBU Papers.

43. "Press Release from Operation Black Unity," 15 Oct. 1969, Container 1, Folder 4, Stokes Papers. On the award of franchises to African Americans see untitled and undated magazine article in Container 1, Folder 3, OBU Papers.

Chapter 7: Re-election

1. *Point of View,* 1 Dec. 1969, "Speech by Robert Kelly at I.C.A. Hall," 8 Aug. 1969, Container 5, Folder 72, Stokes Papers.

2. *Cleveland Plain Dealer,* 9 Aug. 1969, 27 Sept. 1969; *Cleveland Press,* 30 Sept. 1969.

3. *Cleveland Plain Dealer,* 27 Sept. 1969. For Stokes's remarks during the debate, see "City Club," 26 Sept. 1969, Container 5, Folder 72, Stokes Papers.

4. *Cleveland Plain Dealer,* 25 Sept. 1969.

5. Ibid.; *Cleveland Press,* 24 Sept. 1969.

6. *Call and Post,* 12 July 1969, 19 July 1969.

7. "Stokes' Kickoff Remarks," 3 Sept. 1969, Container 5, Folder 68, Stokes Papers; Sidney Spector to Stokes, 8 July 1969, Container 5, Folder 69, Stokes Papers. For Stokes's own assessment of his two years in office, see "The Stokes Record," n.d., Container 5, Folder 72, Stokes Papers.

8. *Cleveland Press,* 4 Sept. 1969.

9. *Cleveland Plain Dealer,* 19 Sept. 1969, 20 Sept. 1969; William Levy to Stokes, "Action Plan for Primary Campaign," n.d., Container 5, Folder 70, Stokes Papers.

10. *Cleveland Press,* 25 June 1969.

11. *Cleveland Plain Dealer,* 26 June 1969, 27 Mar. 1969; *Cleveland Press,* 10 Apr. 1969.

12. *Cleveland Press,* 8 Sept. 1969.

13. *Cleveland Plain Dealer,* 3 Oct. 1969.

14. *Cleveland Press,* 13 Oct. 1969, 20 Oct. 1969.

15. *Cleveland Press,* 25 Oct. 1969.

16. *Cleveland Plain Dealer,* 27 Oct. 1969.

17. *Cleveland Press,* 2 Nov. 1969.

18. *Cleveland Press,* 17 Oct. 1969.

19. "Campaign Strategy—Special to the West Side News," n.d., Container 5, Folder 72, Stokes Papers; "Stokes for Mayor Staff Meeting," 12 Oct. 1969, Container 1, Folder 11, Stokes Papers; Bill Levy to Carl Stokes, "PR Strategy for General Election," n.d., Container 5, Folder 72, Stokes Papers.

20. *Cleveland Press,* 14 Oct. 1969, 23 Oct. 1969.

21. *Cleveland Plain Dealer,* 22 Oct. 1969, 27 Mar. 1969; *Cleveland Press,* 21 May 1969.

22. *Cleveland Plain Dealer,* 17 Oct. 1969; *Cleveland Press,* 2 Oct. 1969.

23. "The Stokes Record"; Bilinski Campaign Materials, n.d., Container 5, Folder 68, Stokes Papers; Murway to Stokes, re: "Taft's City Club Remarks," 23 Oct. 1969, Container 5, Folder 68, Stokes Papers.

24. "Stokes City Club Address," 1 Nov. 1969, Container 5, Folder 72, Stokes Papers; *Cleveland Plain Dealer,* 22 Oct. 1969, 23 Oct. 1969, 28 Oct. 1969, 1 Nov. 1969; *Cleveland Press,* 3 Nov. 1969; "Campaign Strategy."

25. *Call and Post,* 1 Nov. 1969.

26. *Cleveland Press,* 5 Nov. 1969, 6 Nov. 1969.

27. During the campaign the FOP placed an ad criticizing Stokes in both the *Cleveland Press* and the *Cleveland Plain Dealer,* and several police cruisers were seen with "Perk for Mayor" bumper stickers (*Cleveland Press,* 26 Sept. 1969; *Cleveland Plain Dealer,* 26 Sept. 1969; "Untitled press release concerning the CPD [Cleveland Police Department] on election day," n.d., Container 5, Folder 68, Stokes Papers).

28. Clarence James to Patrick Gerity, 4 Nov. 1969, Container 81, Folder 1577, Stokes Papers; *Call and Post,* 25 Oct. 1969; Arnold Pinkney, interview by Dick Murway, Cleveland, Ohio, 1971, Container 7, Folder 105, Stokes Papers; Carl B. Stokes to Police Chief Gerity, 4 Nov. 1969, Container 81, Folder 1577, Stokes Papers; "Memo from the Mayor's office concerning illegal activity by the police," 5 Nov. 1969, Container 81, Folder 1577, Stokes Papers; Sidney Spector, interview by Dick Murway, Cleveland, Ohio, 1971, Container 7, Folder 105, Stokes Papers; Sgt. Richard Barrett, interview by Dick Murway, Cleveland, Ohio, 1971, Container 6, Folder 97, Stokes Papers; Clarence James, telephone interview by author, 26 Feb. 1998.

29. Barrett interview; *Call and Post,* 15 Nov. 1969; James interview by author; Pinkney interview. This was not the first time that members of the police department had intimidated black voters. In the November 1961 city elections black voters complained of similar tactics. For more on that incident, see "NAACP Protests Voter Intimidation," n.d., Container 42, Folder 1, Cleveland Urban League Papers, Western Reserve Historical Society. All the affected polling precincts were in all-black wards.

30. "Conversation between Angie Pogonowski and unidentified male," 4 Nov. 1969, Container 81, Folder 1555, Stokes Papers.

31. *Call and Post,* 15 Nov. 1969.

Chapter 8: The General

1. Arthur LeMon to Stokes, "Operation Black Unity Wants Gerity Fired," 9 Dec. 1969, Container 89, Folder 1752, Stokes Papers.

2. *Call and Post,* 20 Dec. 1969, 31 Jan. 1970; *Cleveland Press,* 16 Dec. 1969.

3. Stokes, *Promises of Power,* pp. 180–82.

4. "Statement by Mayor Carl Stokes," 12 Dec. 1969, Container 52, Folder 967, Stokes Papers; Stokes, *Promises of Power,* p. 182; *Cleveland Press,* 19 Jan. 1970. Before McManamon left, he completed a lengthy report on the status and conduct of the police department. See "Safety Department Report," n.d., Container 61, Folder 1150, Stokes Papers.

5. *Call and Post,* 24 Jan. 1970, 31 Jan. 1970, 7 Feb. 1970; *Cleveland Press,* 9 Jan. 1970; Stokes, *Promises of Power,* pp. 181, 183.

6. *Cleveland Press,* 2 Feb. 1970, 3 Feb. 1970; *Cleveland Plain Dealer,* 3 Feb. 1970.

7. WJBK-TV, channel 2 (editorial), 4 Feb. 1970, Container 81, Folder 1578, Stokes Papers; Stokes press release re: Ellenburg, n.d., Container 82, Folder 1612, Stokes Papers; *Cleveland Press,* 2 Feb. 1970, 3 Feb. 1970; *Cleveland Plain Dealer,* 3 Feb. 1970; Stokes, *Promises of Power,* p. 187.

8. Stokes, *Promises of Power,* p. 188; *Cleveland Plain Dealer,* 3 Mar. 1970; *Cleveland Press,* 3 Mar. 1970; "Statement on Ellenburg's resignation," 4 Feb. 1970, Container 81, Folder 1578, Stokes Papers.

9. "Ellenburg's resignation"; *Time,* 16 Feb. 1970; *Call and Post,* 7 Feb. 1970.

10. Thomas Monahan, interview by Dick Murway, Cleveland, Ohio, 1971, Container 7, Folder 104, Stokes Papers.

11. Monahan interview; "WKYC-TV Editorial #26," 2 Apr. 1970, Container 88, Folder 1749, Stokes Papers; *Call and Post,* 1 Aug. 1970, 4 Apr. 1970, 20 June 1970, 8 Aug. 1970; Stokes, *Promises of Power,* pp. 191–92, 195–96; *New York Times,* 28 June 1970.

12. Lt. Gen. Benjamin O. Davis to Carl B. Stokes, 29 June 1970, Container 81, Folder 1567, Stokes Papers; *Call and Post,* 1 Aug. 1970, 4 July 1970; *Cleveland Plain Dealer,* 30 June 1970; Rev. Arthur LeMon to Carl B. Stokes re: situation at "79th and Rawlings," 29 June 1970, Container 88, Folder 1746, Stokes Papers.

13. *Call and Post,* 11 July 1970; *Cleveland Press,* 2 July 1970, 20 July 1970, 22 July 1970.

14. *New York Times,* 28 June 1970; Stokes, *Promises of Power,* p. 190.

15. *New York Times,* 28 June 1970; Nelson and Meranto, *Electing Black Mayors,* p. 346; Benjamin O. Davis, *Benjamin O. Davis, Jr., American,* pp. 346–48;

16. B. O. Davis, *Benjamin O. Davis.*

17. Ibid., pp. 346–48; Stokes, *Promises of Power,* p. 200.

18. "Transcript of Press Conference on Ben Davis," 27 July 1970, Container 82, Folder 1612, Stokes Papers; *Cleveland Press,* 28 July 1970.

19. *Cleveland Press,* 28 July 1970, 29 July 1970; *Cleveland Plain Dealer,* 28 July 1970, 29 July 1970; Clarence James to General Davis, 21 Apr. 1970, Container 81, Folder 1567, Stokes Papers.

20. "Statement by Mayor Carl Stokes," 29 July 1970, Container 81, Folder 1574, Stokes Papers; *Cleveland Plain Dealer,* 27 July 1970; *Cleveland Press,* 28 July 1970.

21. *Cleveland Plain Dealer,* 27 July 1970, 28 July 1970, 29 July 1970; *Cleveland Press,* 28 July 1970, 29 July 1970, 30 July 1970; "Mayor's Reports on Conversations with Safety Director Regarding 'Enemies of Law Enforcement,'" 29 July 1970, Container 81, Folder 1574, Stokes Papers; "Statement by Mayor Carl Stokes," 29 July 1970; Nelson and Meranto, *Electing Black Mayors,* p. 347.

22. *Call and Post,* 1 Aug. 1970; "WKYC-TV Editorial #76," 29 July 1970, Container 81, Folder 1574, Stokes Papers; *Cleveland Press,* 30 July 1970; *Cleveland Plain Dealer,* 30 Aug. 1970; *Call and Post,* 1 Aug. 1970.

23. Zannes, *Checkmate,* p. 224; *Cleveland Plain Dealer,* 29 July 1970.

24. Anonymous to Stokes, 1 Aug. 1970, Phipps to Stokes, 29 July 1970, Underwood to Stokes, n.d., all in Container 25, Folder 441 (this folder also contains numerous letters from Davis supporters), Stokes Papers; letters to the editor from Daisy Craggett and Margaret Patton, both in *Call and Post,* 8 Aug. 1970.

25. *Florida Sentinel-Bulletin,* undated clipping in Container 25, Folder 441, Stokes Pa-

pers; Carl Stokes to Julian Bond, n.d., Container 25, Folder 441, Stokes Papers. After the Davis controversy Stokes made no more efforts to gain control of the police department. Rather, the Community Relations Board attempted to improve the relationship between the black community and the police by flirting with the idea of "sensitivity training," for lower-ranking officers (Rev. Arthur LeMon to Baxter Hill, 14 Aug. 1970, Container 58, Folder 1093, Stokes Papers).

Chapter 9: Council Wars

1. *Cleveland Press,* 12 Nov. 1969, 14 Nov. 1969, 18 Nov. 1969.

2. Ibid.

3. *Call and Post,* 29 Nov. 1969.

4. John Cole, interview by Richard Murway, Cleveland, Ohio, 1971, Container 6, Folder 98, Stokes Papers; Clarence James, interview by Richard Murway, Cleveland, Ohio, 1971, Container 84, Folder 1655, Stokes Papers; *Call and Post,* 6 Dec. 1969, 20 Dec. 1969; City of Cleveland, Equal Employment Opportunity Program, n.d., Container 88, Folder 1744, Stokes Papers; Anthony Garofoli, interview by author, Cleveland, Ohio, 26 Feb. 1998. Even before the ordinance passed, Stokes warned all contractors with contracts of $10,000 or more that they needed to have more black workers on their payroll. "Minutes of the Community Relations Board," 11 Apr. 1968, Container 88, Folder 1745, Stokes Papers;

5. Stokes, *Promises of Power,* pp. 124–25.

6. *Cleveland Press,* 15 Nov. 1967; Stokes, *Promises of Power,* p. 26. In fact, on his first day in office in 1967 he awarded a $60,000 contract to Madison, Madison, & Madison, a black architectural firm, to draw up plans for a multiservice center in Hough.

7. *Call and Post,* 25 Apr. 1970, 2 May 1970, 16 May 1970; Nona Cole, interview by Richard Murway, Cleveland, Ohio, 1971, Stokes Papers; LeMon to Stokes, re: Baxter Hill, 25 May 1970, Container 88, Folder 1748, Stokes Papers.

8. "1970—Housing for Cleveland," 16 Mar. 1970, Container 88, Folder 1733, Stokes Papers; *Cleveland Plain Dealer,* 5 July 1970, 13 July 1970; *Business Week,* 18 July 1970; *Cleveland Press,* 8 July 1970.

9. *Cleveland Plain Dealer,* 28 July 1971.

10. *Cleveland Plain Dealer,* 13 July 1970.

11. *Cleveland Plain Dealer,* 11 June 1970, 12 June 1970, 13 June 1970; *Cleveland Press,* 13 June 1970, 16 June 1970; *Call and Post,* 13 June 1970, 20 June 1970; Stokes Press Release re: Stanton, 16 June 1970, Container 58, Folder 1091, Stokes Papers; Stokes to Stanton, 17 June 1970, Container 58, Folder 1091, Stokes Papers; Black and White Clergy to Stanton, 20 June 1970, Container 58, Folder 1091.

12. *Call and Post,* 4 July 1970; *Cleveland Press,* 17 June 1970, 1 July 1970, 8 July 1970; *Cleveland Plain Dealer,* 17 June 1970, 9 July 1970, 11 July 1970; Welfare Federation to James Stanton, 17 July 1970, Container 29, Folder 530, Stokes Papers; Don Morrow, HUD acting regional administrator, to Stokes, 22 Jan. 1971, Container 89, Folder 1753, Stokes Papers; Stokes to Anthony Garofoli, 23 Jan. 1971, Container 89, Folder 1753, Stokes Papers; "Summary of Programs of which Cleveland is deprived by virtue of notification from Department of Housing and Urban Redevelopment," n.d., Container 89, Folder 1753, Stokes Papers.

13. *Cleveland Press,* 9 Oct. 1969, 9 June 1970, 4 Jan. 1971, 5 Jan. 1971; *Cleveland Plain Dealer,*

4 Oct. 1969; *Call and Post,* 9 Jan. 1971; "Three Board Members Must Go," re: CMHA Board, n.d., Container 29, Folder 530, Stokes Papers; Krumholz, *Making Equity Planning Work; Call and Post,* 9 Jan. 1971.

14. "A Public Statement by the Advisory Board of the Cleveland Metropolitan Housing Association," Container 29, Folder 530, Stokes Papers; *Call and Post,* 9 Jan. 1971, 23 Jan. 1971; *Cleveland Press,* 4 Jan. 1971; *Cleveland Plain Dealer,* 5 Jan. 1971.

15. *Cleveland Press,* 20 Jan. 1971, 21 Jan. 1971; *Call and Post,* 20 Mar. 1971.

16. "A Summary of Programs Which Cleveland Is Deprived," n.d., Container 52, Folder 974, Stokes Papers; Morrow to Stokes, 22 Jan. 1971, Container 52, Folder 972, Stokes Papers; Stokes to Morrow, 25 Jan. 1971, Container 52, Folder 974, Stokes Papers; Stokes to Garofoli, 23 Jan. 1971, Container 52, Folder 974, Stokes Papers.

17. "Payroll Information: Comparison of Municipal Employees—Expenditures by Type, Expenditures by Organizational Unit," 30 May 1970, Container 23, Folder 402, Stokes Papers; file on "Police Costs 1968–1970," n.d., Container 55, Folder 1031, Stokes Papers; flyer on "Safety Budget: 1960 and 1970," n.d., Container 55, Folder 1031, Stokes Papers; "Effect of Reciprocity on Municipal Income Tax Receipts, 1969," n.d., Container 74, Folder 1411, Stokes Papers; "The Effect of Structural Changes in Taxation and the Regressivity of the Property Tax with Respect to Income: Cleveland, 1970," n.d., Container 70, Folder 1344, Stokes Papers; *Cleveland Plain Dealer,* 30 June 1970.

18. Clarence James to Philip Dearborn, re: "Municipal Tax Increase, Reciprocity Credit," 10 July 1970, Container 74, Folder 1411, Stokes Papers; "Task Force Membership," n.d., Container 57, Folder 1111, Stokes Papers; Task Force to Stokes, re: "Tax Reform," 21 July 1970, Container 74, Folder 1411, Stokes Papers; Stokes to A. A. Sommer, task force chair, 24 July 1970, Container 74, Folder 1411, Stokes Papers; "Frequently Asked Questions Regarding the .8% Income Tax Increase," n.d., Container 23, Folder 402, Stokes Papers. Unlike other major industrial cities, Cleveland did not undergo rapid plant relocation and deindustrialization until the mid-1970s, primarily because of its diverse industries. The city experienced its first wave of massive job loss between 1947 and 1967 as 53,000 jobs were eliminated. But the experience in the late 1960s was not as drastic. For instance, between 1966 and 1970, 125 firms representing 6,188 employees left the city; however, 187 businesses came into the city limits, bringing 7,654 jobs. For more on employment data and plant relocation, see City Planning Commission, *Jobs and Income,* and "Unemployment and the Cleveland Economy," n.d., Container 52, Folder 981, Stokes Papers.

19. "Remarks by Mayor Carl Stokes," 24 July 1970, Container 52, Folder 970, Stokes Papers; *Cleveland Press,* 24 July 1970; *Cleveland Plain Dealer,* 25 July 1970.

20. *Cleveland Press,* 23 July 1970, 11 Aug. 1970, 10 Sept. 1970, 13 Sept. 1970; editorial reply by Dennis Kucinich, 11 Aug. 1970, WJW-TV8 (Cleveland), Container 74, Folder 1411.

21. John Liebtag, interview by Richard Murway, Cleveland, Ohio, 1971, Stokes Papers; William "Sonny" Harris, interview by Richard Murway, Cleveland, Ohio, 1971, Stokes Papers; flyer on Issue #7, n.d., Container 55, Folder 1031, Stokes Papers; Memo to Task Force members, re: "Door-to-Door Canvassing," 27 Oct. 1970, Container 55, Folder 1031, Stokes Papers; "Fact Sheet for Issue #7," n.d., Container 74, Folder 1418, Stokes Papers; "Exemptions Under Proposed City Income Tax," n.d., Container 23, Folder 402, Stokes Papers; Jacqueline Sanders to Walter Burks, 21 Aug. 1970, Container 59, Folder 1111, Stokes Papers; Pat Nuccio to Tax Campaign Members, 18 Sept. 1970, Container 59, Folder 1111, Stokes

Papers; "Remarks by Mayor Carl Stokes—Town Hall Meeting," 20 Oct. 1970, Container 55, Folder 1031, Stokes Papers; *Cleveland Plain Dealer,* 30 Oct. 1970.

22. Greater Cleveland Growth Association memo, 2 Oct. 1970, Container 59, Folder 111, Stokes Papers; *Call and Post,* 24 Oct. 1970, 31 Oct. 1970.

23. *Cleveland Plain Dealer,* 3 Nov. 1970.

24. *Cleveland Plain Dealer,* 3 Nov. 1970, 5 Nov. 1970.

25. *Call and Post,* 30 Jan. 1971, 6 Feb. 1971; *Cleveland Plain Dealer,* 2 Feb. 1971, 1 Feb. 1971.

26. *Call and Post,* 13 Feb. 1971; *Cleveland Press,* 3 Feb. 1971, 4 Feb. 1971; *Cleveland Plain Dealer,* 3 Feb. 1971, 4 Feb. 1971.

27. Stokes, *Promises of Power,* p. 140.

28. *Call and Post,* 27 Feb. 1971; *Cleveland Press,* 23 Feb. 1971; *Cleveland Plain Dealer,* 23 Feb. 1971; "Transcript of Council Meeting," 22 Feb. 1971, Container 52, Folder 975, Stokes Papers.

29. Stokes, *Promises of Power,* pp. 166–67.

30. Statement by Carl B. Stokes, re: Decision not to seek a third term, n.d., Container 52, Folder 976, Stokes Papers.

31. *Cleveland Plain Dealer,* 17 Apr. 1971.

32. *Cleveland Plain Dealer,* 18 Apr. 1971. Also see Container 27, Folder 492, Stokes Papers, for series of letters from both supporters and critics regarding his decision not to seek a third term.

33. Ibid.

34. "Remarks by Stokes to NOACA," 15 Oct. 1968, Container 51, Folder 960, Stokes Papers; *Stokes v. NOACA,* "Legal Brief," n.d., Container 33, Folder 603, Stokes Papers; Stokes to Samuel Jackson, 18 Feb. 1970, Container 33, Folder 603, Stokes Papers.

35. Minutes of the NOACA Meeting, 26 Mar. 1969, Container 33, Folder 603 Stokes Papers; NOACA Chronicle as of May 1971, Container 52, Folder 978, Stokes Papers; Krumholz, *Making Equity Planning Work,* pp. 74–79.

36. *Stokes v. NOACA,* "Legal Brief"; Stokes to S. Jackson.

37. NOACA Chronicle; *Planning Magazine,* Sept. 1971, p. 134; NOACA Proposal for a 52-Person Board, n.d., Container 33, Folder 602, Stokes Papers; "NOACA News," Nov. 1970, Container 33, Folder 603, Stokes Papers; Krumholz to Stokes, "re: Progress Report on NOACA Negotiations for Board re-organization," 29 Sept. 1970, Container 33, Folder 603, Stokes Papers; "Position of the City of Cleveland Regarding NOACA as of 8/27/70," Container 33, Folder 603 Stokes Papers; Krumholz to Stokes, "re: First Meeting with NOACA Re-Organization Committee on 8/19/70," 24 Aug. 1970, Container 33, Folder 603, Stokes Papers; "Minutes of the Negotiating Committee, 8/27/70," Container 33, Folder 603, Stokes Papers; "Suggested Remarks at NOACA Meeting, 7/1/70," Container 33, Folder 603, Stokes Papers; NOACA to Stokes, 30 Apr. 1970, Container 33, Folder 603, Stokes Papers; Krumholz, *Making Equity Planning Work,* p. 85.

38. "Resolution of the NOACA Board," 1 Mar. 1971, Container 33, Folder 602, Stokes Papers; memo on "Reapportionment of the Northeast Ohio Areawide Coordinating Board," n.d., Container 33, Folder 602, Stokes Papers; Stokes to Harold Brichford, 16 Mar. 1971, Container 33, Folder 602, Stokes Papers; *Planning Magazine;* Brichford to Stokes, 13 July 71, Container 21, Folder 504, Stokes Papers; "The City of Cleveland's Complaint Against NOACA," n.d., Container 21, Folder 504, Stokes Papers.

39. Stokes to Romney, 21 June 1971, Container 21, Folder 504, Stokes Papers; statement

drafted by Stokes administration to U.S. Civil Rights Commission and Department of Housing and Urban Development, 21 June 1971, Container 21, Folder 504, Stokes Papers; Brichford to Rep. Louis Stokes, 13 July 1971, Container 21, Folder 504, Stokes Papers; "Cleveland's Case against NOACA," 1 July 1971, Container 21, Folder 504, Stokes Papers; Press Release, re: "NOACA," 15 Sept. 1971, Container 52, Folder 82, Stokes Papers.

40. *Playboy,* Jan. 1971.

41. Ibid.

42. Ibid.

43. Ibid.

Chapter 10: *The Twenty-first District Caucus*

1. Nelson, "Cleveland: The Evolution of Black Political Power," pp. 176–78; *Cleveland Press,* 26 May 1970; Geraldine Williams, interview by William E. Nelson, Cleveland, Ohio, 1971, in author's possession; Arnold Pinkney, interview by Richard Murway, Cleveland, Ohio, 1971, Container 7, Folder 105, Stokes Papers. The name of the organization reflected the 400,000 African Americans in the Twenty-first Congressional District.

2. Pinkney interview by William E. Nelson, n.d., in author's possession; *Cleveland Plain Dealer,* 12 May 1970.

3. Pinkney interview; "Statement by Arnold Pinkney," 20 May 1970, Container 10, Folder 162, Stokes Papers; *Cleveland Press,* 12 Feb. 1970; *Cleveland Plain Dealer,* 12 May 1970, 17 May 1970.

4. *Cleveland Press,* 14 May 1970; *Call and Post,* 23 May 1970.

5. *Cleveland Press,* 14 May 1970, 16 May 1970, 18 May 1970; *Cleveland Plain Dealer,* 17 May 1970; Pinkney interview by Nelson; *Call and Post,* 23 May 1970; Stokes, *Promises of Power,* p. 242; "Statement by Arnold Pinkney."

6. *Cleveland Press,* 18 May 1970.

7. *Cleveland Press,* 23 May 1970, 30 May 1970; *Cleveland Plain Dealer,* 23 May 1970.

8. *Call and Post,* 23 May 1970; *Cleveland Press,* 20 May 1970, 26 May 1970, 27 May 1970; *Cleveland Plain Dealer,* 23 May 1970.

9. *Cleveland Press,* 19 May 1970, 25 May 1970, 28 May 1970; *Cleveland Plain Dealer,* 26 May 1970, 28 May 1970, 29 May 1970; *Call and Post,* 30 May 1970.

10. *Cleveland Press,* 7 July 1970, 8 July 1970, 27 Aug. 1970, 28 Aug. 1970, 14 Sept. 1970, 17 July 1970, 28 Sept. 1970; *Cleveland Plain Dealer,* 28 Aug. 1970, 30 Aug. 1970, 29 Sept. 1970; Nelson, "Cleveland: The Rise and Fall of the New Black Politics." p. 194.

11. *Call and Post,* 24 Oct. 1971, 31 Oct. 1970.

12. "21st Congressional District Caucus Endorsements," 28 Sept. 1970, Container 52, Folder 971, Stokes Papers; *Cleveland Press,* 30 Sept. 1970; *Call and Post,* 24 Oct. 1970.

13. *Call and Post,* 15 Oct. 1970.

14. Nelson, "Cleveland: The Rise and Fall of the New Black Politics," p. 195; Pinkney interview by Nelson.

15. *Cleveland Plain Dealer,* 4 Nov. 1970; *Cleveland Press,* 7 Nov. 1970, 18 Nov. 1970.

16. *Cleveland Press,* 9 Nov. 1970, 14 Nov. 1970.

17. *Cleveland Press,* 2 Dec. 1970; *Cleveland Plain Dealer,* 3 Dec. 1970; *Call and Post,* 12 Dec. 1970.

18. *Cleveland Press,* 29 Apr. 1971, 1 May 1971; *Call and Post,* 1 May 1971.

19. *Cleveland Press,* 7 May 1971.

20. *Cleveland Press,* 26 June 1971, 28 June 1971, 29 June 1971; *Cleveland Plain Dealer,* 29 June 1971.

21. *Cleveland Press,* 16 June 1971, 17 July 1971; *Cleveland Plain Dealer* 17 July 1971; Nelson, "Cleveland: The Rise and Fall of the New Black Politics," pp. 187–205; Pinkney interview by Nelson.

22. *Cleveland Plain Dealer,* 14 Aug. 1971.

23. Pinkney interview by Nelson; Geraldine Williams interview by Nelson.

24. *Cleveland Plain Dealer,* 13 Aug. 1971, 26 Sept. 1971; *Cleveland Press,* 13 Aug. 1971, 24 Sept. 1971; Carl Stokes to Anonymous "Friends," 25 Sept. 1971, Container 39, Folder 721, Stokes Papers.

25. *Cleveland Press,* 29 Sept. 1971; *Cleveland Plain Dealer,* 30 Sept. 1971.

26. *Cleveland Press,* 29 Sept. 1971.

27. Estelle Zannes, *Checkmate in Cleveland,* pp. 246–47; *Cleveland Plain Dealer,* 14 Oct. 1971; Pinkney interview by Nelson.

28. Transcript of Stokes radio ad for Pinkney, n.d., Container 39, Folder 716, Stokes Papers; *Call and Post,* 6 Nov. 1971; *Cleveland Press,* 3 Nov. 1971, 4 Nov. 1971, 5 Nov. 1971; *Cleveland Plain Dealer,* 3 Nov. 1971, 4 Nov. 1971; Pinkney interview by Nelson; Nelson, "Cleveland: The Rise and Fall of the New Black Politics"; Zannes, *Checkmate in Cleveland;* Hugh Corrigan, interview by William E. Nelson, n.d., Cleveland, Ohio.

29. Stokes, *Promises of Power,* pp. I-6, I-7.

30. Nelson, "Cleveland: The Rise and Fall of the New Black Politics," pp. 197–98.

31. Ibid.

32. Stokes, *Promises of Power,* pp. I-24, I-25.

33. Nelson, "Cleveland: The Evolution of Black Political Power," pp. 178–84.

Conclusion

1. For more on the collective experiences of black mayors, see Biles, "Black Mayors"; Nelson, "Black Mayoral Leadership"; Preston, "Black Mayors: An Overview"; Eisinger, "Black Employment in Municipal Jobs." For works on Maynard Jackson and Atlanta see Mack Jones, "Black Mayoral Leadership in Atlanta"; Clarence Stone, "Race and Regime in Atlanta"; and Bayor, *Race and the Shaping of Twentieth-Century Atlanta.* For a good historical overview of the experiences of black mayors, please consult Colburn and Adler, *African-American Mayors.* This volume includes essays on Richard Hatcher, Tom Bradley, Maynard Jackson and Andrew Young, Harold Washington, Coleman Young, and others.

2. See Teaford, "'King Richard' Hatcher"; Rich, "The Politics of Detroit" and *Coleman Young and Detroit Politics.*

3. Friesema, "Black Control of the Central Cities." For details on the economic conditions that Wilson Goode confronted, see Bauman, "W. Wilson Goode," and Ransom, "Mayor Wilson Goode of Philly." For the situation in Newark see Woodard, *Nation within a Nation.*

4. Biles, "Black Mayors"; Starks and Preston, "Harold Washington"; Hirsch, For an

excellent study of the relationship between black mayors and police departments, see Saltzstein, "Black Mayors and Police Policies."

5. Teaford, "'King Richard' Hatcher"; Bauman, "W. Wilson Goode"; Hirsch, "Simply a Matter of Black and White."

6. Nelson, "Black Mayoral Leadership," p. 194.

7. For more on Bradley's and Arrington's respective administrations, see Sonenshein, *Politics in Black and White;* and Franklin, *Back to Birmingham.*

Bibliography

Manuscript Collections

COLLECTIONS AT THE WESTERN RESERVE HISTORICAL SOCIETY

Anthony J. Celebrezze Papers
Bruce Klunder Papers
Carl B. Stokes Papers
Cleveland Mayoral Papers
Cleveland NAACP Papers
Cleveland: Now! Papers
Cleveland Urban League Papers
Clifford E. Minton Papers
Community Relations Board Papers
Hough Area Development Corporation Papers
Lowell Henry Papers
Operation Black Unity Papers
Ralph Locher Papers
Ralph Perk Papers
Rev. Wade H. McKinney Papers
Russell H. Davis Papers

COLLECTIONS AT MOORLAND-SPINGARN RESEARCH CENTER, HOWARD UNIVERSITY

William O. Walker Papers

CLEVELAND PRESS ARCHIVES, CLEVELAND STATE UNIVERSITY

Alexander H. Martin Files

Oral Interviews

BY THE AUTHOR

Freeman, Donald, 25 Oct. 1997
Garofoli, Anthony, 26 Feb. 1998
James, Clarence "Buddy", 24 Feb. 1998 (by telephone)
Jones, Harllel, 25 Feb. 1998
Krumholz, Norman, 27 Feb. 1998
Robinson, Lewis, 27 Oct. 1997
Tolliver, Stanley 4 Nov. 1997
White, George, 24 Oct. 1997

BY WILLIAM E. NELSON (UNDATED INTERVIEWS IN THE AUTHOR'S POSSESSION)

Bell, Harry Alexander Thomas
Butts, Charlie
Corrigan, Hugh
Hendrix, Isabel
Pinkney, Arnold
Tall, Booker
Williams, Geraldine

RALPH J. BUNCHE ORAL HISTORY COLLECTION, MOORLAND-SPINGARN RESEARCH CENTER, HOWARD UNIVERSITY

Arki, Jay
Brother Breeze
Brother Diablo
Butler, Ancusto
Clement, Kenneth
Cooper, Ernest
Ealy, Jonathan
Gunn, Richard
Klunder, Joanne
LeMon, Arthur
Mason, Phillip
Murway, Richard
Rawlings, Charles
Robinson, Beth
Robinson, Lewis
Unger, Paul

SCHOMBURG CENTER FOR RESEARCH IN BLACK CULTURE, HARLEM, NEW YORK

Clement, Kenneth
Stokes, Carl

BY RICHARD MURWAY IN STOKES PAPERS

Barrett, Richard
Bauerlein, Robert
Baugh, Edward J.
Bean, Don
Burks, Walter
Chernoff, Marvin
Cole, John
Cole, Nona
Dearborn, Phillip
Ellis, Richard
Gaskill, William C.
Green, Richard
Harris, William "Sonny"
Hill, David
James, Clarence "Buddy"
Keever, John
Krumholz, Norman
Laisure, Earl
Liebtag, John
Mack, Bosie
Matt, Henry
McManamon, Joseph
Midolo, Anthony "Tony"
Monahan, Thomas
Murway, Richard
Pinkney, Arnold
Spector, Sidney
Stefanski, Benjamin, Jr.

Federal Bureau of Investigation Files

62-HQ-111875 Carl Burton Stokes

Books, Articles, Unpublished Papers, and Reports

ACLU of Greater Cleveland. "A Showing of Probable Cause: Documentary Evidence Tending to Show Criminal Activity by Cleveland Police during the Glenville Incident, July 23, 1968, in Support of the Charge That Responsible Local Officials Have Failed to Investigate Where Probable Cause Exists." 1968. Stokes Papers.

Allen, Robert. *Black Awakening in Capitalist America.* New York: Anchor Books, 1970.

Avery, Elroy. *A History of Cleveland and Its Environs.* New York: Lewis Publishing, 1918.

Baldwin, James. *The Fire Next Time.* New York: Dell, 1962.

Barbour, Floyd B., ed. *The Black Power Revolt.* Boston: Porter Sargent, 1968.

———. *The Black Seventies.* Boston: Porter Sargent, 1970.

Bartimole, Roldo. "Keeping the Lid On: Corporate Responsibility in Cleveland." *Business and Society Review/Innovation* 5 (Spring 1973): 96–103.

Bauman, John F. "W. Wilson Goode: The Black Mayor as Urban Entrepreneur." *Journal of Negro History* 77 (Summer 1992): 141–58.

Bayor, Ronald H. *Race and the Shaping of Twentieth-Century Atlanta.* Chapel Hill: University of North Carolina Press, 1996.

Benton, Elbert J. *Cleveland: Cultural Story of an American City.* Cleveland, Ohio: Western Reserve Historical Society, 1944.

Biles, Roger. "Black Mayors: A Historical Assessment." *Journal of Negro History* 77 (Summer 1992): 109–25.

Boskin, Joseph. "The Revolt of the Urban Ghettos, 1964–1967." *Annals of the American Academy of Political and Social Science* 382 (1969): 1–14.

Brisker, Lawrence. "Black Power and Black Leaders: A Study of Black Leadership in Cleveland, Ohio." Ph.D. diss., Case Western Reserve University, 1977.

Browning, Rufus, Dale Marshall, and David H. Tabb, eds. *Racial Politics in American Cities.* New York: Longman, 1990.

Campbell, Thomas. "Cleveland: The Struggle for Stability." In *Snowbelt Cities: Metropolitan Politics in the Northeast and Midwest since World War II.* Ed. Richard Bernard. 109–36. Bloomington: Indiana University Press, 1990.

Campbell, Thomas, and Edward Miggins, eds. *The Birth of Modern Cleveland.* Cleveland, Ohio: Western Reserve Historical Society, 1988.

Carmichael, Stokely, and Charles V. Hamilton. *Black Power: The Politics of Liberation.* New York: Vintage, 1967.

Chapman, Edmund. *Cleveland: Village to Metropolis.* Cleveland, Ohio: Case Western Reserve University Press, 1964.

Chatterjee, Prenab. *Local Leadership in Black Communities.* Cleveland, Ohio: Case Western Reserve University Press, 1975.

Cho, Yong Hyo. "City Politics and Racial Polarization: Bloc Voting in Cleveland Elections." *Journal of Black Studies* 4 (June 1974): 396–417.

Cleveland Citizens Committee. "Hough Grand Jury Report on the Superior/Hough Disturbances." Undated. Available at the Cleveland Public Library.

Cleveland City Planning Commission. *Jobs and Income: An Analysis of Employment in the Cleveland Area.* Vol. 1. 1973. Available at the Cleveland Public Library.

Cleveland Community Relations Board. *To Promote Amicable Relations: Thirty-Year His-

tory of the Cleveland Community Relations Board. Cleveland, Ohio: Community Relations Board, 1975.

Colburn, David R., and Jeffrey S. Adler, eds. *African-American Mayors: Race, Politics, and the American City*. Urbana: University of Illinois Press, 2001.

Condon, George. *Cleveland: The Best Kept Secret*. New York: Doubleday, 1967.

Congress of Racial Equality and Cleveland Citizens Committee. "Final Report of the Citizens Panel on the Hough/Superior Disturbances." 1968. Available in the History Department, Cleveland Public Library.

Cooper, Ernest C. *The Negro in Cleveland: An Analysis of the Social and Economic Characteristics of the Negro Population, 1950–1963*. Cleveland, Ohio: Cleveland Urban League, 1964.

Cuyahoga County Grand Jury. "April 1969 Term, to the Honorable George J. McMonagle Presiding Judge, April 1969 Term, from Joseph Nook, Foreman." Stokes Papers.

Cuyahoga County Grand Jury. "Report of the Special Grand Jury Report Relating to the Hough Riots." 1966. Available in the History Department, Cleveland Public Library.

Davis, Benjamin O., Jr. *Benjamin O. Davis, Jr., American: An Autobiography*. Washington, D.C.: Smithsonian Institution Press, 1991.

Davis, Russell H. *Black Americans in Cleveland*. Washington, D.C.: Association for the Study of Afro-American Life and History, 1969.

———. *Black Americans in Cleveland from George Peake to Carl Stokes, 1796–1969*. Washington, D.C.: Associated Publishers, 1985.

———. "Cleveland in 1912–1961: An Account of the Cleveland Branch of the NAACP." Undated ms. Russell H. Davis Papers, Western Reserve Historical Society.

———. *Memorable Negroes in Cleveland's Past*. Cleveland, Ohio: Western Reserve Historical Society, 1969.

Dulaney, W. Marvin. *Black Police in America*. Bloomington: Indiana University Press, 1996.

Dunfee, Charles. "Harold H. Burton, Mayor of Cleveland: The WPA Program, 1935–1937." Ph.D. diss., Case Western Reserve University, 1975.

Eisinger, Peter. "Black Employment in Municipal Jobs: The Impact of Black Political Power." *American Political Science Review* 76 (1982): 592–606.

Franklin, Jimmie Lewis. *Back to Birmingham: Richard Arrington, Jr., and His Times*. Tuscaloosa: University of Alabama Press, 1989.

Friesema, H. Paul. "Black Control of Central Cities: The Hollow Prize." *Journal of the American Institute of Planners* 35 (1969): 75–79.

Garrow, David. *Bearing the Cross: Martin Luther King and the SCLC*. New York: William Morrow, 1987.

Gerber, David. *Black Ohio and the Color Line*. Urbana: University of Illinois Press, 1976.

Grace, Alonzo. "The Effect of Negro Migration on the Cleveland Public School System." Ph.D. diss., Case Western Reserve University, 1932.

Grimshaw, James. *Bitter Fruit: Black Politics and the Chicago Machine, 1931–1991*. Chicago: University of Chicago Press, 1992.

Gruss, Angela. "An Historical Investigation of the Influx of the Negro in Cleveland into Its Cultural Pattern." Master's thesis, St. John's College, Cleveland, Ohio, 1949.

Hadden, Jeffrey K., Louis Masotti, and Victor Thiessen. "The Making of the Negro Mayors, 1967." *Trans-action* 5:3 (Jan.–Feb. 1968): 21–30.

Hampton, Henry, and Steve Fayer, eds. *Voices of Freedom: An Oral History of the Civil Rights Movement from the 1950s through the 1980s.* New York: Bantam Books, 1990.

Hill, Herbert. "Demographic Change and Racial Ghettos: The Crisis of American Cities." *Journal of Urban Law* 44 (1966): 231–85.

Hirsch, Arnold. "Harold and Dutch Revisited: A Comparative Look at the First Black Mayors of Chicago and New Orleans." In *African-American Mayors: Race, Politics, and the American City.* Ed. David Colburn and Jeffrey Adler. 107–29. Urbana: University of Illinois Press, 2001.

——. *Making the Second Ghetto: Race and Housing in Chicago, 1940–1960.* Cambridge, U.K.: Cambridge University Press, 1983.

——. "Massive Resistance in the Urban North: Trumbull Park, Chicago, 1953–1966." *Journal of American History* 82 (March 1995): 522–50.

——. "Simply a Matter of Black and White: The Transformation of Race and Politics in Twentieth-Century New Orleans." In *Creole New Orleans: Race and Americanization.* Ed. Arnold Hirsch and Joseph Logsdon. 262–319. Baton Rouge: Louisiana State University Press, 1992.

Hodgart, Robert. "The Expansion of the Negro Ghetto in Cities of the Northern United States: A Case Study of Cleveland, Ohio, and University Park, Pennsylvania." Master's thesis, Pennsylvania State University, 1968.

Holt, Thomas, and Elsa Barkley Brown, eds. *Major Problems in African-American History.* Vol. 2. Boston: Houghton Mifflin, 2000.

Hunter, Deborah. "The Aftermath of Carl Stokes: An Analysis of Political Drama in the 1971 Cleveland Mayoral Campaign." *Journal of Black Studies* 8 (Mar. 1978): 337–54.

Jirran, Raymond. "Cleveland and the Negro Following World War II." Ph.D. diss., Kent State University, 1973.

Jones, Adrienne Lash. *Jane Edna Hunter.* Washington, D.C.: Associated Publishers, 1987.

Jones, Mack. "Black Mayoral Leadership in Atlanta: A Comment." *National Political Science Review* 2 (1990): 138–44.

——. "Black Political Empowerment in Atlanta: Myth and Reality." *Annals of the American Academy of Political and Social Science* 439 (Sept. 1978): 90–117.

Keagan, Frank. *Blacktown U.S.A.* Boston: Little, Brown, 1971.

Keller, Edmund J. "The Impact of Black Mayors on Urban Policy." *Annals of the American Academy of Political and Social Science* 439 (Sept. 1978): 40–52.

Kerner Commission. *Report of the National Advisory Commission on Civil Disorders.* Washington, D.C.: Government Printing Office, 1968.

Kilson, Martin. "Political Change in the Negro Ghetto, 1900–1940s." *Key Issues in the African-American Experience.* Ed. Nathan Huggins, Martin Kilson, and Daniel Fox. 167–92. New York: McGraw Hill, 1971.

King, Martin Luther, Jr. *Where Do We Go from Here: Chaos or Community?* Boston: Beacon Press, 1967.

Kleppner, Paul. *Chicago Divided: The Making of a Black Mayor.* DeKalb: Northern Illinois University Press, 1985.

Krumholz, Norman. *Making Equity Planning Work.* Philadelphia: Temple University Press, 1990.

Kusmer, Kenneth. "Black Cleveland and the Central-Woodland Community, 1865–1930."

In *Cleveland: A Metropolitan Reader,* Ed. W. Dennis Keating, Norman Krumholz, and David Perry. 265–82. Kent, Ohio: Kent State University Press, 1996.

———. *A Ghetto Takes Shape.* Urbana: University of Illinois Press, 1976.

Lackritz, Marc. "The Hough Riots." Unpublished ms. 1968. Available at Cleveland Public Library.

Lawson, Steven F. *Running for Freedom: Civil Rights and Black Politics in America Since 1941.* New York: McGraw Hill, 1997.

Lemann, Nicholas. *The Promised Land: The Great Migration and How It Changed America.* New York: Alfred A. Knopf, 1991.

Lester, Julius. *Revolutionary Notes.* New York: R. W. Baron, 1969.

Levine, Charles H. *Racial Conflict and the American Mayor.* Lexington, Mass.: Lexington Books, 1974.

Loeb, Charles. *The Future Is Yours.* Cleveland: Future Outlook League, 1949.

McAdam, Doug. *Political Process and the Development of Black Insurgency, 1930–1970.* Chicago: University of Chicago Press, 1982.

Malcolm X. *Malcolm X Speaks: Selected Speeches and Statements.* Ed. George Breitman. New York: Merit Publishers, 1965.

Malvin, John. *Autobiography of John Malvin.* Cleveland, Ohio: Leader Printing, 1879.

Masotti, Louis. "The Making of the Negro Mayors, 1967." In *Roots of Rebellion: The Evolution of Black Politics and Protest Since World War II.* Ed. Richard P. Young. 219–38. New York: Harper and Row, 1970.

Masotti, Louis, and Jerome Corsi, eds. *Shoot-out in Cleveland: Black Militants and the Police, July 23, 1968: A Staff Report to the National Commission on the Causes and Prevention of Violence.* Washington, D.C.: Government Printing Office, 1969.

Meier, August, and Elliott Rudwick. *CORE: A Study in the Civil Rights Movement, 1942–1968.* New York: Oxford University Press, 1973.

Nelson, William E., Jr. "Black Mayoral Leadership: A Twenty-Year Perspective." In *Enduring Tensions in Urban Politics.* Ed. Dennis Judd and Paul Kantor. 450–57. New York: Macmillan, 1992.

———. "Black Mayors as Urban Managers." *Annals of the American Academy of Political and Social Science* 439 (Sept. 1978): 53–67.

———. "Cleveland: The Evolution of Black Political Power." In *The New Black Politics Revisited.* Ed. Lenneal J. Henderson Jr. and Paul L. Puryear. 172–99. New York: Longman, 1987.

———. "Cleveland: The Rise and Fall of the New Black Politics." *The New Black Politics: The Search for Political Power.* Ed. Michael B. Preston, Lenneal J. Henderson Jr., and Paul L. Puryear. 187–208. New York: Longman, 1982.

Nelson, William E., Jr., and Philip Meranto. *Electing Black Mayors: Political Action in the Black Community.* Columbus: Ohio State University Press, 1977.

Perry, Huey L., and Alfred Stokes. "Politics and Power in the Sunbelt: Mayor Morial of New Orleans." In *The New Black Politics: The Search for Political Power.* 2d ed. Ed. Michael B. Preston, Lenneal Henderson, and Payl Puryear. 222–55. New York: Longman, 1987.

Phillips, Kim. *Alabama North: Black Migration, Community, and Activism in Cleveland, Ohio.* Urbana: University of Illinois Press, 1999.

Porter, Philip. *Cleveland: Confused City on a See-saw.* Columbus: Ohio State University Press, 1976.

Preston, Michael B. "Black Mayors: An Overview." *National Political Science Review* 2 (1990): 131–37.

Ptacek, Ted. "A Comprehensive Study of the Growth and Development of the Cleveland, Ohio School System." Master's thesis, Kansas State University, 1934.

Ralph, James Jr. *Northern Protest: Martin Luther King, Jr., Chicago, and the Civil Rights Movement.* Cambridge, Mass.: Harvard University Press, 1993.

Ransom, Bruce. "Mayor W. Wilson Goode of Philadelphia: The Technocrat." *National Political Science Review* 2 (1990): 183–87.

Rich, Wilbur. *Coleman Young and Detroit Politics.* Detroit: Wayne State University Press, 1989.

————. "The Politics of Detroit: A Look Ahead." *National Political Science Review* 2 (1990): 176–82.

Rose, Kenneth. "The Politics of Social Reform in Cleveland: Civil Rights, Welfare Rights, and the Response of Civic Leaders." Ph.D. diss., Case Western Reserve University, 1987.

Rose, William Ganson. *Cleveland: The Making of a City.* Kent, Ohio: Kent State University Press, 1990.

Rustin, Bayard. "From Protest to Politics." *Commentary* 39 (Feb. 1965): 25–31.

Saltzstein, Grace Hall. "Black Mayors and Police Policies." *Journal of Politics* 51 (Aug. 1989): 525–44.

Sonenshein, Raphael. *Politics in Black and White.* Princeton, N.J.: Princeton University Press, 1993.

Starks, Robert, and Michael Preston. "Harold Washington and the Politics of Reform in Chicago, 1983–1987." *Racial Politics in American Cities.* Ed. Rufus Browning, Dale Marshall, and David H. Tabb. 88–107. New York: Longman, 1990.

Stokes, Carl B. *Promises of Power: Then and Now.* Cleveland: Friends of Carl Stokes, 1989.

Stone, Chuck. *Black Political Power in America.* New York: Dell, 1970.

Stone, Clarence. "Race and Regime in Atlanta." *Racial Politics in American Cities.* Ed. Rufus Browning, Dale Marshall, and David H. Tabb. 125–39. New York: Longman, 1990.

————. *Regime Politics.* Lawrence: University Press of Kansas, 1989.

Sugrue, Thomas. "Crabgrass-Roots Politics: Race, Rights, and the Reaction against Liberalism in the Urban North, 1940–1964." *Journal of American History* 82 (March 1995): 551–78.

————. *The Origins of the Urban Crisis: Race and Inequality in Postwar Detroit.* Princeton, N.J.: Princeton University Press, 1996.

Swain, Johnnie Dee. "Urban Decline and the Underclass." *Journal of Black Studies* 24 (Sept. 1993): 16–28.

Swanstrom, Todd. *The Crisis of Growth Politics.* Philadelphia: Temple University Press, 1987.

Tall, Booker. *John O. Holly, 1903–1974.* Cleveland: U.S. Postal Service, 1988.

Taylor, Clarence. *Knocking at Our Own Door: Milton A. Galamison and the Struggle to Integrate the New York City Schools.* New York: Columbia University Press, 1997.

Teaford, Jon C. "'King Richard' Hatcher: Mayor of Gary." *Journal of Negro History* 77 (Summer 1992): 126–40.

Tyson, Timothy. *Radio Free Dixie: Robert F. Williams and the Roots of Black Power*. Chapel Hill: University of North Carolina Press, 1999.

U.S. Commission on Civil Rights. *Hearing Held in Cleveland, Ohio, April 1–7*. Washington, D.C.: Government Printing Office, 1966.

———. Ohio Advisory Committee. Cleveland Subcommittee. *Cleveland's Unfinished Business in its Inner-City: A Report*. Cleveland: Cleveland Subcommittee, 1968.

Upton, James. "Urban Violence: A Case Study of Three Cities." Ph.D. diss., Ohio State University, 1976.

Van Tassell, David, and John Grabowski, eds. *Cleveland: A Tradition of Reform*. Kent, Ohio: Kent State University Press, 1986.

———. *The Encyclopedia of Cleveland History*. Bloomington: Indiana University Press, 1991.

Viehe, Fred. "Carl B. Stokes: The First Black Mayor of a Major City." October 1989. Unpublished paper presented at the Duquesne Forum, Oct. 26, 1989. In the possession of the author.

Warren, Robert Penn. *Who Speaks for the Negro?* New York: Random House, 1965.

Weber, David. "Negro Voting Behavior in Cleveland." Master's thesis, Kent State University, 1971.

Weinberg, Kenneth. *Black Victory*. New York: Quadrangle Books, 1968.

Welfare Federation of Cleveland. "The Central Area Study." 1944. Unpublished ms. Available at Cleveland Public Library.

Whittelsey, George. *Early History of Cleveland*. Cleveland: Publishing Company, 1867.

Wilson, Julia Boatwright. "Cleveland: The Expansion of a Metropolitan Area and its Ghettos." John F. Kennedy School of Government, Harvard University, Cambridge, Mass., 1991.

Wilson, William Julius. *The Declining Significance of Race*. Chicago: University of Chicago Press, 1978.

Woodard, Komozi. *A Nation within a Nation: Amiri Baraka (LeRoi Jones) and Black Power Politics*. Chapel Hill: University of North Carolina Press, 1999.

Wye, Christopher. "At the Leading Edge: The Movement for Black Civil Rights in Cleveland." In *Cleveland: A Tradition of Reform*. Ed. David Van Tassell and John Grabowski. 113–35. Kent, Ohio: Kent State University Press, 1986.

———. "Don't Spend Your Money Where You Can't Work Movement." Undated ms. Christopher Wye Papers, Western Reserve Historical Society.

———. "Midwest Ghetto: Patterns of Negro Life and Thought in Cleveland, Ohio, 1929–1945." Ph.D. diss., Kent State University, 1976.

———. "The New Deal and the Negro Community: Toward a Broader Conceptualization." *Journal of American History* 59:3 (1972): 621–39.

Zannes, Estelle. *Checkmate in Cleveland*. Cleveland. Ohio: Case Western Reserve University Press, 1972.

Zinz, Kenneth. "The Future Outlook League of Cleveland: A Negro Protest Organization." Master's thesis, Kent State University, 1973.

Index

Walker, William O., 22, 41, 55, 66, 104; criticism of Cleveland Police Department, 142–43
Washington, Harold, 196–97
Weaver, Robert, 54, 69
Weismann, Robert, 164, 166
White, George, 102–4, 110
White, Jay, 114–17, 119
White, Michael R., 189
White, Paul, 62, 65, 153

Williams, Geraldine, 39, 55, 171; dismissal of, 65–66
Witzke, Dormand, 62
Wolfe, Willard, 84

Yates, Mary, 185
Young, Andrew, 197
Young, Coleman, 196

Zone, Michael, 69

LEONARD N. MOORE is an assistant professor of history and director of African and African-American studies at Louisiana State University.

The University of Illinois Press
is a founding member of the
Association of American University Presses.

Composed in 10.5/13 Minion
with Minion display
by Celia Shapland
for the University of Illinois Press
Designed by Paula Newcomb
Manufactured by Thomson-Shore, Inc.

University of Illinois Press
1325 South Oak Street
Champaign, IL 61820-6903
www.press.uillinois.edu